THE
COCKROACH
HALL OF
FAME

and 101 Other

Off-the-Wall Museums

THE COCKROACH HALL OF FAME

and 101 Other Off-the-Wall Museums

SANDRA GURVIS

A CITADEL PRESS BOOK
PUBLISHED BY CAROL PUBLISHING GROUP

A Citadel Press Book
Published by Carol Publishing Group
Citadel Press is a registered trademark of Carol Communications, Inc.
Editorial Offices: 600 Madison Avenue, New York, N.Y. 10022
Sales and Distribution Offices: 120 Enterprise Avenue, Secaucus, N.J. 07094
In Canada: Canadian Manda Group, P.O. Box 920, Station U, Toronto, Ontario M8Z 5P9
Queries regarding rights and permissions should be addressed to Carol Publishing Group,
600 Madison Avenue, New York, N.Y. 10022

Carol Publishing Group books are available at special discounts for bulk purchases,
for sales promotion, fund raising, or educational purposes.
Special editions can be created to specifications. For details, contact:
Special Sales Department, Carol Publishing Group,
120 Enterprise Avenue, Secaucus, N.J. 07094

Designed by Jessica Shatan

Manufactured in the United States of America
10 9 8 7 6 5 4 3 2 1

Library of Congress Cataloging-in-Publication Data
Gurvis, Sandra.
    The cockroach hall of fame : and 101 other off-the-wall museums /
Sandra Gurvis
        p.   cm.
    "A Citadel Press book."
    ISBN 0-8065-1501-5
    1. Museums—United States—Miscellanea—Directories.   2. United States—Popular
culture—Miscellanea—Directories.   I. Title.
AM11.G87 1994
069'.025'73—dc20
                                                            93-42126
                                                            CIP

*This book is dedicated to
the memory of my parents,
Dr. I.R. and Regina Goldberg.*

Contents

THE SOUTH 57

Acknowledgments

Any publishing venture is a collaborative undertaking, and I would like to thank the following: Robert Shook for his initial advice and insight; my agent, Bert Holtje, who guided the manuscript through the rocky shoals of publishing; Linda Deitch; Mickie Gurvis; Una and Dave Knight; Sherry Beck Paprocki; Linda Forristal; Harriet Baskas; and Nancy Frazier, editor of *Museum Insights* for suggesting various and sundry museums; Corinne Sinai who bailed me out when I did a really stupid thing with my computer and lost several chapters; and June and Jim Beard for all their assistance in Tennessee.

Last, but not least, I'd like to thank my wonderful editor Eileen Schlesinger Cotton for her absolutely appropriate suggestions and constant support. And, of course, my family—husband Ron and children, Amy and Alex—who always offered a ready smile, help, and love.

THE
NORTHEAST

Connecticut

♠ Old Lyme: THE NUT MUSEUM

Visitors to the Nut Museum in Old Lyme, Connecticut, can stick their heads inside the eight-foot nutcracker at the entrance, play a sort of "Name That Nut" with masks created by curator Elizabeth Tashjian, and be serenaded with a little "nut" music. "Nobody ever thinks about nuts," croons Miss Tashjian, clad in an Armenian robe that honors the fact that the most popular nuts come from Asia Minor. "Nuts can be so bee-yoo-tee-ful if looked aright / Take some home and handle them properly, artistically . . . ."

Although it might appear that the petite curator of indeterminate age might be just a few pecans shy of a fruitcake, her philosophy makes a nutty sort of sense. "My tours are tailor-made according to mentality and age bracket so everyone gets something out of them," she says. "The museum is meant to be viewed seriously—with the corners of the mouth upturned. But it is also supposed to celebrate creativity, compassion, and joy."

Founded in 1972, the Nut Museum is located on the first floor of Miss Tashjian's cool, dark Victorian mansion, which is surrounded appropriately enough by walnut, hazelnut, and chestnut trees. Inside you'll find nuts ranging from the tiny African baobab to the world's largest nut, a thirty-five-pound double coconut, which grows only on two small islands in the Indian Ocean. "It resembles human buttocks," she points out coyly, adding, "We all came from the same shell."

Because the price of admission includes one nut, Miss Tashjian has been the recipient of many unusual donations; one man jokingly offered his wife. Along with a metal nut—the kind that goes with a bolt—and a whiff of nutmeg, she's been given nut jewelry, nut spoons, nut furniture, and miniatures carved in nuts.

"Someone sent me earrings made from hickory shells," Miss Tashjian recounts. "But one was stolen by a squirrel. So if you see a

The world's largest nut, a coco-de-mer, "sits" in its place of honor at the Nut Museum. (*Photo courtesy of the Nut Museum.*)

squirrel wearing an earring, you'll know where he got it." Although she still has about a hundred different kinds of nuts, squirrels and chipmunks have presented a slight inventory control problem. "Sometimes I forget to put the glass back on the exhibit cases, and those fleet-footed little rascals come in and loot." She keeps hoping they'll get the hint and eat the nuts from the trees in the yard instead. "But I think they're trying to start their own museum."

Inside the museum, a quartet of nut people slice black walnuts in one tiny scene, while in another a wedding takes place. Miss Tashjian's extensive nutcracker collection includes models requiring the use of the knee (so you can sunder some cartilage, too), a cast-iron squirrel, an acorn, an aviator wearing goggles, a ten-foot-high traditional nutcracker, and one from the Philippines "that's on the naughty side, so I don't often bring it out." Tashjian will also sometimes wear the Mask of the Unknown Nut "to honor those who are unrecognized and unappreciated."

She's created her own nut-related artwork as well. Her outside sculptures *Nuts Nourish Man* and *Nuts Grow in the Garden of Eden* deal with the women's movement and the contemporary male preoccupation with sex, respectively. The former is a metal female torso with coconuts for breasts, while the latter, a tin-and-nut rendering of male genitalia, "was carved by talented squirrels."

Along with gentle jokes, Tashjian will crack nuts, but she says "I have to eat them with my eyes closed because, before I know it, I'll have opened a whole row and will be admiring their beauty." The seed of her obsession was planted early: "My family always liked nuts, and, early on, I discovered them not only as edible delights but paintable subjects." And she's a one-food artist. "I can't bear looking at carrots and apples, although of course I eat them." Future plans include a one-woman show and a nut theme park to rival Disney World. Whether or not the public's ready to digest all that may be another story.

The Nut Museum
303 Ferry Road, Old Lyme, CT 06371
((203) 434-7616

LOCATION: West of New London off I-95
HOURS: May–November; Wednesday, Saturday, Sunday, 1:00–5:00 P.M.;
   or by appointment
ADMISSION: A slight fee and a nut

♦ Terryville: THE LOCK MUSEUM OF AMERICA

How fitting that Tom Hennessy, lock designer and curator of the Lock Museum of America in Terryville, Connecticut, holds the keys to some of the most important locks in the world. After all, he's spent a career locked onto his goal of increasing public appreciation of the history and artistry behind not only locks, but safes, padlocks, safe plates, doorknobs and escutcheons, handcuffs, leg irons, exit devices, and door closers.

Rather than bolting from such a seemingly mundane accumulation, more and more people are stopping by to view what, according to Hennessy, is a vital key to America's past. "At one time, locks were the largest industry in Connecticut," he observes. "Although they're not as romantic as, say, the clocks and guns that were also produced here, they are important and necessary and the craftsmanship is remarkable."

The museum started out modestly. "We had a small store," recalls Hennessy. "On one side was my private collection and on the other were locks from the Eagle Lock Company." The store is gone, but the museum has continued to grow, now housed in its own building with eight display rooms.

Along with a seven-thousand-pound, five-foot-tall, three-foot-diameter 1910 safe that's shaped like a cannonball, the museum has part of a four-thousand-year-old wooden pin tumbler lock made in Egypt. Although appearances of locks have changed, a few basic mechanisms have endured throughout the ages. "The ancient Romans had warded locks," Hennessy continues. These worked by matching cuts in the key to obstructions inside the lock. The museum's collection of one hundred warded German locks dates from 1500 to 1700. The more complicated lever tumblers came into being in the late eighteenth century and were the first locks utilized in colonial America. Tumblers of different heights corresponded with cuts in the key.

But the real breakthrough came in 1865 with Linus Yale, Jr., according to Hennessy. "He developed the mortise cylinder pin tumbler, considered the greatest invention in lock making." This same principle is still used in many locks today. Consumers no longer had to carry around cumbersome iron keys (which at least didn't get lost or forgotten as easily). Along with the original patent model of Yale's design, the museum has a mechanical hand and arm that demonstrate exactly how the complicated pin tumbler works—a different spin to the hands-on display.

The museum's various chambers unclasp the mystique around assorted locks. The Eagle Lock room features over one thousand locks and keys made from 1854 to 1954. "At one time, Eagle was the largest trunk and cabinet lock maker in the world," notes Hennessy. The company built a so-called manipulation-proof safe in 1865 and a lock with what appears to be a swastika, which at first was believed by

Hennessy to have been meant for a German customer, "but further research showed it was an Indian sign, produced in 1907." Ah, closure.

The bank lock room contains bank locks, vault locks, safe locks, and time locks and is sure to give pause to those who hide their savings under a mattress. A two-hundred-number dial combination lock manufactured in 1865 and a vault lock used in the White House during the Lincoln administration are other highlights; as are a menacing-looking agglomeration of handcuffs and leg irons. The original doorknobs from the state of Connecticut capitol building, colonial hardware, and a wooden stock lock add to the combination.

The museum also has information on patents, as well as lock catalogs, books, and periodicals. One wonders though, how does Hennessy keep all those keys straight?

The Lock Museum of America
130 East Main Street
P.O. Box 104, Terryville, CT 06786
((203) 589-6359

LOCATION: **About 25 miles west of Hartford on Route 6**
HOURS: **May–October; Tuesday–Sunday, 1:30–4:30 P.M.**
ADMISSION: **Admission is charged**

Maine

♠ Freeport: THE DESERT OF MAINE

It's a beautiful, sunny day and you're surrounded by a silky, shimmering desert. Dunes of drifting sand add to the tropical ambiance, and you're seized with the urge to jump into a bathing suit and sip an oddly colored beverage with an umbrella in it. One slight problem though: This particular strip is in Freeport, Maine, and it's ten

Visitors pass the only camel found at the Desert of Maine. (*Photo courtesy of the Desert of Maine.*)

degrees above zero, with two feet of snow predicted for tonight. Life can be a beach at the Desert of Maine.

The Desert is billed as a "living museum." "This is a totally natural phenomenon," states Carolyn Dobson, who, along with her husband Sid, owns the museum. "It's an actual desert, with most of the elements of its Asiatic counterparts, such as the Gobi or Sahara." The only camel, however, is a plastic one that greets visitors.

And no, it's not man-made, although from above the thirty-five-acre stretch resembles a giant litter box surrounded by trees. "Geologists established that a glacier slid through here about eight thousand years ago at the end of the Pleistocene period," explains Carolyn. "It formed a lake, which eventually evaporated, leaving behind sand and mineral deposits in an approximately thirty-mile radius."

Later eras produced a thick layer of topsoil that completely covered the wasteland underneath. The unsuspecting William Tuttle family settled there in 1797 and raised healthy harvests of hay and potatoes for several generations. However, massive land clearing, failure to rotate crops, and overgrazing by cattle resulted in erosion.

Around the turn of the century, a patch of sand showed up. As any male (or female) who's lost hair knows, once a bald spot begins . . . it's only a matter of time. "The wind blew the sand around, and by 1919 what was an eight-foot stretch had grown to dozens of acres," states Carolyn. So "the Tuttles surrendered, leaving the Desert to its destiny."

Shortly after the Tuttles departed for destinations unknown, a Mr. Henry Goldrup purchased their farm, turning it into a tourist attraction. The Dobsons obtained the Desert in the early eighties, spiffing it up and adding new exhibits.

Geologists and students can drift for hours, analyzing the sands and various minerals. The rest of us, however, need to be entertained while marveling at the really weird feeling of being in a desert amid pine forests, colorful flowers, bubbling brooks, and rolling hills. To that end, the Dobsons have refurbished the original Tuttle barn. Built over two hundred years ago, it retains its hand-hewn timbers, wooden pegs, and mortise work. Inside are ancient pieces of farm equipment, such as a harrow, tractor, and hay rake that have been uncovered by the shifting sands.

Every summer the Dobsons hire sand artists who produce various shapes and patterns in glass bottles and pictures. "All of the colors are completely indigenous to the Desert, even though we've temporarily 'lost' the veins of grey and pure white." Sand comes in more than boring beige: "Based on the texture or level of coarseness, it can be pink, black, red, or even green."

Still another collection at the Desert consists of over five hundred different vials of the stuff, from deserts, beaches, and even from former President Eisenhower's golf course. People bring the Dobsons sand samples from all over the world.

But none is so fine as the Desert of Maine's. "Because it was basically silt, when it blows it builds a barrier, causing the Desert to constantly shift," points out Carolyn. As a result, the dunes get higher and the hollows deeper.

The Desert reaches its powder-like tentacles beyond its borders and continuously reveals other spots for miles around, a sort of Expand-a-Desert. "According to our estimates, the dunes will be up to the tree line [about one hundred feet] in fifty years or so. They're at eighty feet now."

When that happens, perhaps the people of Maine should give up their maple sugar and lumbering enterprises and concentrate on selling surfboards and string bikinis.

The Desert of Maine
95 Desert Road, Freeport, ME 04032
℃ (207) 865-6962 OR (508) 824-0188

LOCATION: Just outside of Brunswick
HOURS: May 10–October 15; seven days a week, 8:30 A.M. to dusk
ADMISSION: Admission is charged

Maryland

♠ Baltimore: The Mount Vernon Museum of Incandescent Lighting

The Mount Vernon Museum of Incandescent Lighting hides its "light" under a bushel. Tucked away on an inconspicuous street in Baltimore, Maryland, it provides visitors with an illuminating perspective. The museum has about seventy thousand light bulbs, most of which still work. Thank goodness it's not on the San Andreas Fault.

The largest bulb ever made, a four-foot-high, three-foot-tall, fifty-thousand-watt colossus shares space with the smallest, a microscopic model the size of pin prick, that is still used to inspect missile parts and for surgery. The former, manufactured to celebrate the fiftieth anniversary of Thomas Edison's discovery, could be lit for thirty seconds, then had to cool for two minutes, and is the only one left of several; the others were broken down to recycle valuable tungsten. The museum also has the world's longest incandescent bulb, which, at three feet, brightened the French steamship *Normandy* in the 1930s. Other luminaries include a cockpit bulb from the *Enola Gay*, the airplane that dropped the first nuclear bomb during World War II; a headlight bulb from Nazi leader Heinrich Himmler's staff car; a bulb from the original torch of the Statue of Liberty; and a fluorescent light from the table lamp under which the Japanese surrendered in 1945 on the USS *Missouri*. Along with the approximately eight thousand on display is a bulb-by-bulb chronology of the development of lighting, starting with Edison's prototypes in the late 1800s.

The bright idea of Dr. Hugh Hicks, a man in his seventies who also moonlights as a dentist, the museum is the culmination of a lifelong passion. "Do you believe in reincarnation?" he asks with a smile. "William J. Hammer, the world's foremost collector of light bulbs and a colleague of Edison's, died the same month I was born."

Dr. Hicks remembers playing with bulbs as a baby. "My family was very tolerant," he recalls of the early years when he began to accrue his cache in the basement. "They couldn't figure me out, but since I wasn't being destructive, they went along with it." He soon had friends saving old bulbs and searching through trash cans for "finds".

One of about thirty-five collectors in the United States, Hicks is considered to be among the best. He is able to pinpoint a bulb's date of manufacture to within a few months. "Things like the shape and

Need a light? Dr. Hugh Hicks has seventy thousand of them. (*Photo courtesy of the Mount Vernon Museum of Incandescent Lighting.*)

base of the lamp, type of filament, and support wires provide clues."

Although he opened his own museum in 1960, a windfall from a fellow collector who passed away and left his hoard of forty-eight thousand bulbs to Hicks in the sixties added greatly to the exhibits. "We had no idea what he had," recalls Hicks. "The bulbs were buried in boxes with layers of newspaper. We'd find ten pieces of junk, then number eleven would be one of Edison's early lamps."

Some of the first Christmas lights have a home here, as do decorative bulbs and lamps. The former include cherub faces, parrots, Chinese lanterns, and Betty Boop; while the latter category encompasses everything from star and grape-cluster shaped bulbs of the late Victorian era to an ornate brass and crystal lamp that illuminated a railroad dining car in the twenties. The museum even has its own "bulb of Damocles," a nine-thousand-watt arc light used for night work at Cape Canaveral. Due to extreme pressure inside the bulb, it must be kept in a special plastic case. "If it broke, everything else would shatter," comments Hicks.

Hicks is still on the lookout for lights, whether they be donated, purchased or "liberated." "In the sixties, I spotted a group of old bulbs along a subway tunnel in Paris. I thought, what harm would there be in taking one?" Alas, the bulbs were wired in sequence so that if one went out, they all did. After removing a bulb and plunging the subway into total darkness, Hicks frantically tried to screw it back in. When that failed he "grabbed two more and took off." A remarkable feat, even for a man who claims he's never broken a light bulb that's gone into his museum.

The Mount Vernon Museum of Incandescent Lighting
717 Washington Place, Baltimore, MD 21201
((410) 752-8586

LOCATION: Downtown Baltimore
HOURS: Seven days a week by appointment
ADMISSION: Donations are welcome

✦ Salisbury: WARD MUSEUM OF WILDFOWL ART

Joseph P. Forsthoffer, public relations coordinator for the Ward Museum of Wildfowl Art in Salisbury, Maryland, once received a phone call from a Hollywood producer enthusiastic about the newly opened facility. "We began discussing the logistics of doing a documentary on wildfowl carving and she suddenly paused," he remembers. "Then she asked, 'But how do you keep the meat from spoiling?'"

Thanksgiving dinner aside, the only "fowl" these carvers take a knife to is wood. In fact, many of the birds look so lifelike they seem ready to take flight. But it's only artistic details these hunters are after.

Like many honorable American traditions, wildfowl carving began with indigenous Indians. "As early as 2000 B.C., Native Americans created wooden decoys to help find food for sustenance," recounts Forsthoffer. "The Europeans adopted the practice, utilizing decoys to obtain large amounts of game, first for the settlement, then even more for metropolitan areas." Foul play.

Over time the craft of wildfowl carving developed into an art. After World War II, however, the end of mass hunting and the proliferation of manufactured decoys threatened its very existence. Then Lem and Steve Ward, two Crisfield, Maryland, barbers who already

Art imitates life, beautifully, at the Ward Museum. (*Photo courtesy of the Ward Museum of Wildfowl Art.*)

had reputations as excellent carvers, decided to fashion decorative ducks intended as sculpture, branching out later to other species.

Their efforts drew an appreciative audience, and by 1968, a group of Salisbury artists, collectors, and community leaders established the Ward Foundation. Along with organizing a small museum at a nearby university, they initiated a competition to encourage budding and experienced artists. In 1992, the present $5.3-million, thirty-thousand-square-foot facility opened its doors. And thousands of carvers from all over the world now flock to participate in the Ward World Championship, which purchases winning entries for the museum's permanent exhibition. Although there are several categories, including one for decoys that float, rubber duckies need not apply.

As visitors enter the museum, they are struck by Lem Ward's masterpieces: two life-sized swans that dominate the lobby. Then, the completely uninitiated might want to stop for a brief video that explains the art form and tells the story behind the museum. From there, most proceed into a sort of timeline that traces the history of decoys. This completely re-created marsh has eerily realistic lighting and nature sounds. "We see this exhibit as a way of introducing people to conservation," explains Forsthoffer. An adjacent presentation stresses the importance of preserving natural habitats.

Visitors can take a gander at the only gallery in the cosmos where decoy ducks and geese are arranged by migratory patterns. "The purpose behind this is to illustrate the geographical and sociological differences in woodcarving."

An exhibit featuring the Ward brothers' carving studio gives insight into the actual creation process, "bridging the gap from the decoy as a working tool to something perceived as art." Here visitors will find the Wards' early decoys as well as later efforts.

Along with the competition winners, the main gallery has close to one hundred carved items, from extremely realistic to interpretive pieces. An eight-foot-tall ferocious hawk swoops down on an unsuspecting pheasant. A piece of gently burled wood suggests a sleeping goose. "Carvers are constantly challenging the art form and experimenting with new techniques."

Although some might turn up their noses at calling these endeavors "art," Lem and Steve Ward and thousands of others would no doubt regard such critics as a bunch of turkeys.

The Ward Museum of Wildfowl Art
P.O. Box 3416
Beaglin Park Drive, Salisbury, MD 21802
((410) 742-4988

LOCATION: One mile south of Route 50
HOURS: Hours vary according to the season
ADMISSION: Admission is charged

Massachusetts

♠ Salem: THE SALEM WITCH MUSEUM

On the surface, Salem, Massachusetts, seems like an ordinary little town, replete with shopping malls, frozen yogurt shops, and fancy restaurants. But look a little closer and, along with historic homes, a quaint commons, and other points of interest befitting one of America's oldest settlements, you'll find symbols of witches on everything from street signs to T-shirts. For a real spook-out, among other sights, there's the Salem Witch Museum.

Housed in an eerie stone church in historic Washington Square, the museum offers a half-hour multisensory presentation with (appropriately) thirteen diorama stage settings. Each scene is lit up and narrated in the three-story nave, or center, of the church. "Along with depicting the full course and aftermath of the Salem witch trials, we try to provide an idea of what life was like in 1692," explains director Patty MacLeod. There's a circle with the names of the executed in the knave; informational signs are scattered throughout.

"There were actually very few keepsakes left," MacLeod goes on. If you're searching for concrete evidence, the nearby Essex Institute has court transcripts, other written records, and a few personal items such as pocket watches and walking sticks. And several blocks away, the Witch Dungeon offers, along with a live reenactments of the trials based on actual court records, a replica of a dungeon with telephone-booth-sized cells and torture devices. Wholesome fun for the entire family.

What exactly happened in the town of Salem over three hundred years ago? The apparently simple facts belie the complexity of events: More than two hundred people were accused of witchcraft, and of the twenty-three convicted, nineteen were hanged. Those who "confessed" were spared, while others who maintained their innocence

The Salem Witch Museum looks as scary as its history. (*Photo courtesy of the Salem Witch Museum.*)

went to their deaths. According to legend, two dogs were also hanged on Gallows Hill as witches (apparently they didn't confess either).

A group of mostly adolescent girls, among them the minister's own daughter, gathered in Reverend Samuel Parris's Salem Village kitchen to listen to the tales of his West Indian slave, Tituba. They also tried their hands at fortune-telling, using various "old wives" methods to see who their husbands might be. "For girls raised in a repressive Puritan background, this was a major risk," relates MacLeod.

"What many people today don't understand was that in the 1600s, everyone was very superstitious, believing in magic and the devil," she continues. So when the girls began to rant and throw fits, old Lucifer was blamed. (Causal theories now range from hormones to clinical hysteria to a contaminated rye wheat crop.) So, with the encouragement of some adults, the girls started pointing fingers. Of course, Tituba was among the first charged, as was Sarah Good, a poor beggar, and Sarah Osborne, who was known to have lived with her second husband *before* they married.

"Initially, most people didn't believe the girls," says MacLeod. "But because the accused were on the outskirts of society, it became easy to justify that they could be possessed."

Political factors were at work as well. The mostly rural Salem Village (now called Danvers) chafed against taxes and encroachment by the larger and more prosperous Salem Town. "With no charter and a government in England, things were in a constant state of turmoil." And there was a land dispute between the parents of one of the girls and a wealthy, well-respected family of three sisters, all of whom were convicted of witchcraft.

Once "witchcraft hysteria" gripped the community and arrests were made, things went straight to hell. Says MacLeod, "Neighbor turned against neighbor and no one felt safe around the girls," whose ravings were taken so seriously by the court that it demanded a retrial when a jury found one of the accused, Rebecca Nurse, innocent. Considered acceptable by the court, "spectral evidence" included the girls' seeing spirits flying around doing such nasty things as biting others.

Eventually cooler heads prevailed, and by the early 1700s legal procedures against witches were declared unlawful by the governor of Massachusetts. But thanks to the Salem Witch Museum and others, it looks like "witchcraft" has settled in for a spell.

The Salem Witch Museum
Washington Square, Salem, MA 01970
((508) 744-1692

LOCATION: About 20 miles north of Boston
HOURS: Open seven days a week, except holidays; hours vary according to season
ADMISSION: Admission is charged

♠ Worcester: THE AMERICAN SANITARY PLUMBING MUSEUM

It's enough to make you flush: an amazing assortment of old toilets, sinks, bathtubs, tools, books, and catalogs plumbing the depths of a trade few can live without. Founded by the late Charles Manoog, a plumbing distributor, based in Worcester (pronounced: Wooster), Massachusetts, the American Sanitary Plumbing Museum has become a sort of Jerusalem for wanna-be plumbers who want to be privy to history before they take the plunge.

With the bulk of its visitors from trade schools, this three-thousand-square-foot museum takes its subject seriously. After all, it's the only repository of its kind "and we want to preserve the changes in products and methods for future generations," points out curator B.J. Manoog, daughter-in-law of founder Charles. Still, "when people come to visit, they have lots of funny stories."

Trying to understand the workings of the exhibits can be draining, so Manoog recommends getting a handle on the highlights. These include:

•A piece of the original wooden water main leading from Jamaica Pond to Faneuil Hall in Boston. "This was installed circa 1652 by Massachusetts's first waterworks company," states Manoog. Uncovered by engineers excavating a tunnel in 1956, the ancient spigot-end piece "provided impetus to start the museum."

•A variety of short hoppers. Basically toilets with above-ground pipes, these "indoor outhouses" were primarily used in the early 1900s. "All waste would then go to the basement where it would eventually have to be emptied." There's even a duplicate of one that's at Mount Vernon, painted in blue with distracting scenes of people, buildings, and forests; a precursor to magazines. George Washington flushed here.

•Examples of early lav (sink) devices. These include a copper pantry sink with a hand pump for obtaining water from a cellar cistern, and 5-foot-long copper lined steel tubs encased in wooden boxes, which disguised above-ground pipes; Victorian-era Jacuzzis without the whirlpool. "You'd pick a tub, then select the frame to go around it," explains Manoog. An elegant steel claw-footed tub boasts copper lining and an oak rim.

•Toilets galore, from an 1891 green and white floral motif model embellished with gold tracings and an oak seat to a grim-looking iron number manufactured in Pittsburgh a few years later for use in a jail cell. With a one-piece, nondetachable seat, "it was designed to deter inmates from using it as a weapon."

There is also a flood of overflow plates from bathtubs. Used to help with drainage, they bore the names of the manufacturers and "were an early form of advertising," observes Manoog.

A lavender pedestal sink is a standout, not only due to its color but because "it was originally in a bathroom that had green and black checked tile walls." A nickel-plated brass faucet has caused an outpouring of debate as to whether or not the attached cup held jewelry or the plug.

Plumb the depths of the museum's downstairs and you'll find an agglomeration of everything including the kitchen sink: gas, kerosene, smudge pot, and oil water heaters; blow torches; threading pipe machines; pipe cutters; and other tools. Okay, so maybe it's not the Burlesque Hall of Fame (see California), but a 1928 "electric sink" offers a glimpse into the future of automated appliances. Two sinks and agitators were utilized for washing dishes *and* clothes. And, along with a complete (1903–29) collection of the *Plumbers Trade Journal*, there's an assortment of appropriate reading matter (i.e., joke books) for those private moments.

Although the museum may unclog misconceptions about what Manoog and others believe is an honorable trade, this is one plumbing facility that doesn't make house calls.

The American Sanitary Plumbing Museum
39 Piedmont Street, Worcester, MA 01610
((508) 754-9453

LOCATION: Off I-290, 42 miles west of Boston
HOURS: Tuesdays and Thursdays, 10:00 A.M.–2:00 P.M.; closed during
    July and August
ADMISSION: Free

New Hampshire

♠ Manchester: THE LAWRENCE L. LEE SCOUTING MUSEUM

Now here's a deal: Not only can you visit the Lawrence L. Lee
Scouting Museum in Manchester, New Hampshire, for free, but
camping on the adjacent grounds costs only fifty cents a night. Picnic
tables, lakeside scenery, and nearby trails make it a natural for family
adventure. Plus, there's the potential for unforgettable campsite
memories: pitching a tent in the rain; cooking a can of beans over
the open fire for dinner because raccoons got into the hot dogs; waking up with the sense that every rock, pebble and stick is embedded
in your back, despite the new $125 down-filled sleeping bag. Per-
haps a nearby hotel room would be a better investment . . . .

Regardless, the Lawrence L. Lee Scouting Museum is a testament
to the durability of the Boy Scout's pledge to be trustworthy, loyal,
helpful, friendly, courteous, kind, obedient, cheerful, thrifty, brave,
clean, and reverent. Although visitors may not be immediately familiar with such names as Lord Robert Baden-Powell, William T.
Hornaday, Dan Beard, and the area's own "Uncle Max" Silber, they
will be upon leaving.

The rough-boarded, knotty pine structure, built (of course) by hand
in 1969 with volunteers, currently houses over three thousand square
feet of displays. These include Cub Scout, Boy Scout, and Explorer
insignia which chart a boy's and, at the high school Explorer level,
girl's progress through the ranks; patrol medallions and flags; awards
and their history; neckerchief exhibits; National and World Jamboree
items; and international collections, such as the world's only complete
grouping of Catholic Boy Scouts of Ireland memorabilia. Life-size

mannequins model vintage and international uniforms, including the full Indian regalia of the elite Order of the Arrow.

The museum isn't just for former and future model citizens, however. Philatelists will bond with the comprehensive stamp collection that highlights the siege of Mafeking (which made Baden-Powell a hero during the Boer War) and Scout issues dating from 1900. Artistic types can appreciate several original paintings of thirties and forties covers of the official scouting magazine *Boys' Life*. And history buffs can admire a nineteenth-century wooden bead from the necklace of Chief Dinizulu of the Zulu tribe. "Only about two hundred such beads are known to exist," states Yvon Brunette, chairman of the museum's operating committee.

The museum's library offers Scouting related periodicals, handbooks, yearbooks, and first-edition nonfiction, as well as the boys' adventure fiction so popular during the early part of this century. There are also books for the handicapped and visually impaired.

The fathers of Scouting are well represented here. At the turn of the century, Lord Robert Baden-Powell organized the first Boy Scout group in Britain, publishing their manual a year later. The idea quickly caught on in the United States and around the world. Ceramic dishes commemorating Baden-Powell's achievements in the Boer War, a flag and ceremonial dagger given to him by the Scouts of Hungary during the World Jamboree of 1933, and his manuscripts, letters, and personal papers are encamped here.

The museum has a famous portrait of Dan Beard and a beaded pouch worn by Beard, the developer of the American Scouting program. It features his biography along with those of other American Scouting founders Ernest Thompson Seton and James West. Visitors can peruse the buckskin shirt, pants, and other personal effects of conservationist and explorer William T. Hornaday, after whom a prestigious Scouting award is named. And just about everyone is familiar with astronaut and former Boy Scout Alan Shepard, the first American in space, who presented the museum with a flag and patch carried during an expedition to the moon.

Also, in the library that bears his name, are the belt buckles fashioned by Nashua industrialist and bronze manufacturer Max I. Silber. First made as a New Hampshire commemorative for a 1950

National Jamboree, the buckles have been produced annually by
Silber for Jamborees and other Scouting commemorations ever
since. Designs range from wagons to buffalo to various Scouting
logos and even to an (almost) funky axe-in-log neckerchief slide. In
order to obtain one, you have to be a Scout, although other souvenirs
can be purchased in the gift shop. Sometimes it pays to "be prepared."

The Lawrence L. Lee Scouting Museum
P.O. Box 1121, Manchester, NH 03105
((603) 627-1492

LOCATION: Take I-293 to Manchester; the nearest city is Nashua, 19
   miles to the south
HOURS: Hours vary
ADMISSION: Free

New Jersey

♦ Camden: THE CAMPBELL MUSEUM
What a self-serving idea for a museum: In 1966, the Campbell's
Soup Company began to set up a collection of three-hundred-plus
tureens, bowls, and utensils. The resulting nonprofit Campbell Museum of Camden, New Jersey, has whetted the public's appetite for
containers more permanent than the styrofoam cup. The tureens
have also satisfied curiosity about customs and manners of a long-
forgotten epoch when dining was a gracious and elegant pastime
rather than fifteen minutes at McDonald's.

   For the uninitiated, tureens—deep covered dishes for serving
soups, stews, and sauces—come in round or oval shapes and are
often accompanied by an equally decorative platter. Although the
collection is made up of "beauties," mostly fancy eighteenth-century

rococo and neoclassical tureens, there are plenty of beasts among them: A rabbit munches on a turquoise leaf, a turkey spreads his tail, a bespeckled mother hen fusses over her chicks.

And those are the "nice" animals. There is also the bull whose sharp, curved-horn handle looks more to be avoided than lifted up; the boar's head with blood dripping out of his mouth; and a fine kettle with blanched-out fish flopping on the lid. One number covered with crustaceans, seaweed, and shells appears as if it's been dredged from the bottom of the ocean. M'M Good!

"The tureens were one of the ultimate status symbols of their time," states Ralph Collier, the museum's president. "They represent some of the best work in European and Chinese porcelain, silver, pewter, and faience [glazed earthenware]." Among the latter, a green-and-yellow woven "basket" topped with a bird nibbling a cluster of fruit might look more in place in Aunt Millie's kitchen than in a spacious museum with red velvet walls. But hey, it's certified as a genuine 1775 Mosbach.

Although tureens gained popularity among royalty in Europe during the late 1600s, "they've been around in various forms for centuries," Collier continues.

The original soup can, accept no imitations. (*Photo courtesy of the Campbell Museum.*)

"Primitive tribes as well as medieval peoples ate soup and stew from communal pots." But it was during the elegant and refined reigns of Louis XIV and Louis XV that soups became a delicacy, creating a hunger, as it were, for tureens. With their fancy flowers, flourishes, and fruits, they also often served as centerpieces. "Having one in the middle of the table meant you had arrived."

Individual artistry makes even the simplest tureens special. New

This rabbit is adorable, but would you want to eat rabbit stew from it? (*Photo courtesy of the Campbell Museum.*)

York silversmith Hugh Wishart created a rare, unadorned tureen with grapes and leaves on the handles for the maternal relatives of George Washington. Another favorite is a neoclassical number crafted by London's Robert Makepeace, upon which only the Tatton family coat of arms is engraved. Among many others, the collection includes pieces by such makers as Meissen, Delft, Wedgwood, and Paul Revere.

Also of interest is the finial, the center ornament on the cover of the tureen. More commonly known as the handle, "The finial sometimes indicated what kind of foodstuffs it contained," observes Collier. Lobsters, artichokes, cauliflower, and sheep gave strong hints as to what was on the menu. But crossed branches, a boy with his dog, or a flower made it anybody's guess. And rabbit stew, chicken soup, or some other delicacy served in the aforementioned "cute animal" containers might induce pangs of guilt rather than hunger.

Tureens are still made and used today. One of the collection's weightiest (almost thirty-five pounds) is the contemporary *Tommy Toad* by Sue Halls of London. The mottled, lumpy frog has a curling tongue that transforms into a ladle when his head (the lid) is lifted. Just open and heat a can of Campbell's soup and you've got a meal fit for a king, or at least a frog prince.

The Campbell Museum
Campbell Soup Company World Headquarters, Camden, NJ 08101
☎ (609) 342-6440

LOCATION: On I-76, 32 miles south of Trenton, across the Delaware
  River from Philadelphia.
HOURS: Monday–Friday, 9:00 A.M.–4:00 P.M.
ADMISSION: Free

✦ Millville: THE MUSEUM OF AMERICAN GLASS

In a state known for its discount malls, high crime rates, and expensive real estate, the Museum of American Glass in Millville, New
Jersey, is a clear standout. Located in Wheaton Village, an eighty-
eight-acre complex of Victorian shops, crafts exhibits, and a glass
factory, it has more than seventy-five hundred pieces of glass on exhibit, from Mason jars to Tiffany masterpieces. Windex, anyone?

Shards of local history are embedded throughout. For instance, the
nation's first successful glass factory was established a stone's throw
away in Salem County. The Wistarburgh Glassworks began producing
everyday items such as windowpanes, bottles, and jars in 1739, visibly
contributing to the colonies' independence. A few years ago, the
museum sponsored a rare exhibit of Wistar glass; a dozen bowls, bottles, and pitchers from the less than twenty period items known to
exist. Thanks to abundant resources of silica sand, timber, and water,
nearly seventy-five factories in southern New Jersey were manufacturing much of the glassware for a growing nation by late 1800s.

The museum's twenty thousand square feet of displays are

This Durand art glass
depicts the variety and
beauty at the Museum
of American Glass.
(*Photo courtesy of the
museum.*)

arranged in mostly chronological order. The so-called Furnace Room offers a variety of American free- and mold-blown glass from the mid to late 1700s. The collection of early Wistar, Steigel, and Amelung pitchers, fruit jars, and window panes doesn't appear particularly awe-inspiring because, as curational assistant Patricia Martinelli points out, "the factories focused on producing useful items that were necessities as well as scarce. Tableware and decorative articles were considered luxuries."

The Bottle Room, with its federal-style decor and chandelier, contains multitudinous flasks, decanters, jars, and jugs. The bottles held everything from food to whiskey to medicines such as Green's Great Dyspeptic Panacea. Included are pickle jars as well as beverage, ink, and perfume containers. "Many are aqua in color, due to the natural iron in the unprocessed sand used in making the glass," notes Martinelli.

"Whimseys"—figures used for advertising and product recognition—can also be found here. Throughout the decades, whimseys have been created by gaffers (glassblowers) during their lunch hours and at the end of the day. "Since much of the glass produced was everyday items, [making it] got boring very quickly," Martinelli observes. Hence, the colorful and imaginative animals, miniatures, and, most importantly, paperweights scattered throughout the museum. "These pieces helped define Victorian, art nouveau such as Tiffany, and even today's contemporary art glass."

The green and white Gazebo Room covers glass produced from the end of the Civil War to the turn of the century. With the discovery of inexpensive fuel and increased competition among manufacturers, "this period saw an incredible amount of creative glass chemistry and decoration," states Martinelli. Here you'll find art glass in amberina (shades of yellowish orange to ruby), peach blow (opaque glass in pastel colors), and other hues, etched and plain "of everything from hairpin boxes to vases to tableware."

A Victorian kitchen exhibit spotlights kerosene lamps, Mason jars, electric light fixtures, and marbles, as well as glass cheese graters and rolling pins. A "What Is It?" case lets visitors figure out such novelties as a colonial-style fly catcher, a cremation urn, glass eye, and an early fire extinguisher.

A dense agglomeration of paperweights ranges from antique and traditional round models to innovative contemporary shapes. The Millville Rose, a flower form inside a glass paperweight shell invented by local gaffer Ralph Barber, is featured here as are some elaborate lampworked and overlay numbers. Originally functional items sold in stationary stores, "paperweights are now considered objects of art and are highly collectible," comments Martinelli. Also, they make great missiles.

Today, glassmaking has evolved into an art, with places like the Wheaton Village factory offering fellowships in exchange for the gaffer's work. For $40, visitors to the factory can also try their hand at a Millville Rose or other paperweight. But it may shatter the misconception that glassmaking is as simple as it looks.

The Museum of American Glass
Wheaton Village, Millville, NJ 08332
((609) 825-6800

LOCATION: 35 miles west of Atlantic City
HOURS: April–December; seven days a week, 10:00 A.M.–5:00 P.M.;
   closed holidays; hours vary in the winter months
ADMISSION: Admission is charged

New York

New York City: THE AMERICAN BIBLE SOCIETY LIBRARY

Fifty thousand books in one library is not uncommon, but fifty thousand different copies of the same tome can be found only in the American Bible Society (ABS) Library and Archives in New York City. Rather than being as dull as a Sunday sermon, the world's largest and most comprehensive collection of Bibles is simply divine.

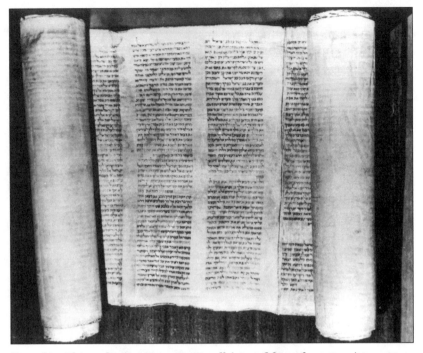

Found in China, the Kei Feng Fu Scroll (circa fifteenth century) is written in Hebrew and is on permanent display in the gallery. (*Photo courtesy of the American Bible Society Library.*)

The Bible has been translated into nearly two thousand languages, and this holy lot ranges from a handwritten (as in before the invention of the printing press) vellum Latin vulgate manuscript from the thirteenth century to a 1685 Bible translated into Algonquin, and on to recent publications of the Holy Word in Nyabwa, eBembe, Burrara, Dooyaayo, Naulu, and Kadiweu. There are comic-book Bibles, shorthand Bibles, and bejeweled Bibles with semiprecious stones and brilliantly colored illustrations. One miniature Bible looks like a locket and has an accompanying magnifying glass.

Transcribed by 31,102 people (not all at the same time), the 1949 Chicago Railroad Fair Bible starts with Genesis ("In the beginning") and ends with the Book of Revelations ("Amen"). It took nearly a year and was written in sequence. Another kind of "chain Bible" was attached to the church pew to prevent the pious from filching it. To paraphrase Batman, Holy Scriptures!

Like its holdings, the ABS also has a long and distinguished history. Founded in 1816, it established the library a year later, with George Bush named as its first librarian in 1836. Really: Along with being an ancestor of the former president, this Bush was a Presbyterian minister and prominent Hebrew scholar. Most of the books were donated by individuals, ABS members, and churches.

Linguistically, Bibles go from Abaknon, a Philippine dialect, to Zuni, a Native American language of New Mexico. Obsolete tongues are also included, such as Esperanto, an artificial international language invented in 1887 by a Polish philologist, as are those spoken by only a few dozen people. Still, the collection is far from complete. According to some estimates there are up to six thousand dialects in the world, and the ABS is in the process of translating Bibles into several hundred native languages.

Candid snapshots illustrate Bible distributors who spread the Word with typical American ingenuity. A turn-of-the-century Coney Island stand offered multilingual scriptures starting at two cents for the Gospels and going up to twenty-four cents for a complete Bible. Anna Scott and her Bible bus traveled throughout the Chicago area during the Depression. "Hess the Bible Man" peddled his heavenly wares in Ada, Oklahoma, from his auto shop cum house. "[Distributors] used any means of transportation—buses, trains, boats, even horseback," explained a member of the museum's devoted staff.

Only a rare few are permitted to actually handle the books. "This isn't a lending library," the staff member notes. Bibles are preserved in a climate and humidity controlled area with some even supported by a special book cradle, a sort of Bible belt.

A second-floor gallery features a faithful reproduction of Johannes Gutenberg's printing press. Visitors can also view leaves from an original Gutenberg Bible. Changing exhibits highlight women in Bible work, first edition holy books, and other aspects of ABS history. A reference service provides just about any scriptural information. Where else could you obtain photocopies of Acts 2:1–13 in Latin, Hebrew, Greek, Japanese, and Russian? A bookstore sells periodicals and you-know-whats in dozens of languages, a veritable Babel of Bibles. But there isn't a Bible in Pig Latin—at least not yet.

The American Bible Society Library
1865 Broadway, New York, NY 10023
((212) 408-1204

LOCATION: Corner of 61st Street, two blocks from Lincoln Center
HOURS: Monday–Friday, 9:00 A.M.–4:00 P.M.
ADMISSION: Free

✝ New York City: THE LOWER EAST SIDE TENEMENT MUSEUM

In 1988, historian and museum founder Ruth J. Abram was searching for a building that would re-create a nineteenth-century tenement in New York City. Unfortunately, it seemed that existing housing had either been renovated to conform with city codes or torn
down, so she and her small staff decided to concentrate on telling
the tenement story without an actual example. "We were looking for
office space and saw a FOR RENT sign here," she says, referring to
the museum's location at 97 Orchard Street.

After deeming it acceptable for administrative needs, Abram and
curator Anita Jacobson asked to see the bathroom. "It was then we
realized we'd stumbled upon exactly what we were seeking."
Although the first floor was used for stores, the upstairs had been
shuttered since 1935 "and was an excellent example of a [prehous-
ing-code] tenement." To borrow a Yiddish expression from one of
the ten thousand tenement inhabitants, who hailed from twenty-five
nations, it was *bashert* (destiny).

This is one museum whose time has definitely arrived. Although
farmhouses and log cabins have long been turned into museums
"our site is the first tenement to be preserved in America and listed
in the National Register of Historic Places," observes Abram.
Instead of hostile Indians, wild animals, and isolation, the teeming
masses faced overcrowding, exploitation (most neither spoke nor
understood English), and culture shock. Not only did they have to
adjust from life in simple villages to the city, but they had to adapt to
the many nationalities—Irish, Polish, German, Greek, Italian,
Jewish, Chinese, African, and English—who shared the streets of
their new land.

The founders had just about given up hope of locating a real tenement for their museum when they stumbled on this genuine article. (*Photo by Wangsheng Li. Courtesy of the Lower East Side Tenement Museum.*)

The museum doesn't look like much and isn't supposed to. The six-story, narrow, worn-red-brick building serves as a reminder that most of America's immigrants started with zero, zilch, *nada*. Between 1880 and 1919, over twenty-three *million* Europeans found their way to America. Nearly three-fourths of them ended up in New York City. Constructed between 1863 and 1864 by Lucas Glockner, a German-born tailor, 97 Orchard Street was intended as apartments for twenty-two families with two storefronts in the basement. Each floor featured four three-room apartments with a about 325 square feet of living space and a single window. At the time, tenements were heralded as a terrific innovation for eliminating the housing shortage.

But the immigrants were nothing if not frugal. "As many as eighteen would eat, sleep, make love, have babies, and die in one unit," points out Abram. Along with studying, sewing piecework, or taking in laundry at home, families often accepted boarders to further supplement income.

"The only light came the window facing another line of tenements," she continues. "And the only heat from a coal-burning stove." Forget amenities like private bathrooms, running water, and ventilation. Those didn't come along until 1901, when legislation forced the addition of indoor sinks, hallway toilets, and interior windows that encouraged circulation, but decreased privacy because now you could see the neighbors in the hall, too.

A closer look reveals a certain beauty in the disrepair, however. The unrenovated apartments have twelve to eighteen layers of carefully chosen paint and linoleum; a marriage contract and photograph of a long-deceased child can also be found. There's a slate sink used by a Chinese laundry as well as a sign on the wall PANTS MADE TO ORDER: $1.50. A display of pictures on the first floor reflects dignity amid the squalor: Fine lace shawls dry above a rubble-filled lot; shined shoes stand next to a can of kerosene that was used to ward off bugs.

The first floor has rotating exhibits, snapshots of tenement existence in the 1930s, as well as a two-sided "urban log cabin" dollhouse portraying 97 Orchard Street in 1870 (water drawn from a common courtyard spigot and hauled upstairs, toilets outside) and in 1915 (indoor plumbing, air shafts). One recently refurbished apartment illustrates the life of a German Jewish single mother in the 1880s who moonlighted as a seamstress, while another depicts living space during the Depression. *Bobbeh* and *Zaideh* (Grandma and Grandpa) would have *kvelled* (smiled radiantly) at their history and humble beginnings so lovingly displayed.

The Lower East Side Tenement Museum
97 Orchard Street, New York, NY 10002
((212) 431-0233

LOCATION: On New York's Lower East Side
HOURS: Tuesday–Friday, 11:00 A.M.–4:00 P.M.; Sunday, 10:00 A.M.–4:00 P.M.
ADMISSION: A donation is suggested

Pennsylvania

♦ Douglassville: THE MARY MERRITT DOLL MUSEUM

It's a true valley of the dolls: French fashion plates model the latest Paris styles from 1850 to 1880. A naked (legs demurely crossed) ivory Ming-dynasty-era doctor's doll is used by a modest Chinese female to show her physician where it hurts. A salesperson's sample kit contains a fully dressed doll, with its Select-a-Head options of blonde, brunette, and straight-haired baby noggins. The flip of a single long skirt transforms a pig's visage on a Pennsylvania Dutch rag doll to that of a human. These represent only a microscopic portion of the five thousand dolls purchased by Mary Merritt in her over forty years of collecting.

About half of these are on display at the Mary Merritt Doll Museum in Douglassville, Pennsylvania. Ranging from a seventh-century bone doll found in an Egyptian pyramid to modern versions, dolls are matched with their corresponding time periods against backgrounds of lace, fans, framed watercolors, doll furniture, and over forty fully decorated miniature rooms and dollhouses.

Okay, so it's not the Museum of the Fur Trade (see Nebraska), but even the macho might find it worth a gander. A re-created Philadelphia toy shop with all manner of 18th and 19th century play-things offers mechanical dolls that smoke, cycle, and perform a myriad of movements to music. There are lead soldiers, Noah's arks, circus and safari sets, hobby horses, and transportation toys. Although an exhibit with the first Barbie and GI Joe, a set of the Dionne quints, and others is targeted to the contemporary minded, fans of Barbie, Ken, Midge, et al., are better directed to the Barbie Hall of Fame in Palo Alto (see California).

Dolls run the gamut from sumptuous French wax mini-mannequins in detailed period costumes to a humble corn-husk peddler with a breadcrumb face. They cook, receive visitors, and recline gracefully in Victorian era houses with gables, mansard roofs, and bay windows; party in an ornate eighteenth-century ballroom with paneled walls and gilt and painted furniture; and tend livestock in a homemade Pennsylvania barn with hex signs. The museum has complete sets of fine china upon which they can take leisurely meals. Seems the dolls have it better than the humans after whom they were patterned.

The first dolls were mostly simple, stiff creations made of wood, wax, and other available materials. The rare Queen Anne models of

the early eighteenth century "were among the first European dolls to wear ornate costumes and have wigs of human hair and expressive faces," points out Marjorie Merritt Darrah, Mary Merritt's daughter, who took over the museum when her mother retired. Other early dolls include milliners' models used in lieu of fashion magazines and peddler dolls with up to 125 kinds of fruits, vegetables, and notions in their satchels.

The Victorian era produced a veritable explosion of dolls. Greiner dolls with blown glass eyes; lifelike wax dolls, descriptively called "pumpkin heads;" bonnet dolls, where the hat or headpiece was permanently molded to the head; and china

The Germans developed jointed dolls with lifelike faces and eyes and mouths that opened and closed. (*Photo courtesy of the Mary Merritt Doll Museum.*)

dolls made to look like celebrities of the day such as performer Jenny Lind and Empress Eugenie were the rage. Bisque dolls were also sought after, particularly those made by a Frenchman, M. Jumeau. Only a few of the largest Jumeaus, thirty-six-inchers, were ever made because it was cumbersome for little girls. The museum's most valuable doll, also of French manufacture, is valued in the $20,000 range.

It was American ingenuity that took "dolldum" a giant step forward—literally. "In 1873, Joel Ellis from Springfield, Vermont, patented a wooden doll with moveable joints," explains Darrah. Clothes could be changed more easily and the doll could "participate" in any number of activities. A few years later, the Germans developed jointed dolls with lifelike faces replete with eyes and mouths that opened and closed. By the turn of the century Albert Schoenhut, a German immigrant, had created a totally flexible doll that could assume any position.

The museum's lobby does a brisk business in buying and selling antique and collectible dolls, clothing, and accessories, as well as stuffed animals and other toys. Dull? Hardly.

The Mary Merritt Doll Museum
R.D. 2, Douglassville, PA 19518
((215) 385-3809

LOCATION: **Between Reading and Pottstown on Route 422**
HOURS: **Monday–Saturday, 10:00 A.M.–5:00 P.M.; Sunday 1:00–5:00 P.M.;**
   closed holidays
ADMISSION: **Admission is charged**

✦ Easton: THE CRAYOLA HALL OF FAME

In June of 1990, Binney & Smith, the makers of Crayola crayons, announced the retirement of eight colors: maize, raw umber, blue gray, yellow orange, violet blue, orange red, lemon yellow, and green blue. They were to be replaced by the upstarts cerulean (a twenty-dollar term for sky blue), vivid tangerine, fuchsia (purplish-red), dandelion, teal blue, royal purple, and wild strawberry.

"The change resulted from interviews conducted with children," explains company representative Mark O'Brien. "They expressed the need for brighter, bolder shades, so we took a close look at our existing palette and, after careful study, determined that certain colors were outdated and dull."

Eight favorite colors were inducted into the Crayola Hall of Fame. (*Photo courtesy of Binney & Smith.*)

Adults regarded this as a national insult tantamount to the reformulation of Coca-Cola, and the resulting cry over the hues was enormous. Protest groups such as RUMPS (Raw Umber and Maize Preservation Society) and CRAYON (Committee to Reestablish All Your Old Norms) (really) quickly formed, bombarding the company with letters and phone calls.

Their efforts helped establish the Crayola Hall of Fame at Binney & Smith headquarters in Easton, Pennsylvania, in 1990, along with the temporary reinstatement of the eight discarded colors a year later. A giant five-foot replica of each crayon is encased behind glass: Push a button and you'll hear adults and children talk about the color. Of lemon yellow, Binney & Smith president Richard Gurin remarks, "We prefer to have one less lemon in our lineup." Fred Rogers of *Mr. Roger's Neighborhood* fame admits to being color blind at the orange-red display, and newscaster Charlie Gibson of ABC-TV laments the passing of blue gray. "How can you do Confederate soldier pictures and Civil War pictures without it?" Kids such as six-year-old Ebony will miss raw umber because "Whenever I drew me, I used [it]" and an adult named Roger (age forty-two) regards maize "as American as mom and Chevrolet . . . apple pie came later."

Plaques describe the evolution of each color, when it was introduced, its primary uses, and similar shades. Visitors can also view a
timeline which, through sample products and photos, traces the
company's colorful history. Binney & Smith began operation in 1864.
"We originally manufactured items in the black and red range, such
as lamp black, charcoal, and a paint with red iron oxide used to coat
barns," states O'Brien.

Around the turn of the century, the company ventured into the
children's art field when they developed a wax crayon. "Although
researchers believed pigments and mixing techniques could be
adapted to a variety of colors, they needed to create synthetic, non-
toxic crayons that could be at times chewed or even digested." More
than one four-year-old has munched on a particularly appetizing-
looking tint.

In 1903, the first box of eight rolled off the assembly line. It cost a
nickel. Today, over two billion crayons are produced annually in a
total of seventy-two colors with eight fluorescent hues. Binney &
Smith also manufactures markers, Silly Putty, clay, and paints in
addition to art kits for budding Rembrandts and Picassos.

A small display also honors Silly Putty, to which Binney & Smith
acquired the rights in 1977. Invented during World War II by accident (researchers were looking for a rubber substitute), this poly-
merized compound bounced into the adult toy market through the
efforts of consultant Peter Hodgson, who molded it into a multimillion dollar egg for all ages.

Along with being sold internationally, Silly Putty has gone to the
moon on Apollo 8, has laid limited-edition eggs in the Neiman-Marcus
catalog for $75 each, and is still being manipulated by baseball, foot-
ball, and tennis players to strengthen their grips. Although Silly Putty
relieves stress, plugs leaks, and levels furniture, it is no longer capable
of lifting images from newspapers that now use cold printing processes
or reformulated inks. Copyright law, 1; big and little kids, 0.

The Crayola Hall of Fame is part of a tour of Binney & Smith's
manufacturing and packaging processes. Participants are given a free
box of crayons at the end of the visit. They are also invited to do a
coloring activity. Not to worry: The folks at Binney & Smith won't
take off points if you stray outside the lines.

The Crayola Hall of Fame, Binney & Smith
1100 Church Lane, P.O. Box 431, Easton, PA 18044
((215) 559-2632

LOCATION: Off I-78, 19 miles west of Allentown
HOURS: Call Monday–Thursday, 10:00 a.m.–2:00 p.m. to schedule tours
ADMISSION: Free

♦ Johnstown: THE JOHNSTOWN FLOOD MUSEUM

What a disaster: A twenty-million-ton ball of water unleashed itself
on the unsuspecting population of Johnstown, Pennsylvania, at 3:10
on the afternoon of May 31, 1889. Two thousand two hundred and
nine people died, tens of thousands were left homeless, and the
flood and its aftermath of fires totally laid waste to a prosperous iron
and steel industrial town. Eight inches of rain in two days precipitated the bursting of an earthen dam at the nearby South Fork
Fishing and Hunting Club, a playground for Pittsburgh's nineteenth-
century elite (Andrew Carnegie, Andrew Mellon, Henry Clay Frick),
and caused one of the biggest scandals of the century.

But if every cloud has a silver lining, Johnstown's may be its Flood
Museum and the attendant tourist attractions that have sprung up
like flowers after a downpour. These include the flood-related
Johnstown National Memorial, overlooking the ruins of the
Southfork Dam; and Grandview Cemetery, which honors unknown
victims with 777 tombstones.

Despite the fact that the flood occurred over one hundred years
ago, a gee-whiz attitude prevails throughout the museum. "People
are still fascinated by the events," the museum's enthusiastic director, Richard Burkert reports. "It has all the elements of a great
drama—a man-made disaster coupled with the forces of nature."
According to Burkert, what happened was basically this: The old
canal reservoir, built several years prior, "was abandoned in the late
1840s and the infrastructure rotted away." Although it was reputed
to be the largest man-made reservoir at that time, when the South
Fork Fishing and Hunting Club purchased it in 1879, they made

Johnstown before and after the flood. (*Photo courtesy of the Johnstown Area Heritage Association.*)

shoddy repairs and didn't even use an engineer. "It was an accident waiting to happen." While the rich enjoyed their private resort with its hunting, sailing, three-story clubhouse, and private cottages, the public wondered what would happen if the *dam* thing burst.

Although the flood resulted in $17 million worth of damage, Johnstown was hardly washed up. "There was an incredible outpouring of assistance," relates Burkert. "The tragedy drew worldwide attention, attracting journalists and relief workers from all over the world."

And, of course, someone had to be blamed. There were dozens of lawsuits. "After a lot of finger-pointing, it was believed the South Fork Fishing and Hunting Club was responsible, and, hence, the wealthy. The flood gives insight into the antielitist mentality of nineteenth-century industrial society." In the end, however, the courts determined it to be an act of God and the lawsuits were dismissed. If all else fails, blame it on the Big Guy upstairs.

Along with traditional exhibits, the museum has an entire sixty-five-foot wide by seventeen-foot tall wall of wooden "wreckage," pieces of locomotives, and other flotsam and jetsam. "People enjoy guessing what the various household items were," says Burkert. The wall serves as a backdrop for a light and sound animated fiber-optics map that re-creates the path of the flood. Along with a description of what happened in each section of the city, it highlights stories of individual heroics, such as a locomotive engineer who tied a whistle to his train to warn those in the eastern valley of the oncoming onslaught.

Several movie choices are offered as well. In addition to an Academy Award–winning documentary about the flood, a short video gives an interesting mini-physics lesson in cause and effect, while another intersperses clips from a 1926 Hollywood production about the event with a Mighty Mouse cartoon in which the resilient rodent rescues the residents of Johnstown.

But perhaps the most telling things on exhibit are the personal mementos, such as six-year-old Mary Waters's dress. "She and her sister disappeared under the water and her father, knowing he could only save one child, grabbed for the feet," explains Burkert. Miraculously, he caught both children and pulled them out. A white pitcher, the only intact thing from a completely demolished residence, and a bell used by one man to locate people trapped in the wreckage are but a few of the many articles on display.

The Johnstown flood may seem a mere trickle compared to today's hurricanes, earthquakes, oil spills, and nuclear disasters, but for nineteenth-century calamities, it can't be beat.

The Johnstown Flood Museum
304 Washington Street, Johnstown, PA 15901
((814) 539-1889

LOCATION: Off U.S. 219, 43 miles west of Altoona
HOURS: Hours vary depending on the season
ADMISSION: Admission is charged

✦ Lititz: THE CANDY AMERICANA MUSEUM

You might have thought the *I Love Lucy* episode at the chocolate factory was the absolute last word on candy making in America, but if you follow the rich, smooth aroma down Route 501 to Lititz, Pennsylvania, you'll find something more: the Candy Americana Museum, a delectable piece of the Wilbur Chocolate Company. Founded in Philadelphia in 1884, the company moved to Lititz in the thirties, filling the air and people's stomachs with confections ever since.

Penny Buzzard, now-retired, and the wife of the former candy company president, began setting up the museum in 1970. She scoured the antique-laden countryside for candy memorabilia, locat-

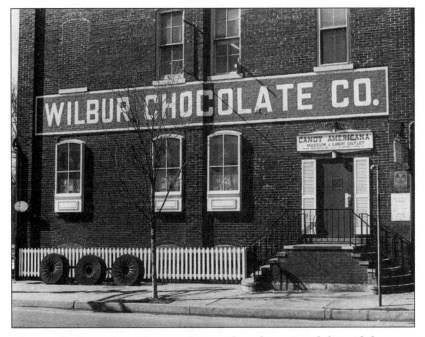

The Candy Americana Museum, home of candy memorabilia and the
Wilbur Chocolate Company, and destroyer of diets. (*Photo courtesy of the
museum.*)

ing such items as a sweets horoscope telling what candies people
prefer based on their birthdays. Like waistlines, the museum has
expanded ever since.

Dietary considerations aside, the Candy Americana Museum provides unique insight into the mystique of concocting chocolate. A
life-size re-creation of a circa-1900 kitchen features a cheerful candy
maker perpetually stirring something in a shiny kettle. His work area
includes a brass blender, dipping table, stove, molds, and other tools.
You can also see live workers in a modern see-through kitchen whip
up the day's batch of goodies.

Miniature candy-making machinery takes up another room. These
include silos where beans are stored, a roaster, a "cracker-fanner"
that separates beans from their shell, and a grinder, as well as other
equipment. A press of a nearby button elicits the history and use of
each item, and a seven-minute video tells how chocolate is transformed from the raw bean to the finished product.

The collections of antique novelty candy containers; cocoa tins; and animal, holiday, and large commercial chocolate molds add flavor to the past. Many of the containers, five hundred wooden and metal vessels, date from the early 1900s and still have the original candy in them. Although this contributes greatly to their value, don't ask to try a piece, since "they are really quite stale," according to Sylvia Roberts, the current manager. Along with long-forgotten names like Iona, Basco, Waverly, Sunrise, and Lignette, colorful cocoa tins attest to the longevity of Hershey, Baker, and, of course, Wilbur.

But the icing on this museum's cake can be found in the accumulation of about two hundred fine porcelain chocolate pots. Dating from the late 1700s, many are hand-painted with floral designs or tipped with gold and come from all over the world, bearing such monikers as Haviland, Limoges, Nippon, and Dresden. Hot chocolate "was served the way tea and coffee are today, with chocolate shops in many European countries," explains Roberts. Nearly all the pots have a small hole in the lid for the insertion of a stirrer, "so the drink will be smooth and well mixed." A few have accompanying cups and saucers, although matched sets didn't become common until later years, when coffee and tea became popular.

Because the working candy factory is upstairs, due to federal regulations, tours are not permitted there. But after visiting the museum, most visitors have had their fill, both educationally and gastronomically. And you can always stop by the neighboring apparel outlet stores, perhaps in anticipation of a larger clothing size.

The Candy Americana Museum
46 N. Broad Street, Lititz, PA 17543
((717) 626-0967

LOCATION: South of I-76 on Route 501.
HOURS: Monday–Saturday, 10:00 A.M.–5:00 P.M.
ADMISSION: Free

♠ Philadelphia: THE CENTER FOR THE HISTORY OF FOOT CARE AND FOOT WEAR

It's a step in the right direction: Go from Arch Street to Race Street (really), up to the sixth floor of the Pennsylvania College of Podiatric Medicine in Philadelphia and you'll stumble upon its footwear collection, the Center for the History of Foot Care and Foot Wear. It contains much more than a footnote: about seven hundred pairs or single shoes dating back to Egyptian burial sandals circa 2000 B.C., although most are from the mid-nineteenth to twentieth century.

The 250 pairs of shoes on display in fifteen showcases range from army jungle boots to celebrity footwear to roller skates to pre-Cousteau iron diving numbers. There are bridal shoes, children's shoes, Earth shoes, Chinese cloth shoes for bound feet, and practical clogs. Eat your heart out, Imelda Marcos (alas, the museum has none of hers).

Rather than being light on its feet, this museum has a leg up on educating the public, with every exhibit thoroughly researched. Faculty members, other muse-

This 6 ½-inch heel made walking a challenge during the Victorian era. (*Courtesy of the Center for the History of Foot Care and Foot Wear.*)

ums, famous people, shoe retailers, and podiatrists bared their soles to contribute to the collection, which opened in 1976.

"We want to raise consciousness about the care of the foot," states manager Barbara Williams. "Poor choices in footwear can adversely affect the entire body." She notes that the Chinese "lotus foot" "was supposed to be erotic. The ideal size of the 'golden lotus' was three inches, with the four-inch 'silver lotus' being less desirable." Through bandages and manipulation, the foot was forced into an abnormally high arch by "middle-class mothers ambitious for their daughters' successful marriage." Try folding your foot to one third its

Entertainer's footwear: Grizzabella's from "Cats," Lucille Ball's, and Ringo Starr's. (*Courtesy of the Center for the History of Foot Care and Foot Wear.*)

normal size and you get the idea. In contrast, a "really big shoe" (not Ed Sullivan's) from a victim of gigantism is also shown.

Toe tappers receive a gentle kick, too. Since the last century, "ballerinas [have] used toe shoes to achieve an illusion of lightness," she goes on. "But [the shoes] do untold harm to the foot, and repeated abuse can result in bleeding." Dancer Judith Jamison avoided them; casts of her undamaged feet are contrasted with a photo of Martha Graham's deformed tootsies.

The man and, particularly, the woman on the street also fell prey to podiatric excesses. The center has examples of the absurdly high "walking maypoles" worn in Renaissance Venice to keep ladies' feet off the unpaved ground; six-and-a-half-inch stiletto heels from the 1890s that refuse to sand up by themselves, although they show signs of heavy wear; and glittering gold "platform shoes" from the disco era, which have just become popular again.

Many visitors hop right over to the racks of notables' shoes: among them, Ringo Starr's black-starred white bucks, Sandy Duncan's green suede Peter Pan peds, Grizzabella's "paws" from *Cats*, Billie Jean King's signed Adidas sneakers, Bernie Parent's skates, and Lucille Ball's $1000 red pumps. Nancy Reagan's gaudy rhinestone heels share space with husband Ron's spit-polished black classics. First ladies Mamie Eisenhower, Betty Ford, and Lady Bird Johnson put their best shoes forward too, as did sports stars Kareem Abdul Jabbar, Mike Schmidt, Jim Ryun, and Steve Ballesteros.

The feet-and-footwear-in-art exhibits are a little more pedestrian. An exploration of the Cinderella/glass slipper phenomenon reveals over five hundred adaptations of the tale. "Foot in mouth" artwork, such as the six toes on William Blake's subject in *Humanity* and cartoons and written works can also be found.

Lasts (but not least) reveal that the earliest shoe shapers were made first of stone and then hardwood. Although they were manufactured by machine as early as 1820, "right and left feet were not differentiated until the Civil War," observes Williams. By the 1850s, however, equipment created standard half-sizes and widths, and by World War II millions of lasts were produced each year. Nowadays, with frequent changes in styles, lasts just don't.

Although the Center for Foot Care and Foot Wear is as comfortable as an old guess-what, walk-ins are discouraged. So if you plan on visiting, please write or call first.

The Center for the History of Food Care and Foot Wear
Pennsylvania College of Podiatric Medicine
8th and Race Streets, Philadelphia, PA 19107
((215) 629-0300

LOCATION: **Downtown**
HOURS: **By appointment only; Monday–Friday, 9:00** A.M.**–4:00** P.M.
ADMISSION: **Free**

♠ Philadelphia: THE MUTTER MUSEUM

A word of advice: Don't go into Philadelphia's Mutter Museum expecting to see fancy costumes, parade memorabilia, and hear various renditions of "Oh! Dem Golden Slippers." That's the *Mummers* Museum, and it's several blocks away. Originally intended as a medical teaching museum at the College of Physicians of Philadelphia, this Mutter is chock full of antique medical instruments; rare anatomical and pathological specimens and anomalies; and assorted other medical curiosities.

Inside the dignified, high-ceilinged galleries you'll find a major attraction, a plaster cast of the nineteenth-century Siamese twins

Chang and Eng accompanied by their attached livers. "After the autopsy, it was found they were joined only by skin and cartilage and shared no common organ," states museum director Gretchen Worden. "Today, [the twins] could have been easily separated."

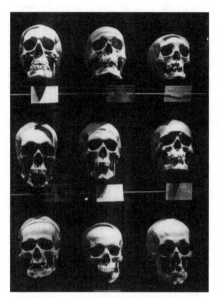

Try to pick out Yorick in this lineup; it's the Hyrtl Skull Collection.
(Photo by G. Loie Grossman. Courtesy of the Mutter Museum.)

The Soap Lady and Mega- ("as opposed to semi") Colon are also crowd pleasers. The Soap Lady is a preserved corpse who looks as though she were auditioning for a musical version of *The Night of the Living Dead*. The soft tissue of her body decomposed after burial into a fatty wax known as adipocere, which is similar in composition to lye soap. There have been some questions about the exact cause and year of her death: "But we do know she was very overweight because of the amount of soft tissues that were preserved," notes Worden.

In life, known under the stage names of Wind Bag or Balloon Man, the owner of Mega-Colon had a rare anatomical disorder that caused severe constipation and an enlargement of the colon, making this skinny guy look several months pregnant. Not surprisingly, he died trying at age twenty-nine with a backlog of forty pounds of fecal matter. An eight-foot-four-inch section of his colon is preserved in the museum and bears more than a passing resemblance to the sand worms in the film *Dune*. "What he needed was a simple resection of the colon," points out Worden. "But in 1892 they didn't do abdominal surgery."

By now, most visitors have surmised the Mutter is more than a cheap way to get grossed out. "A lot of what we have is a testimony to the progress of technology," Worden explains. "Not only do we want to enlighten the public about medicine and illness and help teach those in the profession, but we assist researchers."

And yes, this museum has the body parts of famous people, a sort of anatomical Hall of Fame. Along with a tumor from Grover Cleveland's jaw, there are bladder stones removed from Supreme Court Justice John Marshall in 1831, as well as a piece of John Wilkes Booth's thorax.

Physicians are recognized here by their innovations: Florence Nightingale's sewing kit, Marie Curie's electrometer, a full scale model of the first successful heart-lung machine designed by Dr. John Gibbon in 1953.

The anomalies of ordinary folks are found here, too: among them a six-inch horn that projected from a woman's forehead and a rib cage that was compressed by a too tightly laced corset. James Cardinal, a hydrocephalic who died in 1825, had a skull that held five quarts of water. "Many people think he looks like Napoleon Solo, the man from U.N.C.L.E.," Worden remarks. A skeleton of a three-foot-six-inch dwarf and her stillborn child stand next to a seven-foot-six-inch Kentucky giant. "He was purchased in 1877 for $50 with no questions asked." (Of course, by then he was dead.)

A cavalcade of latex eyeballs clarifies various optical diseases. Along with a grouping of deformed fetuses used for the study of birth defects, a gang of 139 skulls (known in the museum as the Hyrtl, not Yorick, Collection) proves that under the skin, we're basically all alike. "By collecting specimens from Central and Eastern Europe, Austrian anatomist Joseph Hyrtl tried to illustrate physical variations among ethnic groups," explains Worden. Although there are some differences, "you can't point to a skull and say that's a Serb or a Croat."

The Chevalier Jackson Collection of swallowed objects also goes down easy. The father of broncoesophagology, Jackson accumulated over three thousand objects in three decades. Along with instruments he helped design to retrieve them, an amazing variety of ingested seeds, nuts, shells, buttons, bones, ammunition, toys, and needles join a rosary, perfect-attendance button, radio knob, and toy opera glasses in this dubious honor.

These examples only scratch the surface (so to speak) of what's in the museum. "You can't prepare someone for what it's actually like," Worden observes. "Each person finds his or her own fascination."

The museum has become such a draw (seven thousand visitors annually) that it publishes its own calendar. It is also the site of local gatherings and is available (really) for weddings and bar mitzvahs. A great idea for party planners who want to save on food bills.

The Mutter Museum
19 South 22nd Street, Philadelphia, PA 19103
((215) 563-3737

LOCATION: At the College of Physicians
HOURS: Tuesday–Friday, 10:00 A.M.–4:00 P.M.; closed federal holidays; group tours by appointment
ADMISSION: Free, but donations are welcome

♠ Strasburg: THE TOY TRAIN MUSEUM

Before most visitors set foot in the Toy Train Museum in Strasburg, Pennsylvania, they'll know they're in a railroad Valhalla. Strasburg also has the Railroad Museum of Pennsylvania, one of the most comprehensive agglomerations of full-size locomotives and "rail-roadiana" in the United States; the Strasburg Rail Road, a steam engine joy ride; and Choo Choo Barn Traintown USA for the kiddies.

Next to the Toy Train Museum is the Red Caboose Restaurant and Motel (717/687–6646) where guests sleep in real cabooses and can take meals in a dining car that moves back and forth and has (but of course) railroad-related songs piped in. By this time, the thoroughly indoctrinated will feel compelled to stop at the Strasburg Train Shop (717/687–0464) and pick up several hundred dollars' worth of model locomotives, scenery, and buildings so they can take the experience home. The shop also accepts mail orders. Talk about being railroaded . . . .

Actually, the ten-thousand-square-foot Toy Train Museum came about because a group of enthusiasts formed the Train Collectors Association (TCA) in the fifties and decided to build a museum in 1977. Floor toys, electric trains, and related accessories track progress from the mid-1800s to the present. "The first trains were hand-powered—the child pushed them," says Anthony D'Alessandro, executive director of the museum. Toys such as record players and telescopes produced by model train manufacturers are on view as well.

Several types of gauges (trains) are represented and exhibit painstaking detail. (*Photo courtesy of the Toy Train Museum.*)

Among many others, there are models by the manufacturers Ives, Marx, Marklin, Gilbert, the better-known American Flyer, and Lionel, today's biggest player. Five operating layouts highlight the development of model trains. With tinplate trains, a roundhouse, and twenties and thirties period structures, the *standard gauge* illustrates the earlier models. The smaller *O gauge* presents the next generation of trains from the forties through the present. "This three-track train is more of a toy," explains D'Alessandro, pointing to the *O gauge*. "It has a lot more accessories," such as industries, a lake with boats, road crews, and a lift overpass that actually works with gongs, bells, and lights. "Many of the landmarks, such as bridges, actually do exist."

Those looking for realism will find it with the *S gauge*. Consisting of American Flyers, this two-track model re-creates a city in the boom years after World War II. "Along with being smaller than earlier versions, the trains are much closer to scale," D'Alessandro adds. With bark chips, mulch, weather-resistant buildings, and embankments, it's obvious the larger *G gauge* is meant for outdoor use. "At night and during inclement seasons [hobbyists] often have the trains run directly into their cellars," making them a "whistle stop" away.

The *choo-choo de resistance* is the recently acquired *HO gauge*. Professionally constructed from a series of articles in *Model Railroad Craftsman*, it depicts the contemporary Lowville and Beaver River Railroad in Lewis County, New York, and includes a town, quarry, dam, and lake. At one point the train disappears into a building only to reemerge in a completely different area. "In addition to being the smallest of our working gauges, the HO is often the most accurate," states D'Alessandro.

Other uncommon trains and accessories abound. A "girl's" set made in the mid-fifties with a pink engine, yellow boxcars, and blue caboose was repainted black by most store owners because it didn't sell. The museum has one of the few in its original colors. A rare train-powered Ferris wheel (Marklin "Wonder Wheels") is also shown. There are also early model stations with separate entrances for blacks and whites, as well as for men and women.

Along with an extensive library and a continuous show of train-related cartoons and comedy films, the museum has a gift shop that offers crystal train sets, railroad memorabilia, and miniatures made of clay, brass, and other materials. Although this museum guarantees it will make you feel like a kid again, it may derail the pocketbook.

The Toy Train Museum
P.O. Box 248
Paradise Lane, Strasburg, PA 17579
((717) 687-8623

LOCATION: Just outside of Lancaster on U.S. 222
HOURS: Hours vary according to the season
ADMISSION: Admission is charged

✦ Williamsport: THE PETER J. MCGOVERN LITTLE LEAGUE MUSEUM

This is the only museum in the world dedicated to a child's game, according to director Cindy Stearns. Located only minutes away from the birthplace of Little League baseball, the Peter J. McGovern Little League Museum of Williamsport, Pennsylvania sits adjacent to Howard J. Lamade Field, the site of the Little League

Baseball World Series Stadium. It scores big with those who play ball.

Since its inception in 1939, Little League has developed from a simple backyard pastime into the world's largest youth sports program, with more than 2.5 million children and 750,000 adult volunteers in nearly forty countries. Talk about a big league record.

This hands-on museum encourages you to touch exhibits, swing bats, and throw balls. Upon entering the colonial-style building, you are immediately immersed in a 15-foot-high by 110-foot-long photographic mural shot from the pitcher's mound. While you're gaping at the thousands of people in the stands, the realization dawns that you're in the middle of a Little League World Series championship playoff. Flags from countries having Little Leagues dangle overhead and there's a scoreboard in left field. A life-size catcher and umpire behind home plate serve as reminders that the fans are waiting for *you* to toss that first ball.

Perhaps it's time to move on to the many displays charting the history and rules of the Little League. A fiberoptic map tells the story via a chronological light show. Hats, bats, caps, balls, and other memorabilia also trace its development. Documentary movies talk about how Little League has helped children, offering tips on batting, pitching, running, catching, and coaching as well. A Play It Safe Room offers educational exhibits on safety equipment, recycling, nutrition, and the dangers of illegal drugs, alcohol, and tobacco.

Camaraderie and sportsmanship among boys of all ages and walks of life are promoted at the Little League Museum. (*Photo by Vannucci Foto-Services. Courtesy of the museum.*)

Then you're tested in the Basic Room via a question-and-answer panel. (Those who "flunk" may feel compelled to start the tour all over again.) Self-activated videos, an oversized coach's manual, and exhibits illustrating the different stages of equipment production further emphasize the fundamentals.

Now it's time to exercise the body—a little. With four batting and pitching safety cages, the Play Ball! area allows visitors ninety seconds to evaluate their skills. Each participant views a video of his or her performance. "This is very helpful in pinpointing mistakes," notes Stearns. The camera also adds ten pounds.

The Showcase Room features major leaguer's memorabilia from their Little League days. Mike Schmidt's and Tom Seaver's baseball caps share space with Steve Stone's uniform, as well as a complete outfit from Gary Carter, who, according to Stearns "was sort of a pack rat."

And the Hall of Excellence honors past and present Little Leaguers, an eclectic mix of role models who have gone on to bigger things: the aforementioned Mike Schmidt and Tom Seaver, as well as Nolan Ryan; major league hunk and actor Tom Selleck; NBA veteran and U.S. Senator Bill Bradley; former Vice-President Dan Quayle; and the most recent inductees, columnist George Will and legendary NBA center Kareem Abdul Jabbar. A Gallery of Achievement showcases leadership from within.

Special issue World Series caps given to local district administrators range from some with simple logos and the year of play to an elaborate depiction of Lamade Stadium commemorating the recent addition of lights for nighttime games. Also on display are Little League World Series uniforms and actual footage of the events.

Non-Little League fans might actually be enthusiastic about baseball by the time they've reached the home stretch. Or, they might strike out and not even get to first base.

The Peter J. McGovern Little League Museum
P.O. Box 3485, Williamsport, PA 17701
((717) 326-3607

LOCATION: On Route 15 in South Williamsport, about 15 miles north of I-80
HOURS: Hours vary
ADMISSION: Admission is charged

Vermont

♠ Shelburne: THE SHELBURNE MUSEUM

Some people collect stamps. Electra Havemeyer Webb accumulated buildings. And cigar-store figures. And weather vanes. And hats and hat boxes. And straightedge razors (no, she wasn't suicidal). And railroad cars, toys, and lanterns. And quilts, fine art, and furniture. And tools for farming, weaving, and printing. Even a huge steamboat (the S.S. *Ticonderoga*), a lighthouse, and a covered bridge. In fact, just about anything that's related to Americana has found its way into the Shelburne Museum—over eighty thousand items in a massive complex of thirty-seven buildings on forty-five acres, near Lake Champlain in Shelburne, Vermont.

Dubbed the Vermont Smithsonian, it's the mother of all eclectic museums. Anyone with an urge to visit at least some of the exhibits mentioned in this book can probably save time and money by perusing the Shelburne's assortments. And these are serious hoards, not just dribs and drabs, for Electra Webb, along with being the daughter of wealthy "sugar king" Henry Osborne Havemeyer and the wife of Vanderbilt descendent James Watson Webb, came from a line of pack rats. She made her first acquisition in 1907 at age eighteen, bringing home a $15 cigar-store Indian and never stopped until her death.

The price of admission covers two consecutive days, because "it's virtually impossible to see everything in just a few hours," remarks Eloise Beil of the museum. Along with truly necessary maps, the museum provides a helpful thematic tour guide (folk art, childhood, tools and trades, etc.).

Most tours begin at the McClure Center, a circa 1901 three-story

The land-locked
Ticonderoga is the last
remaining vertical
beam side wheel ship
in America. (*Photo
courtesy of the Shelburne
Museum.*)

round barn, one of the few left in America. An eight-minute intro-
ductory slide show is a must for those who don't want to experience
sensory overload once they start roaming the grounds. From there,
you'll spot the Herschell carousel and a horseshoe-shaped circus
building. Inside the latter is a 525-foot-long model circus parade as
well as a 3500-piece Kirk Brothers toy circus. A complete collection
of old time circus posters and carousel figures rounds out the "show."

Next stop: the 1890 Victorian railroad station. Once the destination of wealthy families summering in Shelburne, the station now
hosts a sumptuous private rail car presented to the governor of
Vermont by Electra's father-in-law. The Central Vermont Railway's
last ten-wheeler steam locomotive can also be found here.

Although transporting various buildings and bridges was a challenge, the S.S. *Ticonderoga* presented a true test of *ingenious
Americanus*. Floated out of the lake into a specially dug, water-filled
basin, it was moved onto a railroad carriage, then towed over cus-
tom-built tracks through frozen swamps, meadows, and around the
schedules of operating trains. Hop aboard: Inside you'll find
Edwardian furnishings as well as a movie with the story of the boat.
An 1871 Colchester lighthouse overlooks the *Ticonderoga*, offering a
safe harbor in the rather unlikely event of a flood. Come to think of
it, the Shelburne *is* a sort of Noah's Ark.

Often the outside of buildings gives little clue as to what's within.
The Stagecoach Inn houses homemade and commercial weather

vanes, Pennsylvania Dutch folk art, ship carvings, trade signs, cigar-store figures, and a variety of sculptures. A New England one-room schoolhouse, general store, apothecary, jail, and doctor's offices are found in other structures; while still more hold costumes, Conestoga wagons, hooked rugs, stencils, saws, and toys.

But the Electra Havemeyer Webb Memorial Building is the corker. Constructed in 1967 by the family in memory of Electra and her husband, it contains not only her collection of twentieth-century paintings and sculpture, but also a re-creation of their luxurious Fifth Avenue apartment. "Most people don't expect to see French Impressionists in a home setting," notes Beil. "But that's the way they were meant to be shown."

"People are always surprised by us, no matter how many museums they've been to," she goes on. "This is an Alice in Wonderland sort of place." There goes the white rabbit into the hat and fragrance building . . . .

The Shelburne Museum
P.O. Box 10, U.S. Route 7, Shelburne, VT 05482
((802) 985-3344 FOR TAPED INFORMATION OR (802) 985-3346

LOCATION: Route 7, Shelburne (you can't miss it)
HOURS: Hours vary
ADMISSION: Admission is charged

THE
SOUTH

Arkansas

⬆ Eureka Springs: THE FROG FANTASIES MUSEUM

It's to croak for: over six thousand frogs of every description, made of every conceivable material. There are clay-pipe frogs that were found in an Oklahoma Indian burial mound; frog tobacco jars from the 1800s; frogs made from Italian crystal and Australian black jade; German beer steins swarming with frogs; and a forty-pound frog made from steel wire, pop tops, hangers, and nails. Oriental frogs abound: three-legged toads from Chinese pagodas, ivory carved frogs, frogs manufactured in occupied Japan. There's a cluster of Kermits, a mass of Mexican dancers (with sombreros and blankets), a gaggle of gorgeous and gaudy frog rings, pins, necklaces, and bracelets. Frogs even hatch out of a giant egg. And to think that the Frog Fantasies Museum in Eureka Springs, Arkansas, began because over half a century ago, Louise Mesa put some money in a gumball machine and out came a you-know-what.

MUSEUM • GIFT SHOP
Famous Collection of over 5000

(Photo courtesy of the Frog Fantasies Museum.)

"My mother already had a frog hanging over the family fishbowl and suddenly there were frogs in the china cabinet, in the upstairs bedroom, and eventually on the entire top floor of my parents' house," recalls Mesa. "They said it was all my fault." A few years ago, Mesa and her husband Pat sprang the museum upon an unsuspecting public, throwing a few frogs of their own into the hopper.

Originally it was intended for children. "We thought it would be a fun and inexpensive thing to do." But, instead, adults went frog-wild: "They spend hours poring over the various displays and spend big money on collectibles in the gift shop."

The Mesas have even organized an annual Frog Fantasies Festival, which sends collectors leaping from all over the United States. "They have to be serious if they come all the way to a place that doesn't even have an airport."

But even the biggest pond has a pecking order, and this one's no exception. Displays are arranged by categories, such as banks, toys, stuffed critters, ash trays, pipe holders, and candles and night lights "that either scare or comfort children." There's a two-story dollhouse

Frogs are everywhere at the museum. They line walls, cases, even windows. Curator Louise Mesa can't get enough. (*Photo courtesy of the Frog Fantasies Museum.*)

completely furnished with frogs and a special frogs-only Christmas tree with blown glass and other ornaments. Mesa has found that her hobby leapfrogs into other's collections, such as Hummel figurines, enameled pottery, salt and pepper shakers, and expensive jewelry.

There are knickknacks made from the skins of real toads "not my favorites, but my parents brought them back each year from Mexico," as well as a pond out back that accommodates the live versions. Mesa welcomes new arrivals, warts and all: "Sometimes people will leave a note—'Here are two tree frogs and three garden frogs.' "

There's a kitchen decorated in modern frog. Toad-splattered cookware sits atop a stove; a bikini-clad frogette warms herself inside; a crocheted leaper sits on the oven door. "There's a whole line of Sears kitchen utensils that have become collectible," notes Mesa. Napkin holders, clocks, steak knives, and paper-towel holders also jump out at visitors.

The bathroom's specially designed for those with frogs on their minds. Along with frog soap dishes, toothbrush holders, towels, and a shower curtain, a bathing suit and a toilet seat practically swim with the creatures. A ceramic frog perches atop the "throne" with a big smile on her countenance. "One visitor came out in tears," of laughter, that is.

The Mesas's hobby has even brought them some (human) celebrities. "Singer Robert Goulet has collected over three thousand frogs and has been very supportive of us." Fortunately, his sideline hasn't rubbed off on his vocal cords. Although Goulet has never visited the museum "we've offered to sneak him in with a blond wig and sunglasses." A Kermit costume might also be appropriate.

Not everyone appears to toady up to the idea. "Sometimes I get some really strange looks," admits Mesa.

Mesa would never bite the frog that feeds her by munching on *cuissess de grenouille* (frog legs). "It would be like eating the family cat. In fact, the other day, I picked up an intelligent-looking frog and said 'Hey buddy, I make a living off of you.'" But she's still not quite ready to kiss it.

The Frog Fantasies Museum
151 Spring Street, Eureka Springs, AR 72632
((501) 253-7227

LOCATION: About 30 miles southwest of Fayetteville
HOURS: Seven days a week, 10:00 A.M.–5:00 P.M.
ADMISSION: Admission is charged

✦ Fort Smith: THE PATENT MODEL MUSEUM

There's an 1876 wooden washing machine that looks like it would chop up rather than clean clothes. An 1867 floating bed has attached oars and provisions in case the ship sinks at night. An eight-inch-by-eight-inch printing press invented in 1873 will work with ink and miniature paper. A transparent window shade, invented in 1856 by E.R. Kernan fulfills every Peeping Tom's fantasy. And one wonders where H.B. Walbridge was thinking of putting the round refrigerator he designed in 1876.

These and eighty-some other working miniature models and pictures of inventions comprise the Patent Model Museum in Fort Smith, Arkansas. Located in a circa 1840s structure believed to have been built by the city's founders, it was renovated by State Representative Carolyn Pollan in honor of the 1976 Bicentennial. Representative Pollan's office is upstairs in the Rogers-Tilles House, as it is called, and, according the museum's brochure, "you are invited to visit with [her] concerning matters of state government." You can complain about taxes and soak up a little history at the same time.

Many of the prototypes are practical items such as egg incubators, wagon jacks, grain scales, and the forerunner of a hand powered washing machine that actually went into production. There's a combination fold-down bed, wardrobe, and bureau; an ironing board

that also doubles as a clothes rack; and an 1869 toy man on a tricycle. Some items, such as an 1880 spring roller shade and a pre-Civil War artificial leg brace, originated by Dr. Benjamin Jewett, are still in use today.

In addition to the prototypes, which were not to exceed twelve square inches according to Patent Office rules, the museum has photocopies of plans and seventeen framed prints of other devices concocted in the early nineteenth century. The latter include portrayals of a gadget to

This early washing machine was a forerunner of things to come. (*Photo courtesy of the Patent Model Museum.*)

demolish bedbugs, of diving equipment that used balloons to raise sunken vessels, and of a massive 1831 fire ladder on which men with top hats sprayed water on the blaze.

It was a conflagration in 1836 that destroyed most of the first patent models. "Prior to that time, patents were registered by the inventor's name and description of the item," explains Dorothy Williams, who works at the museum. "But after the fire it was decided that, since ten thousand new inventions had been recorded since the establishment of the Patent Commission in 1790, a numeric system was needed and Patent No. 1 was issued."

The museum has an unnumbered metal fireplace and a brick-making machine believed to have survived the blaze. Its earliest numbered patent, 326, is for an 1837 paddle wheel.

The industrial revolution of the 1800s caused a torrent of patent applications, up to fourteen thousand a year by 1870. So, with the exception of flying and perpetual motion machines, the requirement for models was discontinued due to space limitations, not only because the Patent Office couldn't hold any more, but because it was being inundated with tourists who wanted to see the amazing inventions. Although blueprints were substituted "the government kept accepting models until 1880 because [prototypes] were instrumental in settling copyright disputes," adds Williams.

In 1925, Congress decided to sell all the designs not kept by the Smithsonian Institution. The rest, some 125,000, changed hands several times until 1941, when Rundle Gilbert of New York state purchased the collection for $4500 at a federal bankruptcy auction. His chief competitor, a junk dealer, "planned to burn the unopened crates and sell the remains to Japan as scrap metal," says Williams. It was at Gilbert's periodic auctions that Carolyn Pollan obtained her collection.

From 1793 to 1880, 250,000 models were filed with the Patent Office. To date, people have applied for over five million patents, many of which now originate from overseas. "These ideas made America the great industrial nation it is today," adds Williams. And to think they were almost recycled into Japanese weapons for World War II.

The Patent Model Museum
400 North 8th Street, Fort Smith, AR 72901
((501) 782-9014

LOCATION: On I-40, about 160 miles west of Little Rock
HOURS: Monday–Friday, 9:00 A.M.–4:00 P.M.; weekends by appointment
ADMISSION: Free

✦ Pine Ridge: THE LUM 'N' ABNER MUSEUM

Okay, so the closest major metropolis (Little Rock) is over one hundred miles away, and the only route to the Lum 'n' Abner Museum in Pine Ridge, Arkansas, is two-lane Highway 88, twenty miles east from Mena, or twenty miles west from Mt. Ida. In fact, Pine Ridge is not really a town at all, just a collection of buildings with a population of about twenty-four "including children and dogs," adds Kathryn Stucker, who along with husband Lon, owns and manages the museum. "We don't even have a school here and I'm the part-time postmaster."

But it *is* home to the Jot 'Em Down general store, which served as grist for the famous *Lum 'n' Abner* radio program of the thirties and forties. Next to Amos and Andy, Lum 'n' Abner were the biggest radio personalities of their day. And anyone who ventures to the store

The original Lum 'n' Abner. (*Photo courtesy of the Lum 'n' Abner Museum.*)

and museum may learn that, in addition to President Bill Clinton, humor is another Arkansas import that made a big national impact.

A sample: "Never put your faith in seed catalogs. That thing with the double barreled name always turns out to be radishes." Although far from sophisticated, Lum 'n' Abner's sly wit and homey anecdotes about the fabricated town of Pine Ridge and its not-so-fictional denizens contained a grain of truth. Originally called Waters, the tiny burg officially changed its moniker to Pine Ridge in 1936 after the success of the daily radio show, a sort of reverse Fifth Amendment.

But Lum 'n' Abner were hardly stereotypical hayseeds. College graduates and the sons of well-to-do businessmen, Chester "Chet" Lauck (Lum Eddards) and Norris "Tuffy" Goff (Abner Peabody) grew up together, playing pranks and doing comedy routines at school and civic functions. Just two "good old boys" sitting around the country store discussing the follies and foibles of their neighbors along with imitating their personalities, voices, and mannerisms,

Lauck and Goff never went back to their day jobs once they began performing. A contract from NBC radio led to fame, fortune, and an eventual move to Hollywood and careers in the movies.

Yet Lum 'n' Abner retained close ties with their Arkansas friends and family, getting the latest scoop about what was going on at barn dances, pie suppers, or around the checkerboard at the Jot 'Em Down store. Goff/Abner, who was younger by five years, passed away in 1978, while Lauck/Lum died in 1980.

The unpretentious museum (could it be anything but?) consists of two adjacent clapboard buildings, the largest of which was the original general store. Along with Lum 'n' Abner movie posters and larger memorabilia, it also sells souvenirs and antiques.

Down the hallway is the museum. Family photos, documents, and other correspondence line the walls, along with a display case of advertising premiums. Listeners could send for a Walking Weather Forecaster (a litmus-paper button), a Horlick's Malted Milk Mixer, various almanacs, and a Let's 'Lect Lum button from 1936, when he ran on the "Demopublican" presidential ticket. (In the true American spirit, the boys paid for this one, as it was done without the backing of a sponsor).

Then visitors can go into the smaller building, which contains stuff—or the nearest available facsimile—from the gen-u-ine Jot 'Em Down. A dusty checkerboard sits near an old potbellied stove and barber chair. Tobacco, shoes, spitoons, and other necessities folks couldn't grow, swap, or make by hand, share shelf space with patent medicines such as Grove's Tasteless Chill Tonic. "It's mostly made from alcohol, and it tastes awful!" comments Stucker, who surely must speak from experience. Mannequins of some of Lum 'n' Abner's more famous personas, as well as newspaper articles and pictures document their stellar careers.

Other rooms display antique furniture and appliances from local homes. A trunk overflowing with World War II clothes, equipment, and Lum 'n' Abner promotional materials on war bonds and rationing illustrates the boys' efforts for the boys.

According to Stucker, recent years have resulted a resurgence of all things radio. "In 1983, the National Lum 'n' Abner Society

[NLAS] was organized." Rather than sitting around a stove, however, devotees swap stories nineties style: networking at a convention in Mena and Pine Ridge.

The Lum 'n' Abner Museum
P.O. Box 38, Pine Ridge, AR 71966
((501) 326-4442

LOCATION: Highway 88, between Mena and Mt. Ida
HOURS: Hours vary
ADMISSION: Admission is charged

Florida

♠ Naples: THE TEDDY BEAR MUSEUM

There are Pooh bears, polar bears, panda bears, and Paddington bears; one-inch bears and those the size of an average grizzly; bears made from marble and bronze; antique, limited-edition, and manufacturer's "theme" bears such as William Shakesbear; bear photos, paintings, posters, and prints; and (of course) a "libeary" for research and story times. You'll find a bruin clown school, a wedding where every pew is filled with you-know-whats, and a trompe-l'oeil cottage where only the bears are really three-dimensional. Teddies picnic on hot dogs and baked beans, parade through a turn-of-the-century town with an "attorney at paw" and "pawdiatrist," and convene a "bear-d of directors" with a "head grizzly," a cigar-chomping general who had to quit because Havanas became too expensive. Also "children kept smashing the cigars and I got tired of replacing them," admits director

George Black Jr., leader of the hug—a hug being a batch of teddy bears similar to a pride of lions. It's almost too much to bear.

That barely scratches the surface of the over twenty-two hundred inhabitants (not including three hundred pieces of art) at the Teddy Bear Museum (formerly Frannie's Teddy Bear Museum) in Naples, Florida. And it's not only for kids. "Teddy bears rank right up there with stamps, coins, and dolls as collectibles," observes Black. "Every weekend there's at least one collector's convention somewhere." A few years ago, Sotheby's auctioned off a rare Steiff bear for $86,000, even though most antiques can be captured for far less.

People often save them as a memento of childhood because "they're soft, cuddly, and very forgiving," continues Black. "When someone has been given a bear as a gift he finds himself confiding in it because it will listen to troubles without commenting." Don't try this with Teddy's live counterpart, however.

It was this appeal that created the museum in the first place. Black's mother, Frances P. Hayes, a widowed philanthropist, fell in love with a plush Teddy given to her by a grandchild in 1985. Along with adding bears furnished by family and friends,

The Chairman of the "bear-d." (*Photo courtesy of the Teddy Bear Museum.*)

she supplemented her growing collection by traveling around the world. Soon her three-bedroom condominium was overrun. She built a permanent "cave" for her charges five years later.

With its rustic setting, soft colors, and natural wood decor, the eight-thousand-square-foot museum resembles a bear's lair. A full-sized tree rises through its center, housing a tiny bear's home with a family of three-inch bears. Look up, and you'll see hot air balloons transporting Teddies in festooned baskets. Bears fly here and there and twirl around in mobiles. Even the bathroom has bears, so visitors won't feel lonely during private moments. A 1906 *Saturday Evening Post* magazine cover, bears from the turn of the century, and a signed first edition copy of *Winnie The Pooh* by A.A. Milne attest to their lasting allure.

Along with fielding about fifty thousand visitors annually, the museum accepts donations of bears in any condition. However, "we decline all taxidermy, as real bears are an endangered species." Sometimes the bears are loaned to children to carry around in the museum. Those desiring to adopt one permanently can visit the well-populated gift shop.

Black recalls an incident in which a seven-year-old wanted to give his Teddy to the museum, stating he was now too old to play with it. "His four-year-old brother was standing right behind him, and you knew the older kid was thinking, 'There's no way my brother's gonna get my toy.' But we took it anyway." Sometimes life can be a bear.

The Teddy Bear Museum
2511 Pine Ridge Road, Naples, Florida 33942
℆ (813) 598-2711

LOCATION: Take Exit 16 off I-75 in Naples
HOURS: Wednesday–Saturday, 10:00 A.M.–5:00 P.M.; Sunday, 1:00 P.M.–
     5:00 P.M.
ADMISSION: Admission is charged

♦ Ocala: THE DON GARLITS MUSEUM OF DRAG RACING

Vroom, vroom. It's off the main "drag" of I-75 on County Road 484, ten miles south of Ocala, Florida. Although the Don Garlits Museum of Drag Racing comes in a plain brown wrapper of a building, there's enough potential horsepower inside to outdistance just about anything on four wheels. Wanna race?

According to general manager Greg Capitano, the human desire to outrun the next guy provided impetus for that all-American sport, drag racing. "If a state had only two cars [the owners] would line them up and see which one would go faster," he asserts. It's a hor-

Don Garlits stands proudly in front of his namesake museum. (*Photo courtesy of the Don Garlits Museum of Drag Racing.*)

monal thing. Thus, after World War II "people began investing money and energy [previously] used for tanks and other vehicles into making cars bigger and faster. Especially on the West Coast, where the industry and money were."

Enter Don Garlits, a "hard-charging kid from Tampa, Florida, who called his race car 'Swamp Rat,'" according to museum literature. "At the infamous Bakersfield, California, U.S. Fuel and Gas Championships, back in the late fifties, they called him Tampa Don, Garbage Don, threw beer cans and shouted insults." Okay, so it wasn't exactly teatime at the Ritz, but Big Daddy Garlits, as he came to be known (not to be confused with Ed "Big Daddy" Roth) triumphed anyway, copping a list of wins and records (170, 180, 200, 240, up to 271.08 mph) that would take up all the space supposed to describe his museum.

He also installed a number of innovations to increase speed and safety, such as revolutionary rear-engine car, developed after a horrific crash in which he lost half his right foot. Other jeered at that invention too, but along with parachutes, roll cages, seat belts, and canopies, it's now a standard safety feature in fuel dragsters. In fact, Big Daddy's gotten so durn respectable his Swamp Rat XXX found a place of honor within the turrets and towers of the Smithsonian.

Opened in 1984, the drag racing museum, a twenty-five thousand-square-foot nonprofit facility is a haven for hot rods, not only Garlit's record-busting pack of Swamp Rats (a name given to all his racing autos) but others as well. Antique (a relative term) dragsters include a rail model from 1941 (rails were often used to construct the cars); the 1957 record holder from an early national meet; and the 1977 race car driven by Shirley Muldowney, the first woman to ever win a major automotive championship.

Garlits has vintage vehicles, too. These range from a wide selection of impeccably restored and original condition 1930s and early 1940s Fords, Chryslers, and Mercuries to "muscle cars" from the sixties and seventies, souped-up models that can be driven on the street. "The frames of many of the older cars were used to make the first dragsters," explains Capitano. "So their inclusion is of historical importance to the museum."

There's car-mobilia from all categories of fellow racers: "pioneer fuelers" Dick Kraft, Emery Cook, and the Bean Bandits; "funny car champions" Don Prudhomme (no relation to chef Paul), Tom McEwen, and Raymond Beadle; "stockers and gassers" Don Carlton, Barbara Hamilton, and K.S. Pittman; and other "personalities" with such descriptive names as TV Tommy Ivo, Jungle Jim Liberman, and Sneaky Pete Robinson.

Each car is lovingly displayed in its own booth, with accompanying photographs and magazine articles attesting to its outstanding performance. Many of the dragsters are outsized with long snouts. There's a ten-foot mother than runs on compressed air ("an unsuccessful attempt to get more combustion"), another with an actual rocket engine ("anything to go faster") and still another that has a wing over a standard engine. "The wing design reduces drag and improves aerodynamics," points out Capitano. "However, when the car goes over 180 mph it begins to lift off the ground." Oops. A "wheel stander"—a Dodge truck that can drive on its two back wheels (the automotive equivalent of a performing dog)—and racing "funny cars"—dragsters with fiberglass bodies of standard autos—round out the collection.

Along with the usual T-shirts and decals, model cars can be purchased at the gift shop. Or, you can wait for the Autoganza, a springtime event that attracts hundreds of real dragsters as well as cars and thousands of spectators. You might meet Big Daddy, too.

The Don Garlits Museum of Drag Racing
13700 SW 16th Avenue, Ocala, Florida 34473
((904) 245-8661

LOCATION: Take county road 484 off I-75, ten miles south of Ocala.
HOURS: Seven days a week, 9:00 A.M.–5:30 P.M.; closed Christmas
ADMISSION: Admission is charged

Georgia

⚑ Columbus: THE LUNCH BOX MUSEUM

Allen Woodall, hoarder extraordinaire (car hood ornaments, political press badges, southern pottery) craved the lunch box collection of Dr. Robert Carr, who'd passed away unexpectedly. "[Dr. Carr] had the premier collection in the country, and, like myself, a lot of people wanted to buy it," recalls Woodall. "But I promised his widow I'd start a museum in honor of him and his family." Today the coveted collection of three thousand boxes and two thousand thermoses lines the walls and wooden shelves of the second floor of SOUTH 106, a Columbus, Georgia radio station Woodall also owns. Naturally, some of the boxes are also in the lunch room there.

Even though he began acquiring lunch boxes only four years ago, Woodall is hardly a dilettante. "I read everything I could about them and the artists who created the lithograph sheets from which they're made," he remarks. Like peanut butter and jelly, Gumby and Pokey,

Roy Rogers and Dale Evans, lunch boxes and thermoses have more value as a team than alone.

They symbolize the *ne plus ultra* in baby-boomer nostalgia. "Lunch boxes go right to the stomach," observes Woodall. "They're what we grew up with and took to school." The TV-shaped containers bearing the likenesses of the Lone Ranger, the Beatles, and

Barbie have evolved from garage-sale curiosities for a quarter, to prizes worth hundreds, and, in the case of a mint condition Jetsons, thousands of dollars.

They also have a certain mystique. Woodall notices it whenever people visit the museum. "Folks get real quiet," he observes. "Then they start pointing to boxes they carried when they were kids or remember some bit of culture or personal

The Lone Ranger rides again at the Lunch Box Museum. (*Photo courtesy of the museum.*)

experience they haven't thought about in years." Along with duplicate boxes, visitors can also purchase T-shirts depicting various boxes or commemorating the Box-O-Rama, an annual gathering of collectors held in Gatlinburg, Tennessee.

Yet they (boxes, not collectors) are of humble origin. And no visit to this museum is complete without indoctrination into this hobby's lore. During the early part of this century, construction workers and miners carried their meals in plain metal tins, as did schoolchildren. In the 1930s, Walt Disney produced a Mickey Mouse lunch pail, which naturally is now extremely valuable. The real bonanza began in 1950 with Hopalong Cassidy—a red or blue metal box with a four-inch decal of the TV hero containing a matching thermos. Aladdin Industries, the manufacturer, sold over 600,000 kits the first year, just as many baby boomers reached school age. It marked the beginning of an era. During the next two decades, over 120 million lunch boxes were purchased in America.

By 1987, however, steel boxes had fallen out of favor. During the early seventies, a group of irate parents in Florida persuaded their state legislature to ban them. "Legend is that one kid clobbered another on the head with a metal box," explains Woodall. Other states followed Florida's example, and more malleable plastic replaced steel. Although the last steel box was, appropriately, Rambo, "you can still find plenty of them around, even on the shelves of old drugstores or in small towns."

Allen Woodall has just about all of them—Toppie, the elephant mascot for Top Value stamps, boxvertisements for Cracker Jack, Fritos, and Frosted Flakes. Now-obscure programs like *Lost in Space*, *Knight Rider*, *Dukes of Hazzard*, and V (remember the ugly aliens?) are captured forever in their mini-TV formats. "Like baseball cards, these are collectibles and a real education," he insists. So come on down, bring a bologna sandwich, and rediscover your roots.

The Lunch Box Museum
1236 Broadway, Columbus, Georgia 31901
((800) 445-4106

LOCATION: Off I-185, 108 miles south of Atlanta
HOURS: Monday–Friday, 10:00 A.M.–5:00 P.M.; or by appointment
ADMISSION: Free

♠ Eatonton: THE UNCLE REMUS MUSEUM

An enormous rabbit with a coat, tie, and pipe sits in the center of Eatonton, Georgia. This bonzo bunny, aka Br'er Rabbit, is a politically correct tribute to the town's literary native son, Joel Chandler Harris. The fascinating and sometimes controversial story behind the droll fables of Br'er Rabbit, Br'er Fox, "de critters"; their narrator Uncle Remus (who was black); and the actual creator Harris (who wasn't) can be found at the nearby Uncle Remus Museum.

Just about everyone's familiar with the Disney movie *Song of the South* which was based on Remus's, er, Chandler's yarns. Because some felt it depicted negative African American stereotypes, the film has been periodically banned, although it's popped up in theaters in recent years. "There's nothing racist about Br'er Rabbit," insists Norma Watterson, the museum curator. "Mr. Harris's stories deal with an old slave who was a composite of people he knew, telling folk tales that had been handed down among generations to a white boy during the mid-1800s."

The chronically shy Harris didn't have an easy ride either. Born in poverty in 1848, never knowing his father, he received an education only because neighbors took pity on him and paid for his schooling. At thirteen he was hired to work at the *Countryman*, the only weekly newspaper ever published on a Southern plantation. The owner, Joseph Addison Turner, encouraged Harris to write, opening up his home, Turnwold, to the talented, impressionable youngster. "It was at Turnwold that Harris began his lifelong friendship with animals and some of the older slaves, such as 'Uncles' George Terrell and Bob Capers," explains Watterson. "They had a gift for storytelling that Harris recaptured on paper." Turner's grandson, Joseph Sidney Turner, provided the inspiration for the Little Boy for whom Uncle Remus spins his yarns. The museum is located at Turner Park, Joseph Sidney Turner's home site.

Br'er Rabbit in his place of honor in the town of Eatonton, Georgia.
(*Photo courtesy of the Uncle Remus Museum.*)

Around the time of the Civil War, Harris ended up at the *Atlanta Constitution*. It was there, at age twenty-eight, that he began to pen the 185 Uncle Remus stories that were to garner international acclaim and translation into twenty-seven foreign languages. Harris also wrote nearly forty novels and a history of Georgia, as well as countless articles.

Rather than being a shrine to the man himself—that can be found at his Atlanta home, the Wren's Nest, where he died in 1908—the museum commemorates Harris's characters. A log cabin made from two original Putnam County slave dwellings, the building resembles Uncle Remus's actual "quarters." The windows contain antebellum scenes of Turnwold, including views of the Turner family riding home in a coach and slaves picking and processing cotton, quite a contrast in lifestyles. Twelve delicate balsa-wood shadow boxes portray the more well known Uncle Remus stories such as "Will-'O-the-Wisp," "Br'er Rabbit's Laughing Place," "The Tar Baby," and "Making a Dollar a Minute."

Other standouts consist of a large portrait of Uncle Remus and the Little Boy and a memento-laden fireplace where much of the alleged storytelling took place. The latter includes slave era pots, pans, chairs, and other household items. There's even a "deceitful jug" like in Harris's tales. "If you want to know what's in it, read the story of 'Uncle Remus and His Deceitful Jug,'" advises Watterson.

The museum also has first editions of Harris's writings, originals of his newspaper and magazine articles, and photos of him with celebrities of the day, such as Mark Twain. Along with copies of Harris's books, the small gift shop sells stationery items, as well as rabbit's feet, a nod to the old Southern superstition that the left hind foot of a graveyard rabbit brings luck. No, thank you.

Nearly fourteen thousand people from around the world visit the museum each year. "Some might not have heard of Joel Chandler Harris or care about Uncle Remus, but they all know Br'er Rabbit," explains Watterson.

Many are African Americans. "Most [blacks] appreciate what we're doing," she continues. "It's part of their history and they're glad someone has saved it for everyone to remember." So what if Uncle Remus has white "roots."

The Uncle Remus Museum
P.O. Box 3184
Highway 441 South
Turner Park, Eatonton, Georgia 31024
((706) 485-6856

LOCATION: About 35 miles south of Macon
HOURS: Hours vary
ADMISSION: Admission is charged

✝ Statesboro: THE U.S. NATIONAL TICK COLLECTION

At first, this collection sounds like a joke: about one million dead ticks sitting in 120,000 vials of alcohol at Georgia Southern University in Statesboro, funded by none other than Uncle Sam. But the United States isn't the only country with ticks up the wazoo: there's a collection at the British Museum of Natural History in London; one in St. Petersburg, Russia; and another in Onderstepoort, South Africa. And along with researchers who hunt and preserve even more of the nasty little buggers, the various collections sponsor exchanges—of both scientists and ticks.

"Ticks are very serious business," emphasizes Dr. James Keirans, a research professor and the curator of the U.S. National Tick Collection. "Among many other afflictions, they carry Rocky Mountain Spotted Fever (RMSF) and Lyme disease, both of which can be harmful to humans if undiagnosed and untreated." And Keirans is all for raising public awareness. "If a tick gets on you, don't burn it or put chemicals on it," he advises. And rather than twisting or jerking it out, "using a pair of tweezers, grasp the tick's mouth part as close to your skin as possible, then slowly pull it straight out to remove as much of the body as you can." Eeeuw.

Keirans also recommends tucking pants in shoes, shirts into pants, and wearing long-sleeved tops in tick-intensive areas (i.e., the edges between woods and fields, especially in the Northeast and Eastern Seaboard where Lyme disease prevails). "If a tick takes hold, it will crawl upward and try to feed. Since you're protected by clothing, you'll only need to check your head and neck when you come inside," he notes, obviously speaking from experience.

Consisting of a rather large room full of wooden and metal cases (the ticks are in vials, which in turn are in bottles, and they're dead; they've been dead for years), the collection features 760 of the 850 known species. The largest is roughly the size of a quarter and the smallest is about one millimeter, small enough to fit on the head of a pin.

According Keirans, ticks haven't changed much throughout the ages. "They look the about the same in prehistoric amber as they do today."

At the turn of the century, when researchers began to nab ticks in investigating RMSF, for identification of species and for taxonomic studies, the collection was hatched in western Montana. Other scientists deposited the fruits of their labors, adding greatly to it and helping to determine the causes of even more illnesses, such as tularemia, Colorado tick fever, tick paralysis, and others. After World War II, ticks from Asia, Africa, Australia, and Madagascar were added, giving the program an international flavor. By the 1980s, the focus had shifted from identifying diseases to molecular research and the collection was moved to Washington, DC, a fitting home for the world's largest and most complete accumulation of despicable bugs (actually, ticks are arachnids).

Researcher and curator Dr. James Keirans puzzles over the mysteries of the U.S. National Tick Collection. *(Photo : by Nick Arroyo.)*

In 1983, the Public Health Service officially donated it to the Smithsonian. Through a five-year, million-dollar grant from the National Institutes of Health and a Smithsonian long-term enhancement loan, the collection was again transferred in 1990 to Georgia Southern University, along with over forty filing cabinets containing virtually every published article on ticks and tick borne diseases. They get around, for a bunch of dead ticks.

The history of each tick—the collection locality, date collected, host organism, collector, species, and an identification number (this *is* the government, after all)—can be found on a card at the collection as well as on the Smithsonian computer. "We find this immensely helpful in our research," points out Keirans. "Not only can we identify ticks from universities, expeditions, and physicians around the world, but it also helps in discovering new species." So the next time you're in the forest and see a strange-looking tick, you know exactly where to send it.

The U.S. National Tick Collection
Institute of Anthropodology and Parasitology
Georgia Southern University
Landrum Box 8056, Statesboro, GA 30460
℃ (912) 681-5564

LOCATION: Off U.S. 301 near I-16
HOURS: Wednesday, 1:30 P.M.–2:30 P.M.; or by appointment
ADMISSION: Free

✦ Summerville: PARADISE GARDEN

Howard Finster is a man of vision(s). On one level, he's a simple
Southern Baptist preacher, mechanic, clock maker, and jack of all
trades, who, if his handwritten autobiography's any indication, has def-
inite need of a spell checker. On another, he's a world-renowned folk
artist, surpassing even Grandma Moses with twenty-seven paintings.

His work hangs in galleries all over the world, including those of
the Library of Congress and the Smithsonian. He's done Easter eggs

for the White House and advertising for Disney, Absolut Vodka,
and MTV. His paintings have
appeared on the covers of record
albums by rock groups REM and
the Talking Heads. His signature
crucifix, "Get Right with God,"
has emblazoned itself on the
national conscience and consciousness. All the elements that
make up Howard Finster come
together in four acres at Paradise
Garden   near   Summerville,

Howard Finster's highly acclaimed
folk art blooms everywhere in Paradise Garden. (*Photo courtesy of
Paradise Garden.*)

Georgia, a pop art Eden with a born-again twist.

The "vision" came in 1976 after Finster, now in his late seventies,
retired from a forty-year, twelve-church stint as a preacher. "For fifteen years he fixed bicycles and lawn mowers, then one day saw a
face on some paint that had come off on his finger," relates grandson
Michael Finster, who toils in the Garden with other family members.
"A feeling came over him to do sacred art, so he went inside and got
a one-dollar bill and painted a picture of George Washington." And
hasn't stopped since, despite a barrage of illnesses. "All he does is
stay in bed and paint. He doesn't even take time out for his family."
Each work is labeled, signed, and numbered.

Finster was no stranger to revelations, however. "At three years old, I saw a clear vision of my sister who had been dead for some time," he writes. That set the tone for his religious life, and with only a sixth-grade education, he began preaching at age sixteen. Along with spreading the Gospel in Georgia, Alabama, and Tennessee, he penned poetry, prose, and songs; farmed; built furniture; and worked as a machinist and in textiles. He's entirely self-taught in all his endeavors and has claimed to take instruction from but one Boss.

Paradise Garden is Howard Finster's gift to the world; he lives nearby. "He purchased it in 1960 and built it up from a swamp, haul-ing in dirt and making walk-ways," says Michael. "People came from all over, bringing truckloads of toys, knickknacks, glass, and old household goods. Anything that's been invented can be found there." But rather than turning into a junkyard, sculptures emerged. Finster sells just about everything he makes right away, and nothing (actually, everything) is sacred: shoes, pic-ture frames, dollhouses, even a "talking" cement lady on a TV set, although most of his paint-ings are on plywood.

Howard Finster began painting after retirement in 1976 and hasn't stopped since. (*Photo : by Ann States.*)

Many of the exhibits (if one can call them that) have to be seen to be believed. A group of famous faces—Jesus, John F. Kennedy, William Shakespeare, and others—pop up like flowers in front of a full-sized church that Finster moved to Paradise Garden and rebuilt himself. Called the World's Folk Art Church, its three stories topped by a dome resemble an oversized rococo wedding cake. Even the sidewalks glitter with inlaid mirrors, colorful pieces of glass, beads, and tools. At various points throughout the garden, hidden cement countenances surprise visitors with their spooky eyes and ferocious expressions. Trouble in Paradise?

A thirty-foot-wide, twenty-foot-high "bicycle tower" consists entirely of welded-together scraps from Howard Finster's shop. "He wanted people to know he was serious about quitting the repair business," Michael half-jokes. Students at Lehigh University in Bethlehem, Pennsylvania, contributed to a cement mini-mountain, which includes their own art, odds and ends (cups, clocks, toy horses, hats), and flags. "People come from all over not only to see what's in the garden but to add their own creations."

And then there's a barn that's chock full of weird stuff. Fronted by an old cotton gin engine (When was the last time you saw one of *those*?), visitors can glimpse (in no order whatsoever) wagon wheels, tea brewers, toasters, can openers, birdhouses, and God knows what else.

A congregation of carved clocks draws the faithful, who still bring their "Finster Specials" in to be autographed by the master. Even before Paradise Garden, "I bought clocks run by electric [sic] and built them," Finster writes. "I made my own printing machines, made my own printing heads, and made all kinds of designs." The clocks' snapshots and elaborate motifs can also be found on spinning wheels, doll beds and chairs, vases, and even on toy cars.

Like the rest of Paradise Garden, the eight-by-ten "bottle house" is a tribute to recycling with its old Pepsi glass containers. Still, Finster's a lifelong fan of Coca-Cola, and along with creating a giant bottle for the company, he has decorated cans and sold them for $35 apiece. "A month's supply of Coke from one empty can," he writes. "That's a good profit." He even draws on empty paint buckets, which then go for $150.

Although it's kind of run down, with parts of the World's Folk Art Museum off-limits and in need of restoration, and snakes, dogs, chickens, and pigeons everywhere, "we still get about 150 visitors a week," states Michael. The gift shop, along with peddling rags, easels, Howard Finster's self-published tomes, and posters, has letters from former President George Bush and First Lady Nancy Reagan casually stapled on the wall. Apparently politics are unimportant in Paradise.

Paradise Garden
Route 2, Box 106-8, Summerville, GA 30747
☏ (706) 857-2926

LOCATION: Take the Adairsville exit off 75N from Atlanta, follow signs to Summerville, turn right on Route 27 and right again on Rena Street
HOURS: Hours vary
ADMISSION: Free

Kentucky

✦ Elizabethtown: SCHMIDT'S COCA-COLA MUSEUM

Almost everyone's familiar with Coca-Cola trays, calendars, drinking glasses, coolers, signs, and, of course, the ubiquitous (before recyclable cans and two-liter containers), distinctly shaped bottle. Thermometers, key chains, leather goods, dishes, playing cards, sheet music, and vehicles large and miniature have also borne the Coke trademark. But it also has appeared on cigar bands, school supplies, candy boxes, and gum wrappers. There's even a toaster that imprints bread with the Coca-Cola logo, a 1905 tray with a topless woman advising consumers to drink "Coca-Cola Highballs" and "Coca-Cola Gin Rickies," and a three-foot-high glass bottle designed by Tiffany. An elegant marble soda fountain made in 1893 for the Columbian Exposition in Chicago, a Depression-era baby doll only available through mail order, and cute little bottle cap earrings can also be found at the thirty-thousand-item Mount Everest of Coke memorabilia: the Schmidt's Museum in Elizabethtown, Kentucky.

Before visitors can enter these hallowed halls of cola, however, they must pass through a sort of time tunnel. Posters line the right side of the corridor leading upstairs, while on the left side are enlarged photos of bottles, starting with the 1940s and going backward. "These are our only reproductions, everything else is the 'real thing.' " says a grinning Jan Schmidt, who along with her husband Bill owns the museum and the adjacent bottling plant, which has been in the Schmidt family for several generations. And they collected the whole shebang on their own; it's independent of the official Coca-Cola museum in Atlanta.

Inside the seventy-five-hundred-square-foot museum the story of Coca-Cola unfolds chronologically with "Doctor" John Pemberton's

Schmidt's Coca-Cola Museum has all the "real things" about Coke. (*Photo courtesy of the museum.*)

invention of the "French Wine of Coca, the Ideal Nerve Tonic" in 1885. Although it didn't cure much, it tasted good. So Pemberton, an Atlanta druggist, reformulated his tonic, leaving out the wine and adding sugar, fluid extract of the kola nut, and a mystery ingredient still used today and still a secret. At the suggestion of his bookkeeper, Pemberton changed the name to the more alliterative Coca-Cola. The Schmidts have a small mirror advertising Pemberton's first attempt, probably the only physical reminder of Coke's obscure beginnings.

Many items in the museum were promotions given or sold to dealers and distributors. Along with a rare 1890 clock, the Schmidts have examples of all the Coke bottles, posters dating from 1895, vending machines and coolers from 1929, wooden and other thermometers, the only known example of a 1901 celluloid-covered boudoir clock, and the most complete collection of Coca-Cola trays in the world. With the latter, "you can practically trace history," points out Jan, noting that while clothes, styles of transportation, and haircuts change, the themes of pretty girls and carefree flirtations do not. However, after the topless tray fiasco by a daring bottler, "Coke went to great lengths to promote an all-American image."

In addition to Coca-Cola seltzer-type bottles meant for home use, the museum has several Hutchinson bottles. "These were made of heavy blown glass with a wire loop holding a lead stopper," explains Jan. "To drink from it, you hit the top of the loop, and it made a popping noise when released." Hence the name *pop*. Bill's grandfather was on the committee that helped choose the prototype for the famous greenish "Mae West" bottle in the early 1900s. "Its shape and ridges made it easy to hold in the dark." All-American, huh?

Historical pieces abound, such as large festoons that hung over soda fountains at the turn of the century, a 1910 celluloid sign offering Cokes with or without an egg, a 1920s dressing screen depicting a Coke for every season, cardboard cutouts of pert girls in 1930s bobs and hats enjoying a glass, even a painted sign rescued from the side of a barn, and a 1948 clock radio. A display of vending machines takes Coke into the late 1960s, when the exhibits stop. "We thought this was a good cutoff point because in 1970, Coke began to standardize its advertising campaigns," states Jan. "Besides, we ran out of space."

"Hardly a person stops by without saying, 'Oh, I remember that!' " she continues. And there's free, ice-cold Coke, Diet Coke, and Sprite to make things go even better.

Schmidt's Coca-Cola Museum
1201 N. Dixie Avenue, Elizabethtown, KY 42701
((502) 737-4000

LOCATION: About 45 miles south of Louisville, off I-65
HOURS: Monday–Friday, 9:00 A.M.–4:00 P.M.; closed Fourth of July,
    Thanksgiving, Labor Day, and Christmas
ADMISSION: Admission is charged

↟ Ft. Mitchell: THE AMERICAN MUSEUM OF BREWING HISTORY AND ARTS

It's beer heaven: an eight-million-dollar complex with an authentically reproduced brewery making German style beers; a "Brew Ha! Ha!" live musical troupe entertaining in a six-hundred-seat, sixty-five-foot-high Great Hall; a genuine pub; and a seasonal outdoor *bier garten*. Located throughout is the world's largest accumulation of beer and brewing memorabilia—125,000 labels, 47,000 coasters, 23,000 bottles, 13,000 cans; numerous match boxes, trays, lithographs, signs, tap markers, foam scrapers; and assorted odds and ends.

Heading (so to speak) up the collection is the "Indiana Jones of Beer," Alan Eames, a renowned expert who travels to the far corners of the earth in search of long-forgotten brews. For those stopping for more than a quick one, there's also an adjacent resort hotel and convention center with pools, bars, tennis courts, taverns, even hair salons.

Beers were advertised using many different gimmicks. (*Photo courtesy of Herb and Helen Haydock.*)

But rather than being a mecca for guys who like to sit around crushing cans against their heads, the American Museum of Brewing History and Arts in Ft. Mitchell, Kentucky, "is for families and people of all ages, and represents a microcosm of this country's founding," Eames asserts.

The reception area houses old brewery equipment from pre-Prohibition days, including bottle and keg fillers, cappers, a fermenting vat, and blenders. "One batch might not be so palatable, so [brewers] mixed several together in hopes the good tasting batches would mask the others," explains Helen Haydock, who along with her husband Herb developed the collection. "Most of the equipment was hand operated, so speed of production depended on the mood of the worker."

Cases housing statues traditionally kept on the back of bars line the concourse leading to the microbrewery. "Basically, these were symbols, such as animals or women, advertising the different breweries, or enlarged labels like Bosch, Miller, or Blatz," Haydock continues. Also included are trays, tin and plaster-of-paris signs, and oil-on-canvas art depicting various drinking scenes, as well as thousands of bottles, miniatures, and cans. "The pre-Prohibition art work is particularly remarkable."

After a guided tour of the microbrewery (a tasting costs extra; sorry, kids, no free samples), visitors can wander through the Great Hall, where the bulk of the current display is kept. With over one million pieces, only 60 percent of the collection can be shown at one time.

"We tried to put related things together," states Helen Haydock. For instance, all novelty items are in a case. These include button hooks, pocket knives, watches and watch fobs, toothpicks, and thimbles produced by various breweries as advertising or for promotions. A beauty section has beer shampoo and beer toothpaste and a sports section displays ice skates and a golf putter. "There was no limit to the kinds of things breweries would produce." Trays, coasters, tap markers, and embossed bottles line the walls in mind-boggling arrays, as do pictorial histories of such well-known companies as Pabst and Schlitz, and lesser luminaries like Piels and Prima.

The Haydocks chose the Oldenberg Brewery for their collection because, although other institutions such as the Smithsonian agreed to take it, "we wanted it to be out where people would enjoy it," says Helen.

Adds Eames: "For a beer historian, it's like walking into a cathedral." Bottoms up, Indiana Jones.

The American Museum of Brewing History and Arts
I-75 at the Buttermilk Pike Exit, Ft. Mitchell, KY 41017
((606) 341-2802

LOCATION: Near the Ohio-Kentucky border
HOURS: Sunday and Monday, 11:00 A.M.–6:00 P.M.; Tuesday–Saturday,
    11:00 A.M.–9:00 P.M.
ADMISSION: Fee charged for tours and tastings

Mississippi

♠ Petal: The International Checker Hall of Fame
Every few years, checkers champs put the pedal to the metal and vie for the crowning glory at the International Checker Hall of Fame in

Petal, Mississippi. Players from around the world roll into this small southern burg to participate in international invitational tournaments. Others come more frequently for a variety of state, regional, and national matches. Often, they don't pay a cent—the tab, which can run to several thousand dollars' worth of prize money for the world matches, is picked up by the Hall of Fame's board of directors, an affiliate of the American Checker Federation. Not bad, for being king (or queen) of a game that's seemingly as easy to learn as it is to acquire.

The power behind this throne is one Charles Walker, a self-made millionaire (insurance) and checkers champ (Florida Open, Irish

The checkerboard floor is used to illustrate the moves in world checker tournaments. (*Photo courtesy of the International Checker Hall of Fame.*)

Open, and innumerable Mississippi contests), who sprang an estimated one million dollars to build Chateau Walker, aka the International Checker Hall of Fame. On the outside, it's decorated in basic fiefdom, a twenty-thousand-square-foot Tudor structure with a seven-story tower, thirty-five rooms, secret passages, and a recently added ten-thousand-square-foot Hall II. The estates of Walker and his married children dot the one-hundred-acre grounds.

But within the main building it's tournament regulation green and beige all over—almost. The basement floor of the tower features a huge sixteen-square-foot playing arena surrounded by a gallery for spectators. There's even a checkerboard motif on the ceiling (in case they repeal the law of gravity?).

The floor playing board is used during world championships, not by the competitors themselves—they have enough to think about, anticipating thirty plus moves ahead—but by a third person who simulates their play via red or white circular pillows. The champion and challenger hunch over a small table at the end of the room and remain uninterrupted and free of distractions. Other checkerboards and tables are available for state tournaments, and portraits of great moments in checkers history adorn the walls—although pictures of two guys scowling across from each other at a table isn't exactly action photography.

Always one jump ahead, Walker also installed several mini-apartments on the upper floors of the Hall of Fame for visiting players. Even though the Walker family originally lived under the same roof as well, since its establishment in 1979, "the Hall just kept growing," states Walker. "So we donated it to the Federation."

Along with portraits of champions, there's another gallery dedicated to promoters and contributors to the game. Advertising memorabilia, barber chairs that accommodated matches along with haircuts, and checkerboards abound. Among the checkerboards are a Hawaiian board and checkers, called *konane*; a World War II German set with swastika-laden pieces; as well as a 144-square Canadian board and a Dutch board with 100 squares (American checkerboards have 64). "The game dates back to the Egyptian era," observes Walker.

The hall of fame has a formidable collection of books and regulations on checkers from all over the world. Starting with the 1756 *First Book of Draughts*, (draughts is the English term for checkers), visitors can learn about the game's many flavors. "There are approximately forty variations," notes Walker. Skills can be tested on computers that offer about half that number, enough to keep anyone busy for a while. The really confident can attempt to beat another computer at Grand Master Checkers, which came in second to the (human) 1990 U.S. Open champ.

But being a checkers maven isn't enough; Charles Walker would like to see chess tournaments at the Hall of Fame as well (he plays that, too). Although a mere babe compared to checkers—chess was invented about one-thousand years ago in India—"chess is often misconstrued as the more intellectually challenging game. But they both require mental skills and should combine their forces to make an even stronger interest group." Memo to chess players: It's your move.

The International Checker Hall of Fame
P.O. Box A, 220 Lynn Ray Road, Petal, MS 39465
((601) 582-7090

LOCATION: Just outside of Hattiesburg, off I-59
HOURS: By appointment year-round; daily during scheduled checkers
    events
ADMISSION: Admission is charged

✝ Vaughan: THE CASEY JONES MUSEUM
When he died, railroad engineer Johnathan Luther "Casey" Jones had no inkling of the "wreckognition" he'd receive as a folk legend/hero. On April 30, 1900, the Missouri native was running a trainful of passengers on the Cannonball Express, trying to make up time on a trip from Memphis to Canton, Mississippi. Intent on reaching his destination, he ignored several signals to halt before ramming into two freight trains near Vaughan, Mississippi. However, seeing that a crash was imminent, he had ordered his fireman, Sim Webb, to jump clear (which he did) and, although Jones perished, all the passengers survived. People really should pay more attention to stop signs.

Such railroad mishaps occurred all over the country during that period and Casey's death rated but a single sentence in a newspaper's brief account. But Casey had friends in low places. Wallace

Unlike the more commercialized Casey Jones Museum in Tennessee, this smaller version also serves as a post office. (*Photo courtesy of the Casey Jones Museum.*)

Saunders, a black man who worked as an engine wiper at the railroad shops had been buddies with Casey, who, according to the literature of the Casey Jones Museum in Vaughan, "admired and respected the men responsible for the upkeep of the locomotives."

Saunders liked to make up songs and, moved by the death of his friend, composed the "Ballad of Casey Jones," serenading anyone who would listen. The tune was later revised and picked up by a vaudeville act, quickly becoming a favorite of entertainers and audiences everywhere. By the end of Word War I, dozens of versions of the song had been published and millions of copies of sheet music sold.

Not too many airline pilots in a crash today would have two—count 'em, two—museums in their honor. One is located in Jackson, Tennessee, and consists of a hotel/restaurant complex built around the Jones homestead with the standard family and period memorabilia. The other can be found at this former railroad depot in Vaughan that serves as a post office, too. A steam locomotive, old No. 841, sits permanently outside.

"We're kind of a small museum," comments curator Hettie Moore. "Originally, we were in Pickins, [Massachusetts] but when the state purchased the museum from a private collector, they had the depot cut in three parts and moved down the highway." By truck, however.

Along with stocking up on stamps and getting to know the locals, visitors can study *Casey's Last Ride*, a diagram of the wreck; learn about a complicated procedure involving a "saw-by" maneuver; ring an engine bell loaded with ten silver dollars ("It has a distinct sound and can be loud when hit just right."); and, if they're not temporarily deaf from the bell, listen to a rendition of the "Ballad of Casey Jones."

"A lot of old timers get up and dance right along with it," says Moore. The words and tune are posted alongside on the wall, so the unfamiliar can join in. Along with pictures and information about Casey, his co-workers, and his engine, No. 382, there are also renderings of the rescued fireman and composer Saunders. In addition, the museum has a photo of country music great Jimmie Rodgers, the "Singing Brakeman."

"Casey got his nickname because when he was a teenager, he moved to Case, Kentucky, for a while," explains Moore. "Shortly afterward, he started working for the railroad." When Jones died at thirty-six, he was married with three young children. "We also have a copy of a song about him composed by his wife." Something about the man just made people want to write music.

Red warning flags of the kind ignored by Casey, telegraphs that sent Morse code messages from one depot to another, and kerosene and later-era lanterns used by conductors to signal departures are also on display. One room with mostly Casey-bilia includes, among other things, a broken black bell reputed to be from his original engine, slightly damaged boards that came off cars involved in the wreck, and a "Sherman necktie," a piece of track that was bent by Union soldiers to derail Confederate trains.

Because the museum is on an actual railroad line, visitors can hear passing trains roaring by if they come at the right time. The spot where Casey met his fate is within strolling distance, three-quarters of a mile down the road. If Casey were around today he'd no doubt advise: Don't walk on the tracks to get there.

The Casey Jones Museum
P.O. Box 605, Vaughan, MS 39179
((601) 673-9864

LOCATION: North of Jackson on I-55
HOURS: Monday–Saturday, 8:00 A.M.–5:00 P.M.; Sunday, 1:00 P.M.–5:00 P.M.
ADMISSION: Admission is charged

North Carolina

♠ Fuquay-Varina: MARVIN JOHNSON'S GOURD MUSEUM

Marvin Johnson's Gourd Museum in Fuquay-Varina, North Carolina, has gaggles of gourds from all over the globe. The thousands of items include doll gourds, drinking gourds, lamp gourds, carved gourds, antique gourds, animal gourds, musical instrument gourds, religious gourds, and gourd toys. And Johnson, a lifelong collector whose Cadillac license plate reads GOURD, has a story for nearly every one of them. "Even as a youngster, I loved gourds." He points to an old-fashioned dipper. "We grew them on our farm and I drank out of this when I was a child."

Even Marvin Johnson's license plate reads GOURD. (*Photo courtesy of Marvin Johnson's Gourd Museum.*)

"Here's a North Carolina heirloom," he continues, indicating a large, hollowed-out number with a faded note and a photograph inside. The picture, over one hundred years old, is of a baby peeking over the top of that very gourd. "Eugenia Price McKenzie of Rutherford County gave us this several years ago. That was her as a child and she lived well into her nineties." Johnson's oldest known gourd is from 1804 and is gold-embossed with the inscription "Grandmother." Hopefully it was a gift, not a portrait.

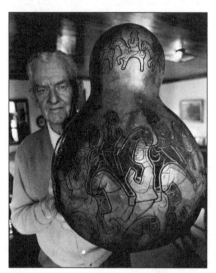

Rather than growing gourds, some people make them into works of art. (*Photo courtesy of Marvin Johnson's Gourd Museum.*)

Many believe the legend that if you give or receive a gourd, it brings health, happiness, and other "gourd" things. However, exactly what a gourd is can be the subject of discord. According to *The World Book Encyclopedia*, gourds are vegetables closely related to squash and pumpkins "that bear fruits of various colors and shapes." However, botanists define them as fruits because they are seed-bearing plants. Johnson and most gardeners agree with the *World Book*, insisting that gourds are a largely inedible vegetable. And no one disputes gourds' usefulness as "prehistoric Tupperware" for holding food and liquids, and for other practical applications in societies around the world throughout the ages.

Although things are rather squashed together, Johnson's museum is a cross section of every imaginable configuration of gourd. Visitors see an unparalleled collection of gourd lamps that light the musty-smelling exhibits. Along with lifelike reproductions of penguins, a rooster, a turkey, dogs, and cats; a gourd rattler looks realistic enough to strike. There's a twisted "gourdian" knot, a hollowed-out gourd with a tiny Nativity scene, and a three-foot-high "gourdgeous girl in gaudy gourd garb." A veritable "gourdchestra" consists of shakers, sitars, guitars, banjos, drums, and a marimba (a type of xylophone). Children can delight in a gourd Ferris wheel and kaleidoscope, in gourd puzzles and dolls, and in storybook characters clad in clothes made from luffa, a type of gourd.

There are also bona fide *objets de gourd*. Johnson displays a carving done by a New Zealand prisoner. "He received a life sentence because he killed the man his former girlfriend chose instead of him." The intricate geometric designs created by a math professor at Ohio State; engravings from an explorer who learned his craft from an obscure New Zealand tribe; and the gourds of Kentucky folk artist Minnie Black can also be found here. (Black has her own gourd museum, which, depending on her health, may or may not be operational.) A delicate Chinese cricket cage, giant African gourds, and plum-size Japanese peace gourds round out the collection.

Johnson, who is in his eighties, receives visitors and phone calls from as far away as New Zealand and Africa. "I've made a lot of friends through this," he observes. "I like to help in any way I can." Rather than vegetating, Marvin Johnson continues to share the fruit of his labors.

Marvin Johnson's Gourd Museum
P.O. Box 666, Fuquay-Varina, NC 27526
((919) 639-2894

LOCATION: A few miles south of Raleigh; at intersection of U.S. 401 and SR 55
HOURS: Open all daylight hours
ADMISSION: Free

South Carolina

♦ Charleston: THE MACAULAY MUSEUM OF DENTAL HISTORY

They appear innocuous enough, the approximately six thousand artifacts and books that make up the Macaulay Museum of Dental History in Charleston, South Carolina. With bone, mother-of-pearl, and ivory handles, many of the dental instruments are aesthetically appealing, as are the carved mahogany and oak cabinets which held them. However, when one considers the fact they were used over

and over on different mouths without sterilization or anesthetics, they take on a different cast.

Located at the Medical University of South Carolina (MUSC), the Macaulay Museum has developed quite a following, thanks to word of mouth. "We've been written up in a few museum guides, although we don't advertise much," comments curator Betty Newsom. Rather than being curious dental students, "most of our visitors are tourists." How do they react to seeing so southern a discomfort amassed in one place? "Actually, most are impressed and many say our collection's nicer than the Smithsonian's." Things look so much easier from the other side of the chair.

This Victorian oak dental cabinet stored all kinds of equipment. (*Photo courtesy of the Macaulay Museum of Dental History.*)

The museum was named in honor of the late dentist Neill W. Macaulay, whose donations, as well as those of his dentist grandfather, the aptly named Dr. John Sharp, make up a goodly portion of the exhibits. The items they collected represent an accumulation of eighty years and most came from the South. Other dentists have added to the collection as well. Dr. J. Gavin Appleby contributed a circa 1895 red plush upholstered semihydraulic dental operating chair, along with century-old hand instruments. According to museum literature, the latter were used "to cut tooth structure and excavate diseased tooth tissue." Without Novocain, of course.

Still, Victorian dentistry wasn't all slash and scream. "Prior to the development of nitrous oxide [laughing gas] in the 1840s, the biggest treatment for decay was removal of the tooth," states Dr. Edward Welsh, Professor of General Dentistry at MUSC, who assists in identifying and procuring artifacts for the museum. "Dentists were among the first to use anesthetics, which made the whole business more tolerable."

The museum also features a one-room dental office of one hundred years ago. With a chair by the window for natural light, a stand-up dental unit, a "modern" foot-powered drill for cleaning out cavities, and a stereoscope so the patient could look at 3-D pictures while awaiting treatment, "it's very authentic," comments Newsom. The hand drill, the foot engine's predecessor, was spun manually by the dentist and was much slower, extending the fun even longer. Included among the memorabilia is a folding dental chair that shows wear and tear from having fallen out of a wagon along country roads. "Traveling dentists went from town to town pulling teeth," states Dr. Welsh. "They often provided the only dental care available and carried their instruments in wooden chests." An early electro-surgical unit, a 1930s apparatus touted as a cure-all for oral diseases, used a heated element to burn away loose gum tissue during surgery and reduce bleeding. "Now most dentists prefer other forms of treatment," he adds. "The [element] can touch the tooth, causing sensitivity." Ouch.

On exhibit is a mill that flattened gold lumps into bands for making crowns; the sheets for fillings were produced by manually beating them. There are also small steel dental keys that fit around the tooth and with a twist, brought it out—an improvement over larger, more awkward forceps—and petite enamel hatchets that chipped away thin pieces of fractured or decayed enamel.

With the potential to give operators high voltage charges, the museum's collection of X-ray machines is rather "shocking." "The tubes invented in the 1890s had no protection," points out Welsh. "So both operators and patients were exposed to radiation, even though early textbooks talk about shielding the former."

The Macaulay Museum is a testament to how far dentistry has come in terms of safety, effectiveness, and comfort levels for patients and even dentists, who prior to modern developments had to be on their feet constantly. Yet despite this, most of us still want to run like hell whenever that whirring little drill is pointed at our mouths. . . .

The Macaulay Museum of Dental History
171 Ashley Avenue, Charleston, SC 28425
((803) 792-2288

LOCATION: Campus of the Medical University of South Carolina
   (MUSC)
HOURS: Monday–Friday, 8:30 A.M.–5:00 P.M.
ADMISSION: Free

Tennessee

♠ Adamsville: THE BUFORD PUSSER HOME AND MUSEUM

The subject of three *Walking Tall* movies and much controversy,
Sheriff Buford Pusser captured the nation's imagination during the
tumultuous 1960s and early 1970s. For some, he symbolized incor-
ruptible law and order, while others regarded him as a few blows shy
of a Storm Trooper. Regardless, he waged a one-man war against
moonshiners, gamblers, prostitutes, and organized crime. And he's a
hero in Adamsville, the "Biggest Little Town in Tennessee" where he
resided most of his thirty-six years.

Adamsville is the site of the Buford Pusser Museum, on Pusser
Street, just down the road from Pusser Park, where you can visit the
cemetery and see where Pusser and his assassinated wife, Pauline,
are buried. The bullets had been meant for Buford; unfortunately
Pauline happened to come along for the ride when he got a call about
some trouble during the early morning hours on August 12, 1967.

Sightseers can also tour the area where Buford started his law
enforcement career; trace the route down New Hope Road where
he and Pauline were ambushed; follow Highway 64 from Selmer

where Buford himself died in a fiery accident in 1974; and see the "crumbling remains of the Shamrock Hotel where he killed Louise Hathcock in a blazing gun battle" (she drew a pistol on him first), this according to Bill Wagoner's locally published memoir, *Buford Pusser, the Blood and Thunder Years*. And you can stay at the Old

Home Motel (901-632-3398, for reservations) where Buford himself resided for a time after his home, now the museum, burned in a fire. Never a dull moment.

Although Pusser reputedly carried a big stick, he did not walk softly. During his terms as local constable and McNairy County sheriff (1962–1970), Pusser booked over seven thousand five hundred prisoners (at the time, Adamsville's population was only about one thousand two hundred); was shot eight times and knifed seven times; destroyed eighty seven whiskey stills in 1965 alone; fought and defeated half a dozen men at once; and, by jumping on the vehicle and smashing the wind-

Buford Pusser poses here with his mother, Helen, who outlived him by 13 years. (*Photo courtesy of the Buford Pusser Home and Museum.*)

shield, subdued a man in a speeding car who tried to run him over. One can only imagine his insurance premiums.

A veritable shrine, the museum/home is maintained exactly as it was when Buford lived in it and is furnished entirely with his and his family's things. "People kept ringing the doorbell at all hours wanting to see Dad's house," recalls Buford's daughter, Dwana Moore. "So when the state of Tennessee expressed interest in making it a museum, the family agreed."

Before taking the tour, most people sit on the green and yellow couch in the shag-rugged living room and watch a video that includes an interview with Dwana and film clips of the man himself free associating about law enforcement, the death of his wife, and assorted other topics. You can then wander through the eight rooms and the garage that holds two of Buford's cars. According to Wagoner's history, Pusser loved automobiles and driving fast and, not surprisingly, was involved in many high speed chases.

Among many other things, the first floor contains photos and school papers from Buford's early life (the caption under his high school yearbook picture reads "more muscle than brain"). The kitchen has copies of poems written by Buford's admirers and the walls leading to the family bedrooms are plastered with family portraits. "The constant threats against Dad and the feeling that something was going to go wrong—and it usually did—made for a very hectic, nerve-wracking life," understates Dwana.

Downstairs you'll find a confiscated whiskey still and drug paraphernalia; Pusser's gun, badge, and big stick collection; and his bunker-like bedroom with its extra-long bed and tall man's clothes. Glass cases hold personal effects such as his wallet with its long-expired drivers' license and American Express card, his toothbrush and toothpaste (very dried out), and gifts from such notables as country-western singer Jerry Reed and right-wing politician Lester Maddox.

The gift shop offers Buford-bilia, busts and figurines, hats, bumper stickers, and belt buckles. It wouldn't be complete without big sticks in three options: small, large, and lapel pins, for those who like the concept but don't want to carry around the real thing.

The Buford Pusser Home and Museum
342 Pusser Street, Adamsville, TN 38310
((901) 632-4080

LOCATION: **Off I-64 in Adamsville**
HOURS: **Hours vary**
ADMISSION: **Admission is charged**

♠ Bristol: THE GRAND GUITAR

Just off exit 11 on I-81 near the Tennessee-Virginia border is a seventy-foot-long, three-story-high guitar. That the Grand Guitar in Bristol is the first thing many people notice when entering

The Grand Guitar draws onlookers from several highways. (*Photo : Joe Morrell.*)

Tennessee is music to the ears of its creator, Joe Morrell. "I wanted to bring attention to the contributions this area has made to country music," he says. "A lot of people are surprised when they learn how many entertainers come from a one hundred-mile radius of Bristol." A map on the wall inside the guitar reveals the origins of such big names as Dolly Parton (Dollywood is just up the interstate), Chet Atkins, Roy Acuff, Andy Griffith, and Ronnie Milsap.

But this colossal clone with an authentically reproduced exterior, fret markers and sound holes that are actually windows, and specially made nylon ropes that mimic strings is hardly a one-note attraction. Inside it you'll find WOPI, the region's oldest radio station, in addition to a collection of rare and unusual instruments, antique recording equipment, and country and western memorabilia. "I spent twenty years thinking about this museum before I actually put it together," remarks Morrell. "I thought, why stick it in a square building? I wanted to get people's attention." With the blessing of the C.F. Martin company, a major player in guitar manufacturing, he designed it to accurately replicate a six-string acoustic model and put the Martin insignia on the handle.

Morrell's medley of over three hundred instruments, located on the second floor of the museum, ranges from autoharps to zithers, with origins in a dozen different countries. Along with full-sized fiddles fabricated from match sticks, there are guitars with turtle-shell bases as well as some made from armadillo hulls and gourds. One display from "The Pick and Shovel Pickers," consists of instruments created from farm tools as well as a "commode flute," a kazoo strapped on a toilet plunger. Along the same vein is a "sit-ar" fashioned from a toilet seat that, according to Morrell, "sounds like s——."

There are also real sitars, along with an Oriental gizmo that looks like a cross between an adding machine and an autoharp. The chords are changed when keys are pressed. A 1910 harp guitar has both straight and bowed necks, the latter serving as a six-string bass. The collection also features a one-of-a-kind four-string guitar designed for a left-handed player along with a guitar shaped like the United States. A cowboy lassos a dogie on the front of an autographed Gene Autry guitar. The museum also has models endorsed by Roy Rogers and Buck Owens. Visitors can see a "ukelin," the melding of a guitar and a ukelele; a celestaphone, a type of zither; and a churango, a ukelele-type instrument found in Peru. Assorted Jew's harps, Hawaiian lap steel guitars, banjos, dulcimers, mandolins, and more add resonance to Morrell's acquisitions.

Morrell also demonstrates how thick old 78 records were generated (manually, by cutting the grooves on the disk) and how wire was used for recording before the advent of tape. "Can you imagine confiscating the Nixon wires?" he asks with a grin. There's a wall loaded with clothes, pictures, and album covers from the likes of singer Jane Fricke; country-music star Vern Gosdin; and the "King of Bluegrass," Jimmy Martin.

Finally, visitors can tarry at the WOPI control room, getting a glimpse of the innards of a radio station. Begun in 1929, WOPI broadcasts pretaped programs twenty-four hours a day during the week with live shows from the Grand Guitar on weekends. "Tennessee Ernie Ford got his start here," Morrell says, pointing proudly to a picture of a much younger version of the late entertainer sitting at the control desk. "And thanks to the Carter family, Jimmie Rodgers, and some others who are now forgotten, the first country records that ever went national were made in Bristol."

Fortunately, Morrell doesn't have to tune his creation. But when he's been up on the roof, he's noticed tourists from both Highway 11 and I-81 photographing his giant. If they don't stop by, he doesn't fret. "Whenever they see us, they think of country music."

The Grand Guitar
875 Kingsport Highway, Bristol, TN 37620
((615) 764-5131

LOCATION: Exit 74 A off I-81 near the Tennessee-Virginia border
HOURS: Seven days a week, 11:00 A.M.–5:00 P.M.
ADMISSION: Free

↟ Chattanooga: THE NATIONAL KNIFE MUSEUM

It's across the street from the largest mall in Tennessee and has nothing but knives. Although some may prefer shopping, the National Knife Museum in Chattanooga may be the better bargain. And it's the only museum in the United States entirely devoted to those sharp little devils that cut our food and have a myriad of other uses.

"Knives have been around since the dawn of humankind," observes Bob Cargill, a veteran collector who also repairs and makes custom knives. Among the approximately twenty thousand points of interest in the museum is a Bronze Age number from a warrior in China circa 231 B.C., swords used by headhunters in the South Pacific, and the world's largest (five feet eight inches, made by Cargill himself) and smallest (one-half inch) knives. And that's barely scratching the surface.

Items will snag the attention of even the littlest blade runner. Along with the knives there is a colorful turn-of-the-century pushcart that was used by street vendors "who made their living by traveling from house to house sharpening scissors and knives," explains Cargill. Unable to hone their skills to meet the cutting edge of technology, these vendors disappeared in the 1950s with the advent of cheaper implements and machines that did the chore automatically.

Another high point is the *Rambo III* display. National Knife Collectors Association (NKCA) member and knife maker Gil Hibben worked with Sylvester Stallone in fashioning a Bowie-style knife that was used for the movie. Along with weaponry such as a crossbow, there is a wooden prototype with Sly's handwritten comments, as well as the original, worth $20,000.

Visitors should prepare to carve out a considerable chunk of time if they want to see everything. Although blades are almost always made of metal, knives can have handles of pearl, wood, abalone, turquoise, ivory, and other materials. "[Knives] made from endangered elements have papers testifying to their legality," states Cargill.

You can find snakes, sharks, bears, and scenes such as George Washington crossing the Delaware engraved in the blades. An incredible array of "hobo knives" range from a simple model with a spoon, fork, and corkscrew to a foot-high, forty-blade gizmo with scissors, files, saws, and other tools obviously not meant to fit into the pocket. There are triangular affairs used by Eskimos, World War II daggers with the Nazi insignia, a multifaceted steel sword and uniform worn by a court peer in nineteenth-century England, and knives denoting the twenty different islands and tribes of Moroland in the Philippines.

Not all knives slice out bone marrow and commit hari-kari, however. An exhibit of delicate-looking, pastel colored glass cake cutlery reflects the more genteel time of the 1800s when ladies used them to serve sweets. Handles with sea shells encased in resin and a titanium model that reflects colors are more to be admired than utilized. "It's not the implement itself, but how it's used," observes Cargill.

He's also pretty sharp at piercing through counterfeits, of which there is a small display. "The manufacturer's insignia is improperly stamped, the knife has extra holes, or the blade is too narrow. Of course, there are three kinds of fakes: obvious, questionable, and fool-us-all." No doubt few, if any, have penetrated the portals of the National Knife Museum.

The National Knife Museum
7201 Shallowford Road, Chattanooga, TN 37421
((615) 892-5007

LOCATION: Exit 5, off I-75
HOURS: Monday–Friday, 9:00 A.M.–4:00 P.M.;
    Saturday, 10:00 A.M.–4:00 P.M.; closed Sunday
ADMISSION: A small admission is charged

✦ Goodlettsville: THE MUSEUM OF BEVERAGE CONTAINERS AND ADVERTISING

By rummaging through trash, Tom Bates made the *Guinness Book of World Records*, became a consultant to Columbia Pictures and other media, and established a thriving museum and publishing concern. This can-do spirit does cans: With the help of his father, Paul, Bates has collected some twenty eight thousand in all, including eight thousand five hundred individual beer cans and eighteen thousand different soda cans. Not to mention the nine thousand individual soda bottles, and assorted bottle openers, advertising signs, glasses, miniatures, bottle caps, promotional arm patches, etc., etc., etc., found in the family's Museum of Beverage Containers and Advertising in Goodlettsville, Tennessee. Many, many more than the proverbial ninety nine bottles of beer on the wall.

Exhibits range from the first beer can ever made (1935, Krueger's Cream Ale) to the first soda can (1938, Cliquot Club) to the most recent issuings from Coke and Pepsi and beverage containers from around the world. More than 90 percent of the items in the collection are no longer produced.

Bates is a walking repository of container lore, which is why he's sometimes asked to provide information on what type of can was used during a certain time period. "The earliest metal cans made beer taste bad, so breweries used kegs or plastic-lined containers," he explains. Soda cans had a tendency to explode: "so the industry stayed away from them until the technology was perfected in the fifties." Odd-looking cone-top cans, shaped like those used today for brake fluid and other automotive products, were popular circa World War II "because they could be run through existing bottle-capping equipment."

The museum is anything but a canned history of the history of cans, although everything is alphabetized and the beer and soda collections are on opposite sides of the twenty-five-hundred-square-foot room. It's easy to be pulled into categories such as animals, sports, flowers, Indians (the Native American kind), and states, as well as into specialized exhibits on manufacturers like Nehi, Orange Crush, and 7-Up. Enthusiasts may hardly be able to contain themselves.

Visitors can see Billy Beer, the brainchild of former First Brother Billy Carter; ale with such unusual names as Bullfrog and Dutch

Lunch; Pussy Pop for cats and K-9 cola for dogs, which Bates's
brother accidentally drank (he survived, although he didn't like the
taste); and Stud Cola from Australia, featuring the motto UNBUTTON
A STUD. Camouflage beer containers issued by the American mili-

These oversized bottle
caps are but a "taste"
of what lies within.
(*Photo courtesy of the
Museum of Beverage
Containers and Advertis-
ing.*)

tary; cans commemorating sporting events and teams; cans promoting the *Happy Days* TV series; and Sunday Funnies cola with cartoon characters such as Hagar, Beetle Bailey, and Blondie can also
be found here. (The latter are not to be confused with Donald Duck
soft drinks, a totally different brand). In this museum, Coke wins
over Pepsi with slightly more cans and the soda wars extend to the
1964 presidential campaign. Billed as the "the right drink for the
conservative taste" candidate Barry Goldwater produced Goldwater
Soda, while LBJ countered with Johnson Juice "a drink for health
care."

Bates has refined his gathering techniques over the years.
Although he and his father obtained many containers by "dumping,"
raking through rubbish piles for interesting cans, they also cull from
flea markets, yard sales, and antique stores. "I've purchased a can for
fifty cents then re-sold it for one hundred dollars," he states. "A lot
of people are interested in collectibles, particularly beer cans."

He feels the museum only has about half of the containers ever
produced, pointing out that there may be hundreds of variations on
a single manufacturer's product. And, like all aficionados, he'd like to
find the collector's Holy Grail: a 1940 Rosalie Beer can worth
$6,000. "There's only one known to exist in mint condition." If it's
out there, Tom Bates is the man for the can.

The Museum of Beverage Containers and Advertising
1055 Ridgecrest Drive, Goodlettsville, TN 37072
((615) 859-5236

LOCATION: Off I-24, north of Nashville
HOURS: Monday–Saturday, 9:00 A.M.–5:00 P.M.; Sunday, 1:00–5:00 P.M.
ADMISSION: Admission is charged

♠ Nashville: THE CARRIAGE COLLECTION

Step onto the grounds at Belle Meade Plantation and be transported
back to the Old South, where farming was a gentleman's occupation
(and a slave's labor), thoroughbred horses were sired without the
benefit of science or genetics, and mint juleps were a drink, not an
artificial flavor.

Built in the 1890s, the Belle Meade carriage house accommodates
an assortment of seventeen vehicles, four of which are "native" to
Belle Meade and were acquired by the plantation's original owners,
the Harding and Jackson families. "This is one of the largest collections in Tennessee and the only on a plantation," observes curator
Janet Hasson. "Until the 1850s, around the time of the industrial
revolution, carriages were considered a luxury only the wealthy and
privileged could afford." The carriages at Belle Meade range from
pre-Civil War to early 1900s.

They have distinct personalities. For instance, an extension-front
brougham is an elegant black number with red trim and beveled
glass windows made in—of all places—Cleveland, Ohio. A peek
inside reveals velvet cushions, sterling silver accents, and the plantation owner's initials on the door, all in excellent condition. "General
William G. Harding, son of Belle Meade founder John Harding, purchased this circa 1895," explains Hasson.

Another Belle Meade original is the vis-a-vis or "face to face"
sleigh, where passengers sat across from each other. Although it is
faded and worn, several of the original carvings on the wooden
frame remain. Throw in horses, snow, and a few buffalo robes, and
it's easy to imagine gliding around the plantation in the wintertime.

The carriage collection at Belle Meade Plantation reflects a more leisured era. (*Photo courtesy of Belle Meade.*)

Like the pony cart purchased at the plantation for children at the turn of the century, it's in the process of restoration.

The C-spring Victoria was the classy brougham's summertime counterpart. This recently refurbished open-air model was purported to have been a favorite of Queen Victoria's. With a folding leather top for inclement weather, black padded leather seats, and red trim, it was considered suitable only for extremely formal calling and special events—no quick runs to the mini-mart. In the late 1800s, victorias started at $1,000, while broughams sold for between $1,000–$2,000. Given the current rate of inflation, the brougham was probably the equivalent of a Rolls Royce or a Ferrari Testarossa.

Other carriages in the collection fulfilled a variety of purposes. The Imperial Park drag (circa 1860) was a four-horse pleasure vehicle utilized exclusively for picnics, parties, and races. "It had a panel that could be converted to a serving table and two fitted lunch boxes with brass handles and places for silver cups and plates," explains Hasson. This precursor to a minibus held fourteen people—four inside and ten on top.

The miniature "break" was a sort of economy-sized sporting vehicle taken to races and other summertime events. Originally designed as a skeleton rig to train horses, open-air breaks were later modified for more casual uses.

Like the carriages, Belle Meade horses were kept in a stable and carriage house complex with gas lights and running water. "Each stall was constructed to protect the animal from rubbing against the rough wood paneling," comments Hasson. Hay and feed were stored in lofts and dropped through chutes at mealtimes. Humans should only have it so easy.

The front carriage room was flanked by the tack areas, which held harnesses and equipment. An early version of a car wash links the stables and carriage house. Just put the carriage underneath, pull a rope, and a ceiling-mounted device sprayed water over it. They didn't even have to wait in line.

According to Hasson, horses and Belle Meade have had a long love affair. In its heyday, the plantation was considered the premier source of championship thoroughbreds, the bloodlines of which can still be found in horses today. "When the plantation was liquidated in 1916, the champion Luke Blackburn was sold to another estate down the road. Until his death, he always faced Belle Meade from his paddock on the riverbank." Somewhere, his descendants are just itching to pull a buggy.

The Carriage Collection
5025 S. Harding Road, Nashville, TN 37205
((615) 356-0501

LOCATION: **On the grounds of Belle Meade Plantation**
HOURS: **Monday–Saturday, 9:00 A.M.-5:00 P.M.; Sunday, 1:00–5:00 P.M.**
ADMISSION: **Admission is charged for plantation tour; Carriage**
    Collection charges no extra admission

♠ Nashville: THE MUSEUM OF TOBACCO ART AND HISTORY

Visitors to the Museum of Tobacco Art and History in Nashville are greeted by a handsome six-foot Indian with a smile on his face and a club in his hand. This cast-zinc warrior typifies the untamed spirit of the Native American and serves as a gentle reminder to keep an open mind about tobacco.

"Tobacco is a truly American product," observes museum director David Wright. "When Columbus made his historic voyage in 1492, the natives of the New World used it every way we do today, from pipe to cigar to snuff to chew to cigarettes." Although Columbus didn't realize those fragrant dried leaves would prove more valuable than his sought-after gold and spices, "[tobacco] soon became the stabilizing cash crop of our economy and its most important export."

This lithograph reflects the artistry found in turn-of-the-century tobacco advertising. (*Photo courtesy of the Museum of Tobacco Art and History.*)

The brainchild of U.S. Tobacco chairman Louis F. Bantle, who purchased and combined several collections, the museum traces the history of tobacco from pre-Columbian times to the present. Wright estimates it has been around for at least three thousand years, "most likely originating in the Andes Mountains in South America. The Indians used many herbs and discovered tobacco had a nice fragrance and could be a stimulant." The museum has an impressive collection of Native American stone and pottery pipes as well as more elaborate peace pipes. The oldest pipe, dating back about one thousand years, is from the Mound Builders of the Ohio Valley.

Visitors get a global view of the art of puffing, chewing, and sniffing. Along with Western civilizations, displays from Africa, the Orient, and northern regions include pipes, snuff boxes, cigar boxes, tobacco jars and boxes, tools, cigar-store figures, and other oddities. The collection of forty meerschaum pipes contains the unparalleled art work of master carver Gustav Fischer, Sr., who plied his trade in the window of a Boston tobacconist, creating lifelike faces, mermaids, and animals. There are exhibits of glass-blown English pipes; "whimsies," intestine-shaped puzzle and snake pipes; and delicate-looking Central European porcelain models all of which were more to be admired than used. Other unusual designs on exhibit include a skull pipe smoked when a man was being pursued by a woman or considering marriage, a pipe portraying a rather risqué lady coming out of a bathtub, and a six-foot-four-inch German regimental model honoring a militia man's lifelong service.

Cigar-store Indians greeted many a frontier shopper. (*Photo courtesy of the Museum of Tobacco Art and History.*)

Like much tobacco art in Western culture, snuff, or finely ground tobacco, has a rather macho legacy. "After dinner, the men would retire to the library and get out the snuff box," explains Wright. This involved a ritual of grating and sifting it until it was fine enough to inhale with a spoon and cleaning one's upper lip with a rabbit's foot when finished. As a result, snuff boxes came equipped with tiny tools and other implements. The museum's menacing-looking Scottish ram's head snuff box undoubtedly served as a conversation piece and a deterrent to the more fragile ladies who might want to try the stuff. S'nuff said.

Along with its regular collection, the museum recently featured an exhibition of figural tobacco jars culled from private and public collections. "These held pipe tobacco and were mostly manufactured in Europe," states Wright. Everything from Satan to smoking monkeys was depicted; "We take one aspect of tobacco history and explore it to its fullest potential."

A blue-and-gold quilt sewn from the silk ribbons used to wrap cigars and "tramp art" of boxes, toys, and cabinets made from wooden cigar boxes can also be found here. "People couldn't afford a lot so they made do with what they had."

Along with utensils for lighting tobacco (the match wasn't invented until 1827), match safes, pipe tampers, and other novelties such as a cigar roulette machine with winnings of up to ten cigars per spin, there are (of course) several cigar-store Indians. These include an 1855 wooden Mohawk chief, a cast metal squaw with a papoose, and a decked-out chieftain holding a handful of cigars pointing the way to the exit. Oh, and smoking *is* permitted in the museum.

The Museum of Tobacco Art and History
800 Harrison Street, Nashville, TN 37203
((615) 271-2349

LOCATION: In the U.S. Tobacco Building, downtown
HOURS: Monday–Saturday, 9:00 A.M.–4:00 P.M.; other times
    by appointment
ADMISSION: Free

♠ Trenton: THE VEILLEUSE-THEIERES COLLECTION

Imagine paying a traffic ticket or attending a Rotary Club meeting in the midst of multimillion-dollar art collection. Created mostly by European ceramists between 1750 and 1860, this assemblage of 525 *veilleuse-theieres*—French for "night-light teapots"—is the world's largest and most valuable. And, rather than being in the heart of a sophisticated metropolis, this teapot tempest is located in City Hall in tiny Trenton, Tennessee, where doors are kept unlocked and visitors can get a key from a "friendly fireman" at the station next door should municipal offices be closed.

A gift to the village from the late Dr. Frederick Freed, a professor of gynecology at New York University and a Trenton native, "it was originally going to be donated to the Metropolitan Museum of Art," recalls Evelyn Harwood, now in her nineties, who is the self-appointed curator and a Freed family friend. "But [Frederick's] brother suggested he leave the teapots to his hometown." Dr. Freed

TRENTON, TENNESSEE
Home of the
World's Largest Collection of
Veilleuses-Theieres

Night-light teapots range from detailed figurines with concealed spouts to plain designs on pedestals. (*Photo courtesy of the Veilleuse-Theieres Collection.*)

agreed, shipping them to Trenton at the rate of fifty a year. "At first, the collection was displayed at the local high school. But we moved it to the municipal building when it was built in 1962."

The eminent Mrs. Harwood, who worked for local government from 1948 to 1970, serving as both city judge and recorder, spouts all sorts of knowledge about *veilleuse-theieres*. "The [teapots] were initially used in sickrooms and nurseries for light, warmth, and to mix medications; and later became popular for serving beverages," she explains. The contents of the pot were heated via a pedestal underneath that contained a shallow dish known as a *godet*. It was filled with either oil with a wick in it or with a candle. "The porcelain was tempered to withstand heat for a long time, although most of the teapots are translucent, producing the soft night-light effect."

Although earlier teapots were made of cruder clay or pottery, many porcelain teapots originated from nineteenth-century France and were the work of ceramist Jacob Petit "who devised the idea of using human or animal personages to disguise the *veilleuses*'s functional nature," she continues. Part of the fun is in spotting the spout: It might be a bobbin of yarn in a woman's hand, a feather in a man's cap, a pitcher held by a goddess perched atop a leaping dolphin, or (literally) hidden up a figure's sleeve.

The collection contains over 130 examples of Petit's work as well as other teapots that came from such far-flung places as Germany, Italy, Thailand, Singapore, Ceylon, Indochina, and Turkey. "People kept them for years and years, so they've known active service," observes Mrs. Harwood. "Some have small chips and cracks," even though the coloring and workmanship seem unmarred to the untrained eye. Two of the teapots were said to have been in Napoleon's family and sport the Bonaparte crest. "Wealthy and aristocratic families purchased the more decorative and ornate *veilleuses*."

Designs range from a wife chasing her husband with a broom to an exceedingly rare and valuable lithopane porcelain figure with detailed religious scenes trimmed in 24-karat gold. They vary from a no-frills white pot-and-base number to elaborate depictions of monks, hunters, castles, and churches. There's a devil in the disguise of a pig on one rococo base that sports a shield depicting Hades; a teapot commemorating the first balloon passage across the English Channel in 1783; one depicting an encounter between Shakespeare's Romeo and Juliet; and another that's a copy of a Normandy house with the chimney as the handle and a crane (as in bird) standing by the entrance.

Trenton celebrates its windfall each May with a Teapot Festival that includes a softball tournament, beauty contest, dance, parade, and (naturally) a tea party. Visitors are always welcome to visit the collection, unless, of course, there's a city council meeting going on.

The Veilleuse-Theieres Collection
309 College Street, Trenton, TN 38382
((901) 855-2014

LOCATION: In the Trenton City Hall on SR-45W, about 30 miles north
    of Jackson
HOURS: Monday–Friday, 8:00 A.M.–5:00 P.M.
ADMISSION: Free

THE
MIDWEST

Illinois

✚ Chicago: THE INTERNATIONAL MUSEUM OF SURGICAL SCIENCE

It certainly looks imposing, a four-story lakeside mansion patterned after a French chateau. Outside stands a statue of a physician supporting a suffering soul with the words *Hope and Help* inscribed underneath. On the second floor of the museum is the Hall of Immortals, containing twelve eight-foot stone figures of healers who made a difference—giants of medicine in more ways than one. Next to it, in the Hall of Murals, vivid paintings depict surgical scenes: One shows the guillotine-like removal of a leg; another, a group of young men washing their hands in a nineteenth-century hospital, a much-ridiculed practice at that time.

Scattered throughout the Italian marble interior of Chicago's International Museum of Surgical Science are amputation kits; various bloodletting devices (which also peeled back skin); four-thousand-year-old skulls that show evidence of trepanning, among the first surgical operations ever performed by prehistoric humans; stone, bronze, iron, and steel implements of surgery and investigation; and probably the world's largest (and perhaps only) collection of gall and bladder stones.

Nearly all of the above mentioned medical procedures were done without painkillers and sterilization. It almost makes you want to shake your doctor's hand or at least increase your health insurance coverage. Until you get the bill, that is.

Yet, unlike the high-profile lifestyles of many current practitioners, until recently this museum had been a well-kept secret. Founded in 1953 by the International College of Surgeons, which has its offices next door, many of the fifteen-thousand artifacts were obtained during its first few years of, ah, operation. The twenty-five rooms of exhibits, mostly organized by country, sat unnoticed for nearly two decades, attracting dust and only occasional passers-by along with medical affiliates of the College.

But the hiring of director Barry Van Deman and his associate Linda Schubert has transfused new life into the museum. "We're re-

The only "fake" in this turn-of-the-century drugstore is the pharmacist; he is a permanent fixture. (*Photo courtesy of the International Museum of Surgical Science.*)

arranging displays according to theme, such as urology, women in medicine, and surgery during wartime," explains the enthusiastic Schubert. "Unlike other medical museums, ours has surgical objects *and* works of sculpture and art."

Like true scientists, Van Deman and Schubert plan on eliminating what doesn't work and keeping the best. The best includes:

• Instruments. These range from a bronze speculum from Pompeii to Civil War amputation knives that still contain dried blood to one of the first stethoscopes from France. Invented in the early

1800s, the stethoscope, a collapsible wooden device, fit into the doctor's top hat. An ancient stone circumcision knife used for Hebrew babies, iron forceps that removed arrows from Roman legionnaires, and early proctology apparatus from India attest to the universality (and discomfort) of certain medical procedures.

A bloodletting collection includes ox-horn cups for suction, a venesection knife that employed different blades for cutting veins, and a fifteenth-century bleeding plate believed to have been used by Lord Lister. "The practice of bleeding persisted well into the nineteenth century," points out Schubert. "People saw it as a panacea for everything from headaches to overeating."

• Devices. The museum almost discarded its working iron lung, a not-so-distant reminder of the horrors of the twentieth-century polio epidemic. "Then we discovered it was one of the few left in the country," comments Schubert. "People are fascinated by it. They turn it on and explain it to their children." What fun.

The extensive collection of X-ray equipment includes the handmade tubes and published articles of the first experimenters, many of whom died because of lack of awareness of the harmful effects. There's also an X-ray shoe-fitter used in stores during the forties and fifties and Victorian-era X-ray-proof underwear.

• Medications. Stacked antique apothecary jars advertise such "cure-alls" as Dr. Schiffmann's Cigarettes to relieve bronchial distress. Handwritten prescriptions and fragrant pharmaceuticals add to the air of authenticity. They are now part of an exhibit that replicates a historic street and includes an 1890s dentist's office and an exhibit of patent medicines.

The museum offers up abundant slivers of history. A scale model of a huge anatomical theater built in 1594 in Italy illustrates the emergence of surgery from the Dark Ages. Previously outlawed dissections of human bodies were held with advanced students in front and plenty of seats in the back for beginning classes as well as for sensation seekers, a sort of gruesome spectator sport. A death mask of Napoleon's face cast by his surgeon, Dr. Larrey, serves as a reminder of the latter's invention of "flying ambulances," horse-drawn vehicles that picked up wounded men on the battlefield rather than leaving them unattended until the skirmish was over.

The only thing this museum still needs is the addition of a woman (or women) to join I-Em-Hetep, author of the earliest known surgical text; Hippocrates, discerner of rational rather than divine causes of human disease; Ignaz Semmelweiss, who deduced the relationship between sanitation and mortality; and the other guys in the Hall of Immortals.

The International Museum of Surgical Science
1524 North Lake Shore Drive, Chicago, IL 60610
((312) 642-6502

LOCATION: **Downtown Chicago**
HOURS: **Tuesday–Saturday, 10:00 A.M.–4:00 P.M.; Sunday, 11:00**
    A.M.–5:00 P.M.
ADMISSION: **A small donation is suggested**

♠ Deerfield: THE TOOTH FAIRY MUSEUM

The Tooth Fairy's not available at the moment, so here's the next best thing: the Tooth Fairy *consultant*, Dr. Rosemary Wells of Deerfield, Illinois. And, unlike one California impersonator who bills herself (really) as Princess Diana Tooth Fairy and walks around in a long gown and tiara, Wells has really sunk her molars into the topic.

Not only has this English Ph.D. written scholarly articles and contributed to books on the origin and myth surrounding TF, as she fondly calls her, him, or it (more on that later), but she's acquired over five hundred dolls, books, cassettes, jewelry, artistic renderings, and other odds and ends. Even the Library of Congress has requested Wells's extensive bibliography. "I have fifty-four books on shedding deciduous teeth and the tooth fairy, more on the subject than they do," she states.

But even Wells, who labors as a desktop publisher and graphic designer when she's not sprinkling fairy lore, admits she may have bitten off more than she can chew. She still doesn't know the answer to the question about the origin of the Tooth Fairy—which sparked her quest in 1972—posed by a student in her scientific writing class at Northwestern University Dental School. "It's a folk tradition that began in this country around the turn of the century," she theorizes.

"It spread by word of mouth," turning into a full-blown urban legend.

Wells perused anything and everything relating to the topic, surveying over two-thousand voluntary respondents about their memories of the rite and the nature of the exchange and talking with anthropologists and other experts (i.e., six year olds).

According to Wells, rituals celebrating the first tooth loss date back to the earliest cultures and involve "throwing [the tooth] up to the sun or at a rodent, usually a mouse; or, during Medieval times, putting salt on or burning it to keep the witches away." The current Tooth Fairy is most likely a combination of the Tooth Mouse, who collected baby teeth of European and Mexican children, and all-purpose good fairies that immigrated to this country with the English, Irish, and Scottish. Getting money for teeth is a distinctly American touch, with twelve cents being the rate of exchange in 1900, rising to meet inflation at the current rate of one dollar. Although candy was offered during earlier times, "TF has also become a symbol of dental hygiene," so the treat is now more likely to be an apple or some other healthy snack.

The Tooth Fairy is also the Howard Hughes of fairies. He/she/it "is open to anyone's imagination. Ask a child what Santa Claus looks like and she can describe him exactly. Ask children about the Tooth Fairy and each comes up with something different. Because there's no set image, TF allows the youngster to develop concepts and imagery."

Wells's collection reflects the Tooth Fairy's eclectic nature. Tooth Fairy angels, children, pixies, and ballerinas, as well as a bag lady and a scowling grouch are scattered throughout one room; a veritable Tooth Fairy treasure trove. They run the gamut of materials, from papier-maché to wood to fabric to clay. "Most Americans see TF as a female, but there are animals, as well as a few men and witches." With the latter though, "particularly in literature, there's a twist, in which good or common sense triumphs."

In the museum, along with songs and T-shirts, as well as boxes, bags, and pillows to safeguard lost teeth, there are Tooth Fairy banks. In one, each tooth is fitted into its proper place in a set of pink gums, affecting a rather bizarre re-creation of the child's smile.

Another, in the shape of a tooth, has a round turntable with a spot for twenty teeth and a place to write a letter to the Tooth Fairy. As the child becomes a teen however, the banks should be removed from public view, lest they disappear under mysterious circumstances.

Wells also encourages individual interpretations by artists. "I set no guidelines," she says. "A true artist loves and welcomes a challenge." She also scours catalogs and crafts fairs and pursues leads supplied by friends and family. "I accept just about everything. Because although it's not my idea of TF, some child, somewhere will think it's just right. I'm happy with them all." Sounds like something the Tooth Fairy might say.

The Tooth Fairy Museum
1129 Cherry Street, Deerfield, IL 60015
((708) 945-1129

LOCATION: On the outskirts of Chicago, off I-294
HOURS: By appointment (contact Rosemary Wells at the museum)
ADMISSION: Free

↟ Des Plaines: MCDONALD'S MUSEUM #1 STORE

This McDonald's offers up history instead of hamburgers. Although it's not *technically* the first McDonald's ever—that honor belongs to two brothers from San Bernardino, California—it *is* the initial effort of the late entreprenuer Ray Kroc, the mastermind behind what has become approximately thirteen-thousand fast-food outlets in over sixty countries. But don't drive up expecting dinner, there's no place to sit and the servers are real dummies.

The Des Plaines, Illinois, McDonald's opened on April 15, 1955. It appears not to have changed a whit. Shiny, vintage Fords, Chevys, Chryslers, and Oldsmobiles are parked in front. (In those days, "Made in Japan" was a joke.) Coin-faced, stump-legged "Speedee" stands underneath the golden arches with a grin and a wink and a fifteen cent sign in his hand (cheeseburgers were eighteen cents).

This McMuseum still hasn't gotten to its second million hamburger (did they ever sell *under* a million?) and through the brightly

The first McDonald's was pure drive-through and had no place to eat.
(*Photo courtesy of the McDonald's Museum #1 Store.*)

lit windows, smiling mannequins are frozen in various cleaning, food preparation, and serving tasks. Next to the red and white tile walls sit two root beer barrels that served the soft drinks and a fishbowl-type globe for orangeade. A tape perpetually blasts "Rock Around the Clock," "Earth Angel," "The Ballad of Davy Crockett," and other period tunes. It feels like one's died and gone to the fifties.

Clad in their pressed dark trousers, neat white shirts with the Speedee patch, aprons, and paper hats, the work force was all male "because it involved lifting one hundred-pound sacks of potatoes and handling heavy equipment, which was considered man's work in those days," explains coordinator Delores Gilchrist. The basement stored extra food, syrups, and condiments, which also had to be lugged upstairs. In 1968, due to refinements, division of labor, and no doubt also to the growing women's movement, the corporation began to hire females. All employees were expected to have "an immaculate appearance, likable personality, and be ready to provide fast service." Yes ma'am.

"Compared to today, where most operations are automated and much of the food is pre-made and frozen, everything was done by hand," she continues. After cutting, potatoes were soaked in water for twenty minutes, rinsed, then air dried and blanched. Rather than being packaged in apportioned pieces, a huge, wheel-shaped cheese slicer cut individual slabs of cheese to top burgers.

Like the menu, which consisted of straight burgers and fries (no healthy salads, chicken, or fish), beverage selection was simple: Coke, root beer, orangeade, or milkshakes. The first two were drawn from barrels: The worker mixed syrup with carbonated water and poured it in. "Each time it tasted different, depending on whether he was being generous with the syrup." A Multimixer whipped up the shakes. "The men would make extra when they weren't too busy and put them in the holding cabinets."

Without the Multimixers, McDonald's as we know it today might not exist. "Dick and Maurice McDonald opened their [San Bernardino] restaurant in 1948," relates Gilchrist. Their self-service, assembly-line system became a hit with families and an order for eight mixers caught the attention of distributor Ray Kroc. He came, saw, and bought, taking the brothers' technological innovations and incorporating his own operating policies of *QSC&V* (Quality, Service, Cleanliness, and Value). Today, restaurant managers train at Hamburger University (really) at company headquarters in Oak Brook, Illinois.

At first, patrons could not dine in. "There was a walk-up window and customers took either took their food home or ate in the car," adds Gilchrist.

A short video about McDonald's, as well as memorabilia including uniforms and posters can be found downstairs, along with a 1955 vintage storage room with Coca-Cola syrup jugs, sacks of potatoes, and stacks of white (hamburger) and yellow (cheeseburger) wrappers. Ray Kroc is a presence here, with pictures of him and the original crew, the first day's ledger, and his various letters to owners and operators. Best of all, the real McCoy is across the street and you now truly *understand* your meal's "roots."

The McDonald's Museum #1 Store
400 North Lee Street, Des Plaines, IL 60016
((708) 297-5022

LOCATION: Northwest of Chicago, Des Plaines is at the junction of I-294 and I-90

HOURS: April–October, 10:00 A.M.–4:00 P.M. most days (call to be sure about hours)

ADMISSION: Free (book tours in advance)

↟ Elizabethtown/Rosiclare: THE HARDIN COUNTY FLUORSPAR MUSEUM

The shiny white trailer with patriotic red and blue bands traverses the state of Illinois bearing news of fluorspar. Rather than being a new kind of mouthwash (although it can be used as a natural method of fluoridating municipal water supplies) or something that glows in the dark (yet the pretty crystals of purple, blue, yellow, pink, green, and other colors can be incandescent in ultraviolet light), fluorspar, aka fluorite, in its purest form is merely a mineral. The fact that it was declared the official state mineral in 1988 by Illinois Governor James R. Thompson is a great source of pride to fluorspar's principal cheerleader, Bob Hardin of Elizabethtown.

"Fifty percent of the nation's supply is mined right here in southern Illinois," explains Hardin, a weathered-looking fellow who's worked in the Ozark-Mahoning mine in Rosiclare for over twenty years. (Both Rosiclare and Elizabethtown are located in Hardin County, but Bob claims no ancestry to the founders after whom the county is named.) Still, "most of the fluorspar comes from China and Spain and, without additional exploration of resources, our supplies will soon run out."

But what the heck does fluorspar *do*? "Basically, it's used to make hydrofluoric acid, the base chemical in elemental fluorine, aerosols, and fluorinated hydrocarbon refrigerants," Hardin replies. Aren't the last two, like, harmful to the environment? "They're being utilized less and less. But fluorspar is needed for refining steel and aluminum and manufacturing glassware, welding-rod coatings, certain types of cements, and Teflon."

Along with promoting his native area as a tourist attraction, Hardin (the man, not the county) takes his rolling museum hither and yon, to schools, county fairs, and even to the big city, Chicago.

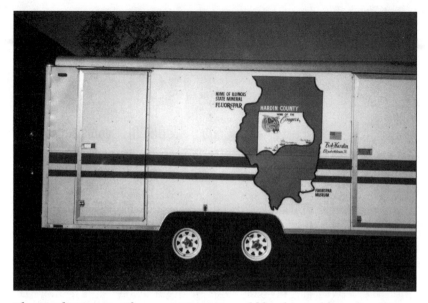

The Hardin County Fluorspar Museum could be the world's only rolling
museum dedicated to a mineral. (*Photo courtesy of Robert Hardin.*)

And it's always a fixture on October 8, Fluorspar Day in Rosiclare.
Along with a painting of the state highlighting Hardin (the county,
not the man) and the local high school mascot, the cougar, the
twenty-foot Wells Fargo unit boasts top-of-the-line carpeting as well
as paneling and lighted display cases that were installed gratis by a
carpenter buddy.

"My first museum, in 1986, had only one door," Hardin recalls.
"You get lots of people going in and out and it becomes real inconve-
nient." The newer model, purchased by Hardin with his own funds
has a separate entrance and exit.

Inside, diamond-shaped cut and rough uncut fluorspar is lovingly
displayed on red cloth. "You have to be real careful with it. The rocks
are so soft you can damage them even when they're wrapped up. I
have to take them out of the display cases every time I go on the road."

When they're available, Hardin offers free samples, which are
about the size of a potato chip. "The people at work are real good
about letting me get some rocks from the stockpile," he says. Although some of the prize specimens were donated, he's hauled hay
in exchange for others. "Instead of buying a bass boat, this has become my hobby. It's my way of having fun."

Other exhibits in this economy-sized museum trace the history of fluorspar (it was first mined locally in 1823) and include photographs, such as that of a 960-foot vein of fluorspar shining in a deep cavity of limestone, and written materials. There's also a description of native points of interest as well as archaeological information that includes local artifacts like a dinosaur bone and mastodon and shark's teeth.

But this museum soon may come to a screeching halt—at least in its present form. Thanks to a donor, Bob Hardin has managed to extract a building in Rosiclare and is in the process of digging up funds for its renovation. Along with a contribution from his employer, he hopes to obtain state monies and have the stationary location operational by 1994. "With the additional space, we can add more specimens, written information, and mining artifacts such as drills and air hammers. Plus, people won't have to worry about hitting their heads on the ceiling."

The Hardin County Fluorspar Museum
Main Street, Rosiclare, IL 62982
((618) 287-3192

LOCATION: On Route 34, 30 miles south of Harrisburg
HOURS: For information contact Bob Hardin at Box 34, Elizabethtown, IL 62931
ADMISSION: Free

♠ Evanston: DAVE'S DOWN TO EARTH ROCK SHOP AND PREHISTORIC LIFE MUSEUM

Talk about firmly grounded: Along with an avalanche of over one thousand plant and animal fossils from nearly every geologic time period, Dave's Down to Earth Rock Shop and Prehistoric Life Museum of Evanston, Illinois, boasts a dinosaur egg with an eighty-million-year-old birthdate and a piece of algae from Wyoming that's 1.5 billion years old.

Covering the Precambrian Age (basically, the beginning of time) through the Pleistocene period, which ended a mere ten thousand years ago, this collection includes a reconstructed Pleistocene cave

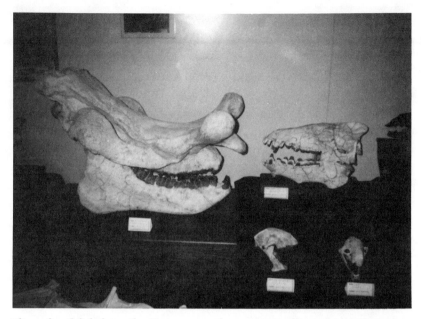

These fossil fish from the Eocene epoch are sixty million years old. (*Photo courtesy of Dave's Down to Earth Rock Shop and Prehistoric Life Museum.*)

bear, a brutish-looking lout; the femur of a dinosaur with tooth marks on it (the beast's grisly fate is always a favorite topic of discussion); and the skull of a hoplophoneus, an ancestor of the saber-tooth tiger, which had huge, dagger-like incisors.

Who on earth dug this stuff up and where did it come from? "Mostly from around here and in the West," replies "Mr. Got Rocks" himself, Dave Douglass, owner of the combination shop/museum. "We also went to Italy, Germany, and China and obtained fossils from other collectors and museums."

"We" initially included Dave and his parents, June and (really) Lincoln Douglass. "I started when I was about eight or nine, when I saw my cousin's rock collection," recalls Dave. "He told me different things about each one and it caught my interest." Rather than gathering moss, the family began taking trips to the local rock-hunting mecca, Braidwood, Illinois, a region rich in fossils. Now a good portion of it has been flooded, however, to make way for a Commonwealth Edison nuclear plant. That's the pits.

During the early sixties, the three Douglasses (or Douglasi, in geologic terms) made their most amazing finds: three entirely new fossils, all of which were about 250 million years old. "It was a humbling experience to discover a life form no one else knew existed," says Dave. As a result, each species was named after the family member who excavated it.

Although Dave planned on obtaining a degree in geology from Northwestern, the road to graduation proved rocky. During his sophomore year, he started an enterprise that would support his expeditions (this being the late sixties, many people must have thought a "rock shop" was a hangout for hippie music lovers who liked to smoke pot). It was so successful he ended up going to school part-time, then dropped out altogether to open up another store in Oregon while his parents handled the Chicago business.

A few years ago, Dave and his wife Sandra moved back to the Windy City, bringing their fossil collection with them. Although they cater to rock hounds and serious collectors, they also offer carvings, Indian crafts, minerals, and precious and semi-precious stones. Dave sells crystals, too, even though he doesn't exactly subscribe to New Age mysticism. "I try to supply what people ask for," he remarks diplomatically.

In the basement museum, visitors can unearth fossils from the Pennsylvanian period of Illinois (about 250 million years ago); mentally gnaw on a two-hundred-pound leg bone of a duckbilled dinosaur; ponder the skull of a titano, an ancestral rhino that came from the badlands of South Dakota about forty million years ago; and roll around with the complete collection of dinosaur eggs. Although he did a lot of the collecting, Dave credits Sandra with the museum's aesthetic appeal: "She designed everything with an artistic flair."

The whole family still digs rock-hunting expeditions. "It's like fishing," he observes. "You go for three days without anything and then you 'catch' something that makes up for the slack." It's a good thing his wife shares his enthusiasm; otherwise, their marriage might be on the you-know-whats.

Dave's Down to Earth Rock Shop and Prehistoric Life Museum
704 East Main Street, Evanston, IL 60202
((708) 866-7374

LOCATION: A few miles north of Chicago
HOURS: Monday, Tuesday, Thursday, and Friday, 10:30 A.M.–5:30 P.M.;
   Saturday, 10:00 A.M.–5:00 P.M.; closed Wednesday and Sunday
ADMISSION: Free

♠ Lemont: THE COOKIE JAR MUSEUM

In 1975, Lucille Bromberek successfully completed a treatment program for alcoholism. Although she had no idea what to do with her life now that she'd recovered, she bolted up in bed one night "because a little voice inside my head told me to start collecting cookie jars." Four years later, she opened the only known cookie jar museum in the civilized world.

"I traveled throughout the country and found them at garage sales, antique shows, and flea markets," she remembers. As her reputation grew, people began sending her C-jars, as she fondly calls them, from all over the United States and abroad. Soon her home was overflowing, not unlike one of her overfilled collectibles.

Today the museum is in an office building and boasts a Wedgewood jar that's over a century old; rare Belleek china shamrock-and-pineapple containers from Ireland; a Crown Milano jar worth $3000; and petite, hand decorated biscuit jars, some of which have gold filigree and others of which are made of exquisite cranberry glass.

"Most C-jars cost from $1 to $2,000, although prices have risen dramatically since I started. Jars I paid $5 for are now worth at least $125." For instance, those made from Depression glass, which was cheap in the thirties, can now fetch up to $8,000. "A few go for as high as $23,000, such as the McCoy 'Aunt Jemima' that belonged to Andy Warhol." That's a lot of dough for something that holds empty calories. Most in the two-thousand-plus collection are from twenty to fifty years old.

But the real fun of the museum is the perusal of Bromberek's piquant groupings. In the the Pig Sty, Miss Piggy shares shelf space with peers dressed in black tie, chef's togs, and a nurse's uniform. There's even a jar depicting a farmer giving slop to the porkers.

Other cookie jar menagerie members include dogs, owls, turkeys, bears, camels, cows, fish, and a whale. "The lambs and the lions and the cats and mice are shelved together and get along beautifully." One of Bromberek's favorites is the "Peek-a-Boo" jar, a ceramic rabbit in pajamas. "They made only a thousand."

The museum has cookie jar trolleys, ships, trains, cars, airplanes, and even a gypsy wagon and a spaceship to help visitors along on their journeys. And, of course, there are the usual seasonal themes: a jack-o'-lantern, a Santa Claus, and a jar commemorating the annual downfall of many a dedicated dieter, Girl Scout cookies.

Nursery rhyme characters range from the old woman who lived in the shoe to the cow who jumped over the moon, and visitors will find Dennis the Menace, Howdy Doody, and W.C. Fields as well. Bromberek has devoted three shelves to a Dutch colony and its population.

Collectors and admirers gobble up Lucille Bromberek's rare cookie jars. (*Photo courtesy of the Cookie Jar Museum.*)

Some of her arrangements tell a story, such as the one in which Cinderella is followed by a castle and then a pumpkin coach. "Turnabouts," with different faces on each side, include Mickey/Minnie Mouse, Papa/Mama Bear, and Pluto/Dumbo.

No cookie jar museum would be complete without homage paid to the treats they hold. A giant Oreo and a Tollhouse cookie, bags depicting Pepperidge Farm and Famous Amos munchies, and the Keebler elf are all represented here. Other enterprising containers include the Quaker Oats box, a Marshall Field's Frango Mint bag, the real-estate logo for Century 21, and an Avon lady calling on a Victorian-style house. For the health conscious, there are strawberry- and green-pepper-shaped jars (at least the *container's* nonfattening). And you can really get caught with your hand in the cookie jars that play music when opened.

Although Bromberek collects cookie cutters, cookie cook books, cookie plates, and measuring spoons that work for other comestibles besides cookies, the jars remain her true passion. "If they could talk, the stories they'd tell!" she half-jokes, "They come alive when I'm not there. The chefs and grannies stir up their favorite recipes for a grand gala affair. They come out of their little house C-jars, go to the barn, turn on the radio C-jar and dance up a storm." She claims she sometimes finds them in different spots in the morning. Well, okay.

Leave the appetite at home, however. "There's not a cookie on the premises."

The Cookie Jar Museum
111 Stephen Street, Lemont, IL 60439
((708) 257-2102

LOCATION: Southwest of Chicago off I-55
HOURS: 10:00 A.M.–3:00 P.M., 7 days a week
ADMISSION: Admission is charged

♠ Wauconda: THE CURT TEICH POSTCARD ARCHIVES

They sit in an unassuming white farmhouse about forty miles north-west of Chicago, a treasure trove of unchained images. Only researchers, some collectors, architectural organizations, illustrators, and publications are permitted access, and even they are limited. The rest of the great unwashed must content themselves with the ro-tating exhibits at the nearby Lake County Museum or visits to any drugstore or gift shop.

But there's a vast difference between today's glitzy photos and the 350,000 original postcards cataloged in the Curt Teich Archives. With duplicates, different angles of the same view, negatives, and job jack-ets tracing the creation of the cards, they number into the millions.

In the early 1900s, when picture and advertising postcards were at their zenith, the Curt Teich Company was the country's largest vol-ume producer. The images reveal America unretouched. The homeyness of Pumpkin Pie Day in a small; turn-of-the century Colorado town; the art deco weirdness of a 1930s Gulf service station shaped like a lighthouse; the glorious tackiness of Lucy the Elephant, a hotel landmark in Atlantic City—all are captured in their prime. Other uncommon, but uniquely American, images include a chorus of singing alligators from New Orleans; "greetings" from Austin, Minnesota, the swine capital of the world; and a wagon holding what appears to be a Florida five-foot grapefruit. "The collection can be more revealing of our culture than many other archives or even books and film media," observes Katherine Hamilton-Smith, curator.

The archive also attests to the racist and sexist underbelly of earlier eras. A picture of a Ku Klux Klan float in a Chamber of Commerce parade, an ad for Coon Chicken restaurants featuring a grinning black face, a picture of a huge lady with "it floats" across

Postcards sent greetings from the biggest cities to the smallest towns. (*Photo Courtesy of the Lake County Museum/Curt Teich Postcard Archives.*)

her bottom, and a cartoon of a woman rebuffing a man who "prefers 'em dumb" are images many would rather forget. Still, Teich also printed cards of a black grocer standing proudly in front of his store in 1906, along with those supporting labor unions and progressive politicians. The collection also has its share of disaster images—train wrecks, collapsing bridges, floods, even the 1906 San Francisco earthquake. "[Postcards] were often the only documentation of a landmark or event," says Hamilton-Smith. "People sent them to keep each other informed about what was happening in the world."

The cards trace the evolution of American life. By the twenties and thirties, cityscapes, such as Chicago's Wrigley Building and New York's Rockefeller Center, supplemented earlier images of Main

Street America and its roadside oddities. "If not for the postcards, these images might be lost forever," adds Hamilton-Smith.

America's love of the automobile was well chronicled: cards advertised car equipment and motor fashions, as well as the overflowing wrecks of Rosey's Auto Graveyard in Vintage, Pennsylvania. During

This alligator chorus reflects the true uniqueness of Teich's postcards. (*Photo Courtesy of the Lake County Museum/Curt Teich Postcard Archives.*)

World War II, the public purchased cards exhorting "Keep 'em Flying!" along with pictures of an Oriental-type sun setting behind the Stars and Stripes. (Japanese manufacturers might have the last laugh on that.) Some of Hamilton-Smith's personal favorites are Leave it to Beaveresque visions of the fifties, such as a woman in high heels and dress taking a ham out of the oven.

Like other memorabilia, postcard collecting (also known as deltiology) has enjoyed a resurgence in recent years, and the Lake County Museum has an excellent selection of reproductions. "Just about everyone has an emotional connection to them, although today people mostly send them when they're on vacation.

"Even school groups find the pictures fascinating," she continues. After they take a tour, youngsters are given a blank postcard and asked to create an image in their lives that would be meaningful fifty years from now. McDonald's restaurants are a common theme, but who can tell which one came from where?

The Curt Teich Postcard Archives/Lake County Museum
Route 176 and Fairfield Road, Wauconda, IL 60084
☏ (708) 526-7878

LOCATION: The museum and archives are in the Lakewood Forest Preserve

HOURS: The archives are available for research only, call (708) 526-8638 for information about access. Museum hours are Monday–Saturday, 11:00 A.M.–4:30 P.M. (on Thursday the hours are extended to 7:30 P.M.); Sunday, 1:00–4:30 P.M.
ADMISSION: Admission is charged

Indiana

✝ Crawfordsville: THE OLD JAIL MUSEUM

On the surface, this large building in Crawfordsville, Indiana, is a nineteenth-century Victorian beauty. Sloping roofs, tiled gables, stone and wooden columns, and "gingerbread" trim recall a more leisured era, when ladies in long dresses and parasols strolled by, ice cream and fried chicken socials were held in the nearby town square, and young men stole kisses from their girlfriends as their horse-drawn surreys rolled past. With countless incarcerations and two hangings, the inside tells a different story.

The Old Jail Museum was the first revolving jail built in the United States and the only of the seventeen rotary jails erected here during the late 1800s that is still operational. The jail is even "turned" twice a year; once for a Labor Day Breakout honoring its reincarnation as a museum, and again for a Strawberry Festival involving the entire community. "People don't actually go into the cells, but watch the [operator] rotate the crank from the basement or the first floor," observes Jane Kessler of the museum. Smart move.

A look at the jail's past adds gravity to the simple pull of a lever. Completed in 1882 for just under $26,000, the three-story structure was fronted by a sheriff's residence that included a stylish parlor,

The Old Jail Museum is the only operating revolving jail in the United States (*Photo courtesy of the museum.*)

dining room, and kitchen on one floor, and four bedrooms upstairs. Behind that was the jail—two floors, each with eight cells in a circle, and a hospital on the third level that was never used because the wooden floor made it a fire hazard. "In those days, jails and sheriff's homes were often combined," states Kessler. "The sheriff's wife cooked for the prisoners and his deputies helped with general maintenance and acted as guards."

The pie-shaped cells revolved around a hollow core that held water pipes and air shafts. Once in the cell, there was no way out, except when the jailer aligned the cell with the single caged opening on each floor. With a single entrance/exit, inmates could basically be left unattended. Or so their jailers thought.

"The sheriff let prisoners out into adjoining spaces for exercise, showers, and meals," reports Kessler. And despite its Spartan motif, the jail was considered state of the art by the standards of the day. Although few homes in those days had indoor plumbing, each inmate had his own toilet—for obvious reasons. Cells were individually heated and ventilated and fresh water was always available. "Sometimes people would do things just to finagle a weekend in jail, especially if the sheriff's wife was a good cook," states Kessler. "It was the cheapest 'hotel' in town."

Still, sometimes gears would jam, making it difficult to rotate the cylinder. Moving the cylinder back and forth became a favorite prisoner pastime, a sort of pre-Elvis "Jailhouse Rock." They'd be stuck for days in their cells while workers scrambled to return the cylinder to the track. Occasionally prisoners got arms and legs caught in the bars while the cells were being revolved. Finally, the core and plumbing began to rust, making it feasible for prisoners to slide down the shaft and flee through the basement. Several escaped in this manner, although all but one were caught.

After ten or fifteen years of use, most rotary jails were disbanded. The Crawfordsville jail remained operational until 1938, after which the cell block was made stationary, doors were cut into each cell, and a catwalk was built around the second floor. It housed short-term prisoners until 1973.

The site of hangings in 1885 and 1886, the museum displays some of the ropes used. Reproductions of the newspapers telling the stories of the executions are available in the gift shop. Tickets were issued for the actual event, with the scaffold left standing as a deterrent to future crime. Today we have cop shows.

"People are enthralled," observes Kessler. "One man even came back with his children to show them the cell where he'd been incarcerated." Now *that's* recidivism.

The Old Jail Museum
225 N. Washington Street, Crawfordsville, IN 47933
((317) 362-5222

LOCATION: Off I-74, 49 miles west of Indianapolis
HOURS: April–October, Wednesday–Sunday, 1:30–4:30 P.M.; or by appointment
ADMISSION: Free

♠ Huntington: THE DAN QUAYLE CENTER AND MUSEUM

You may not personally get to meet former Vice-President Dan Quayle—as hundreds did during the October 1993 dedication of his new museum in Huntington, Indiana—but you can have the next best thing: your picture taken next to his cardboard likeness. Still, "It's about three inches shorter than Dan's actual height," points out a museum employee. "Someone cut the feet off." Oh, well.

Be warned: Huntington residents are not amused at jibes about their favorite native son. (Although in the spirit of true minorities, they can joke about him among themselves.) They take their Quayle very seriously, and once you get to know his museum, you may find he's not such a bad fellow.

Located in a four-thousand-square-foot former Christian Scientist Church that was constructed in 1919, this not-for-profit museum was

organized by a group of civic leaders who call themselves the Dan Quayle Commemorative Foundation. Hey guys, he's not even dead yet.

"This museum serves a dual purpose—to document the history of the vice-presidency and to tell the story of Dan Quayle," explains board member David Schenkel. Visitors are guided to the second floor where they can read all about vice-presidents, including the fact that until the early 1800s the vice president

The Dan Quayle Center and Museum—the only museum in the world honoring a U.S. vice-president. (*Photo courtesy of the museum.*)

was the individual who got the second most electoral college votes (sort of like being the runner-up in a beauty pageant). But conflicts over party loyalties and vagaries over succession resulted in the president choosing his own running mate. The five Indiana vice presidents are highlighted, including Thomas R. Marshall (1913–1921) coiner of the memorable phrase, "What this country needs is a good five-cent cigar." There are also a box of cigars and a vice presidential flag, among other things.

Most people come for the Quayle stuff, however, and there is plenty, beginning with a reproduction of his birth certificate, moving on to baby pictures, and even a lock of hair from his first haircut. You'll find his Little League uniform, childhood letters, a sweatshirt

This display highlights the Veep's early years—including his tiny foot and handprints, made at birth. (*Photo courtesy Matt Farmer.*)

with DANNY stitched across the front. Family Christmas cards document his growth and a brief move to Scottsdale, Arizona, where he excelled on the golf team (a precursor to future political networking). The museum has eleven thousand items, although only about one hundred are on display. "They mostly came from the family, friends, and the Transition Office in Washington, DC," reports Schenkel.

Grade school report cards portray Dan as an A and B student, and although his Indiana University law degree was chewed by family dog Barnaby, it's still valid. "The family was upset," recalls Schenkel. "So Marilyn gave Barnaby away."

Another section illustrates his political career, from his rise to the U.S. House of Representatives in 1976, to his being the youngest person in Indiana to be elected to the Senate four years later. He was reelected in 1986 by a landslide. George Bush picked him as a running mate in 1988 and the rest is well-known history and perhaps a bit of disinformation.

Still, Dan had some help along the way. His maternal grandfather, Eugene Pulliam, was a wealthy and influential publisher of several newspapers in Indiana and Arizona. And Dan worked at the Huntington Herald-Press as general manager along with having a law office with Marilyn until his political career took flight.

T-shirts, hats, buttons, even a chair from Nick's Kitchen in Huntington where Dan announced various candidacies can be found here. The exhibit ends with an exquisite reproduction of a Fabergé egg depicting Quayle's vice-presidential swearing-in. "It was given to him by the state of Indiana," comments Schenkel. Still, the museum is funded by private monies and claims to be apolitical.

The rotating exhibits downstairs depict Dan on the job, noting that he visited forty-seven countries during his stint as vice-president and pointing out that he was a member of the National Security Council and also the first chairman of the National Space Council (Murphy Brown would have fun with that). At this writing, visitors can view memorabilia such as a New England Patriots jersey given to Quayle by Teddy Kennedy and gifts from various governments like a black lacquer jewelry box from Korea and a colorful Kinte cloth from Nigeria. (Presents in the latter category officially belong to the National Archives and not to the Quayles.)

The gift shop sells authentic limited-edition vice-presidential cuff links and tie bars ($150) and pins ($100). Less pricey items include mugs, pencils, T-shirts, and an autographed novel penned by Marilyn Quayle and her sister, Nancy Northcutt. Huntington also offers the "Quayle Trail", a walking/driving tour of Quayle hot spots, such as the *Herald-Press* building, the church where Dan and his family worshiped, and his childhood home.

Who knows? You may find yourself rooting for him.

The Dan Quayle Center and Museum
815 Warren Street, Huntington, IN 46750
((219) 356-6356

LOCATION: West of I-69 off U.S. 224
HOURS: Tuesday–Saturday, 10:00 A.M.–4:00 P.M.; Sunday, 1:00–4:00 P.M.
ADMISSION: Free

♠ Martinsville: DRAKE'S MIDWEST PHONOGRAPH MUSEUM

This record-breaking collection includes phonographs that play on chocolate, tinfoil, rubber, and plastic; victrolas running on treadles, springs, and batteries; a garish-looking lamp gramophone and one that's inside a player piano; animated jukeboxes with dancing figures and flashing lights; and the mother of all record players, the very first chronicler of sound, an 1858 phonautograph. Even more of a blast: just about all of the over six hundred different "talking ma-

For a nickel, this gramophone not only offered music but a gum drop. (*Photo courtesy of Drake's Midwest Phonograph Museum.*)

chines" at Drake's Midwest Phonograph Museum in Martinsville, Indiana, actually *work*.

"What we can't find in original parts, we put together ourselves," states Kathleen Drake, widow of Dr. Ellery Drake, the surgeon who jockeyed the disc players into the museum. But most are for display only, for although Dr. Drake's fascination with phonographs began in his childhood when he could listen to but not touch his great-uncle's, "many are one-of-a-kind and very fragile," adds Kathleen, using sound logic.

There's a really groovy disc collection, which numbers in the tens of thousands. "We have all but 110 of the original 4,120 commercial recordings made by Edison." The museum's oldest disc dates back to 1886 and is made of cardboard.

Basically arranged in chronological order ("we change the exhibits periodically for variety"), the first selections consist of Scott's barrel-shaped phonautograph, which records but does not play sound, and a reproduction of Edison's first working attempt from nearly twenty years later. "The prototype's in the Smithsonian, but we have several 1878 models," says Drake. According to her, Leon Scott, who coincidentally hailed from Martinsville, France, invented the phonautograph "to prove that sound could be recorded, although of course no one believed him at the time." We can thank him for Guns 'N' Roses, bubble gum music, and "Feelings."

Older than spring wound record players, battery operated machines had listening tubes that could qualify as early headsets. "The tubes gave a better tone quality than the best horns. But batteries were messy and difficult, so manufacturers converted to windup motors, which were popular until the 1920s."

Still, "most early machines used exterior horns to disperse sound," Drake goes on. Along with wooden horns, colored "morning glory" horns with flowers, and dual horns that amplified, but did not make stereo sound, the museum has a six-foot trumpeter that could barely fit through the door. "Edison made a horn that ran a city block, but it wasn't practical because sound vibrations only go so far." Cameraphones—small portable phonographs—were also popular during the early part of the century.

Many of the phonograph cases were made of burnished wood, while others consisted of crystal and mirrors with a glass turntable "that was supposed to produce crystal-clear tones," explains Drake. An escalloped gold leaf number with scenic oil paintings turns the volume way up on flamboyance, and an "illustrated song machine" features 3-D postcards with music, a very early precursor of MTV. Occasionally the phonographs went incognito: an oriental Victor model with a lid posed as a small pagoda; a French talking doll concealed a small record player in her stomach; another Edison hid inside a sewing machine. Others are camouflaged behind rolltop desks or in pianos. "People wanted them to blend into their parlors."

The tables turned somewhat differently with jukeboxes. "Coin record players were developed in the 1890s, with the term *jukebox* being created in New Orleans around 1915," she continues. The museum's include a Wurlitzer with colored lights and a curtain that opens to reveal a miniature bandstand that plays when a record starts. Another tentacle-like device utilizes rubber hoses so each individual at the table can listen to the song. Also, if you don't like the music, you can hit the person who selected it with your hose. A See-burg offers a variation on the one-record per turntable with its stack of records on a single spindle all rotating at the same time.

In order to avoid patent disputes, each record player manufac-turer had a different name for its machine. Victor had the talking machine, or Victrola; Berliner used Gramophone; and Columbia went with similar-sounding Graphophone. Edison coined the more common phonograph. But they sound about the same, and tales spun about their origin continue to be on many an oldies lover's hit parade.

Drake's Midwest Phonograph Museum
2255 SR 252, Martinsville, IN 46151
((317) 342-7652

LOCATION: Off S R 37
HOURS: Call for hours
ADMISSION: Admission is charged

♠ Wakarusa: The Bird's Eye View Museum

DeVon Rose is living proof of the paraphrased maxim, "If you build it, they will come." His field of dreams, the Bird's Eye View Mu-seum, consists of a two-hundred-square-foot replica of the Wakarusa, Indiana, business district as it appeared during the 1950s and 1960s. The four square blocks of his miniature municipality con-tain office buildings, businesses, churches, and homes. Along with electricity and a turning barber pole, the lilliputian locality has a laundromat with washers and a Chevrolet car lot. Only it's on a scale of one inch for every five feet, a *fifth* the size of your average doll-house.

Sixty-something-year-old Rose, an architectural draftsman by trade with no formal art training, has been working his miniscule magic since 1961. "My sons asked me to construct a building for their railroad set," he recalls. Rather than slapping some paint on a

shoe box, he decided to reproduce the six-structure Wayne Feed
Mill complex in his hometown of Wakarusa.

For nine months, he toiled. He duplicated the corrugated sheet-
metal siding by using the grooved linings of pencil lead boxes. He
fashioned minuscule windows and doors that opened and, utilizing
thread, wooden dowels, popsicle sticks, and toothpicks, created gen-

The Exchange State
Bank in Wakarusa,
circa 1964. (*Photo
courtesy of the Bird's Eye
View Museum.*)

uine-looking phone lines. He put dirt and stones underneath the
railroad tracks to make them seem like the real thing. "It took over
forty hours to get the shingles for the green roof on that office over
there," he explains, pointing to a diminutive structure that looks as
though it's been beaten by the weather for years. "I cut the shingles
out of cardboard and painted 'em so they look like asphalt. I also use
a lot of brown shoe polish for an aging effect."

The only non-Wakarusa structure in this tiny museum is Bonneyville Mills. Constructed in 1832, the mills were operational when
Rose duplicated them in the mid-sixties and had plans to clone Bristol as well. Now Bonneyville Mills are part of a county park and
several buildings have been torn down.

"When you look back, this is actually history," observes Rose.
"Wakarusa's a small town, no more'n one thousand five hundred
people. But it's peaceful and we appreciate tradition." Some of his
reproductions, including a railroad depot and an outhouse, are on
display at the Wakarusa Historical Society Museum.

"I just go ahead and build, no matter how long it takes," he continues. "I take bits of odds and ends and it eventually resembles the

thing I'm copying." He also visits the structure he intends to replicate, recording every architectural and topographical idiosyncracy.
"If people see me copying in Wakarusa, they hurry and clean up
[their exteriors]. They know I'll show the building exactly the way it
is, down to a crack in the wall or an overflowing trash can." One lady
refused to allow him access until she got her porch fixed.

Friends save fruit crates and popsicle sticks for him and "glue and
shoe polish don't cost much. It took more money to fix up my basement for the museum."

Construction follows a certain logic in Rose's mini-macrocosm.
Sawdust becomes stucco, woodburned cardboard is transformed into
brick, clear plastic makes up windows. He obtained stained glass
windows for the Bible Baptist Church by "cutting up different colored cellophane candy wrappers and pasting 'em on plastic." Trees
consist of "leaves" of spray painted steel wool; branches and trunks
are made from the wires inside automobile tires. "I burn the rubber
off the tires and just let the wires age and get rusty." The coloration
and type of foliage around the buildings exactly matches the original.
Sequins become stop lights and window screens are converted into
chain link fences. Art duplicates life and branches never, ever touch
power lines.

"It'll probably take me another eight to nine years to finish the
rest of uptown," Rose says. "I'd also like to sell ceramic buildings of
the displays."

Still, most visitors appreciate the Bird's Eye View Museum the
way it is. "One old guy came in and told me I forgot something on
the feed mill," he recalls. "When I asked him what that was, he
pointed to the roof and said, 'Pigeon s——.' I told him, 'Hey, I got to
stop somewhere.'" So what's that dog doing by the fire hydrant?

The Bird's Eye View Museum
325 S. Elkhart Street, Wakarusa, IN 46573
((219) 862-2367

LOCATION: Off SR 19, about 15 miles northeast of South Bend
HOURS: Monday–Friday, 8:00 A.M.–5:00 P.M.; Saturday, 8:00 A.M.–noon
ADMISSION: Admission is charged

Iowa

↑ Cedar Falls: THE ICE HOUSE MUSEUM

The circular Ice House Museum in Cedar Falls, Iowa, is truly well-rounded, with collections of dairy equipment, sewing and washing machines, carpentry tools, antique telephones and switchboards, cars, and horse drawn vehicles such as a black (not yellow) school bus. Old-time farm implements include—politicians and lawyers take note—a Litchfield manure spreader. That's in addition to the blacksmith, butcher, and leather goods shops; the broom-making machine that still produces souvenirs; World War I and II displays; an early road grader; and a boat commemorating the time when the icehouse was a boat-storage facility that had been leased from the city for a one dollar per year. Oh, and then there's the museum's main focus, the harvesting and storage of natural ice.

Although executive director Rosie Peterson states that tours take about an hour, she also comments, "You could spend half a day here and not see everything." Most people come for the truly cool, six-hundred-square-foot ice processing display.

"This industry existed in almost every town in America in the last half of the 1800s and early 1900s," points out Peterson. Workers "would locate an area on the river every winter, watching and measuring it until the ice was fourteen to eighteen inches deep." Then they'd start sawing blocks that often weighed up to three hundred pounds, sending them down a pre-cut channel toward the icehouse. A conveyor ran from the river to the door on the house, bringing the giant cubes inside. And to think pushing a button on many refrigerators today can obtain their mini, many descendants.

The icemen would "cometh" door to door, dropping off the amounts requested via signs in customers' windows. Along with a collection of these cards, the museum has ice picks from the days when they were considered household tools rather than potential

The unique round shape of the ice house is reminiscent of barns of the period. (*Photo courtesy of the Cedar Falls Historical Society.*)

murder weapons. "People would get ice a couple of times a week, just enough to prevent their food from spoiling," Peterson notes.

Built in 1921, the Cedar Falls icehouse replaced an earlier version that, incredibly, burned down. "The [original structure] was made of wood and sat next to a barn," explains Peterson. "By October, when a fire resulted from an overturned kerosene lamp, the ice supply was low and had been packed in sawdust for preservation." Despite the intense heat, a few chunks still remained after the conflagration, which took less than an hour.

The replacement, copied from the round barns popular in that era, was one hundred feet in diameter with thirty-foot-high walls made of hollow clay tiles reinforced by steel ties. Along with the capability of storing up to eight thousand tons of ice, the building materials provided excellent insulation.

A mural of the Cedar River in winter forms the background for an array of nineteenth-century tools and implements used to cut natural ice. Along with an ice wagon (horses not included) and blocks of fake ice, there is a life-size photograph of a man using a harvester. Visitors can have their pictures taken standing next to him. It appears realistic enough from a distance to make you want to grab your coat. The most common iceboxes used by the public share space with a scale model of the icehouse when it was in full operation in the twenties.

Visitors can also "chill out" with a collection of early refrigerators, including the Herrick made in nearby Waterloo, a Frigidaire, a General Electric, even a Coolerator. With its icebox with a door for outside deliveries, old fashioned coal cooking range, perforated tin pie safe to keep food from spoiling, and hand-operated cistern pump, the 1920s kitchen draws appreciation for modern conveniences even from reluctant homemakers. You can catch a slide show on "Ice Harvesting" that gives an overview of the industry in the United States and one called "Ice Cutting on the Cedar," that tells the story of the Ice House Museum.

After that, go for a cup of hot chocolate.

The Ice House Museum
Cedar Falls Historical Society
303 Franklin Street, Cedar Falls, Iowa 50613
((319) 277-8817 OR 266-5149

LOCATION: Downtown Cedar Falls at First and Clay Streets
HOURS: May 1–October 31; Wednesday, Saturday, and Sunday, 2:00–4:30 P.M.
ADMISSION: Free

✝ Newton: THE MAYTAG EXHIBIT

It's logical that the Maytag Exhibit, part of the much larger Jasper County Historical Museum, should be located in Newton, Iowa, the Washing Machine Capital of the World. After all, Newton has been home to nine different manufacturers of washing machines at various times, including, of course, Maytag.

Along with tour guides who explain the story of the machines in great and loving detail, there are the devices themselves. They represent a microcosm of home engineering developments of the last century, elevating the lifestyle of the homemaker from a scrubwoman with dishpan elbows to a domestic artiste with a few extra hours for grocery shopping, driving the children to various activities, and working in an office.

Not all the machines are Maytags. One of the first, built in 1898 by the Hawkeye Incubator company, was known as a rachet-slat washing machine. This circular wooden model operated using a tub, a drum, and a manually powered lever. "You put the clothes in the drum, then add the hose, soap, and water," explains museum director Hans Brosig. A milk-stool agitator, also created by the same company which by now had changed its name to the paradoxical One Minute, rotated back and forth in the tub, making it a little easier for the operator to clean clothes.

By 1907, two Minute men had invented an electric motor for the machine. When management decided production would be too expensive, the inventors formed their own enterprise, Automatic Washing Machines. Still another ingenious contraption made by a company called Woodrow had a faucet on the bottom. Rather than dumping the water out manually, the woman (and it was *always* a woman) simply tilted the barrel. "Of course you couldn't completely empty the machine or the slats would dry out and it would leak like an empty rowboat."

Maytag began agitating the industry in 1907 too. Started in 1893, in Newton, the company had primarily produced farm implements. Its first venture into washing machine, the Pastime, was a basic hand-powered wooden tub which was soon superseded by an electric machine (1911). Maytag took a giant leap forward three years later with the Maytag multi-motor. "This self-starting gasoline engine was a great convenience for rural people who had no electricity." Maytag also developed a swinging reversible wringer that could be positioned from any angle and worked forward and backward. "Many companies paid a royalty so they could use it on their washers."

Brosig likes to point out that while competitors made their tubs out of copper in the twenties, Maytag was the first to take advantage of aluminum, which, along with being sturdier, didn't turn green (taking the laundry along with it). They also invented a gyrafoam agitator powered from the bottom of the machine instead of from the top, a soft "balloon" wringer roller that saved buttons and fingers, and a one-piece die-cast tub design that was utilized until 1983.

Maytag also devised laundry detergent ("Soap makers caught on quickly after that"), a commercial washer that used plastic tickets instead of coins ("It didn't last long because the laundromat owner had to be there constantly to give out the tickets."), and a machine that churned butter, made ice cream, or ground meat while you did the laundry (it only accomplished one of the three at a time, though). All of these innovations helped take their rivals to the cleaners.

Postwar prosperity brought automatic washers and dryers (1949) into homes and the technological improvements continued: the "halo of heat" dryer, which spread warmth throughout the tub instead of from one central location (1956); the push-button washing machine that allowed users to select their wash cycle; the electronically controlled dryer which "sensed" when enough moisture had been removed from the load (1961).

The company's other products—oil cans, wrenches, lawn mowers, racing cars for children, dishwashers, and garbage disposals—are also on display. "Because of our production methods, we had detailed knowledge of aluminum casting, which was very helpful during World War II," adds Brosig.

Visitors not overloaded on history by the Maytag Exhibit can stop by the main museum's forty-foot-long bas-relief sculpture that depicts the annals of Jasper County. Exhibits at the museum also include a drugstore, one-room country schoolhouse, and a rebuilt 1875 barn. And these represent only a tiny portion of its offerings. Those who manage to see *everything* at the Jasper County Historical Museum can truly say they've been through the wringer.

The Maytag Exhibit
Jasper County Historical Museum
P.O. Box 854
1700 S. 15th Avenue W., Newton, IA 50208
((515) 792-9118

LOCATION: Off I-80, east of Des Moines
HOURS: May 1–October 1, seven days a week, 1:00–5:00 P.M.; group
   tours by appointment
ADMISSION: Admission is charged

♠ Spillville: THE BILY CLOCKS

Joseph and Frank Bily truly mastered time, carving intricate wooden clocks with moveable figures and music. Their father, John, thought they were slightly cuckoo and felt they should devote themselves entirely to their "real" jobs of farming and carpentry. But the brothers persisted in their carving during the long, idle Iowa winter afternoons and evenings. Although they passed away in the mid-1960s, their artistry remains on permanent display in a Victorian-era home once occupied by Czech composer Antonin Dvorak when he stayed in Spillville, Iowa.

With its well-kept streets, manicured parks, tidy public square, and bandstand that's hosted innumerable tributes to returning war heroes, this picturesque village is a hotbed of Americana. Founded in 1854 by Joseph Spielman, and settled mostly by fellow Czechs, the town's name was later Americanized from Spielville to Spillville. It was here that An-

The Village Blacksmith clock, done between 1942 and 1943, and inspired by Longfellow's poem, was the last major project of the Bily brothers. (*Photo courtesy of the Bily Clocks exhibit.*)

tonin Dvorak, "tired from a year's work as director of the New York Conservatory of Music and homesick for the companionship of his countrymen" (according to a descriptive brochure), came in the summer of 1893 with his family. Along with adding the finishing touches to his *New World Symphony*, he is said to have found inspiration for his *Humoresque* pianofortes, and to have composed the lesser-known *American Quartette* while in Spillville too. He liked it so much he returned the following summer for a two-week vacation.

Visitors might not be as enthusiastic about Spillville—how many hours can one spend staring at a rock with *Humoresque* engraved on its side at the Dvorak Memorial in Riverside Park or meandering around the gothically imposing St. Wenceslas Church, with its 1876 pipe organ that was played by Dr. Dvorak himself? But the forty clocks and two model churches in the Bily exhibit are sure to be fascinating.

The Bily brothers' tools were nearly all homemade, while almost all of their clockworks and chimes came from a factory. Although they primarily used native walnut, butternut, maple, and oak, some of their earlier attempts are made of imported cherry, mahogany, boxwood, and white holly. Many of the clocks are several feet tall, weighing hundreds of pounds. They built the first one around 1913, so some musical discs are nearly one hundred years old.

"You truly can't appreciate the clocks until you see them in action," states exhibit manager Joyce Fuchs. The Bilys' initial tickers, such as the *Grand Tower Clock* and the *Creation Clock*, were quite ornate, patterned after the European Gothic cathedral style. Later endeavors represented specific persons, places, or events. In the *Apostle Clock*, the twelve apostles parade every hour within a large churchlike structure. *The American Pioneer History Clock* has fifty-seven panels showing symbols of U.S. history: the Liberty Bell, the Mayflower, cowboys on the range, and many others. While playing "America," the moving part depicts the four ages of humans, from childhood to geezerdom.

An airplane-shaped *Lindbergh Clock*, with a carving of the aviator's head inside it, commemorates his historic flight. The *Parade of Nations Clock* features a moving globe with people holding hands; the *Statuary Clock* offers busts of Thomas Edison, Michelangelo, and Spillville founder Joseph Spielman, along with other national and local notables. Obviously the brothers admired these folks: a small orchestra inside the clock performs "Praise to the Lord."

Among the cream of the clocks is the *Village Blacksmith*, their last major project, which was done between 1942 and 1943. Based on the poem of the same name by Henry Wadsworth Longfellow, it has a realistic-looking bellows, forge, and anvil; a collection of tools that were carved before being placed individually on the back wall; and a hat that can be removed from the farmer's head and put on the blacksmith's. "You can even see the stitches in the patch on the

farmer's pants," points out Fuchs. "My Old Kentucky Home" is ren-
dered while the blacksmith hammers on the plowshares.

The Bily brothers did not want to sell or break up their collection.
Upon their deaths they had arranged to donate it to the town of
Spillville where it remained in the Dvorak building. As if to cement
the deal, they carved a violin-shaped clock featuring Dvorak's head.
What a harmonious bunch.

The Bily Clock Exhibit, Spillville, IA 52618
((319) 562-3569

LOCATION: At Waterloo, take 63N to 24E near Atkinson
HOURS: Hours vary
ADMISSION: Admission is charged

Kansas

♦ Abilene: THE MUSEUM OF INDEPENDENT TELEPHONY

The Museum of Independent Telephony (pronounced tel-eph-a-
nee) was organized by some pretty smooth operators. Among its
approximately four thousand artifacts are five hundred phones of all
eras, shapes, and sizes; a re-creation of a nineteenth-century telephone exchange; vintage pay stations; dozens of rare and valuable
glass and ceramic insulators; and a collection of telephone-related
sheet music. Visitors can actually talk to one another on the antique
telephones, play operator on a magneto (pronounced mag-nee-to)
switchboard, be at the receiver-end of various telephone songs, and
make calls from an old wooden phone booth that even preceded
Clark Kent.

"People in small cities, towns, and rural areas were clamoring for

telephone service, so to speak," explains curator Peg Chronister with
a smile. "Bell only went into the larger cities, so local citizens organized Independents all over the country, even though they had little
money and staffing."

This museum's on a party line, so to speak, sharing a building with
the Dickenson County museum. Artifacts and written material were
donated from its sponsor, United Telecom, from other Independents, and from private groups and individuals.

"Most instruments have seen actual service," says Chronister. A
wall-to-wall rogue's gallery of phones depicts their evolution, beginning with Bell's first attempt in 1875 over which he could hear voice

This telephone time-
line runs from Bell's
early attempts to to-
day's latest models.
(*Photo courtesy of the
Museum of Independent
Telephony.*)

sounds but not understand words and ending with touch-tone and
cordless models. Other phones include "command dialers" that re-
spond to verbal instructions and a rare circa-1900 hanging phone
that is bolted from the ceiling. Resembling an upside-down coffee
can, "the phone was used by people who didn't want to leave their
work places to make or receive calls. The can had weights on it so
you could adjust it to reach your ear or position it up out of the way."
In the early days, people often journeyed to the corner drugstore, a
hotel, or to the telephone office to make or receive calls.

But the commercial telephone's real roots can be found in a special exhibit on loan from the Smithsonian Institution. Consisting of
models from the late 1870s, the display includes a small Butterstamp
phone in which users pushed a button to get the operator, gave him
or her the exchange, and then moved the receiver from mouth to ear
in order to have a conversation. "It was similar to operating a CB
radio in which you had to tell the other person it was his turn to talk,"

comments Chronister. Also included in the exhibit are the "thumper," which vibrated instead of ringing to let people know there was a call and the "coffin," which, in addition to looking like one, was the first phone design to utilize bells and a separate box for talking.

The museum's old telephone office has crank style phones, a magneto switchboard, a rolltop desk, a cot for the operator to nap on, and a lantern, shovel, and gloves "in case the switchboard caught fire during an electrical storm and the operator had to smother it with sand," says Chronister. A Calculagraph clock that measured the duration of long distance calls was actually used for sixty years. "In 1892, it cost five dollars for a five-minute call from New York to Chicago." At least something's cheaper these days.

Which explains why a few of the museum's coin operated pay stations have slots for silver dollars, along with openings for nickels, dimes, quarters, and fifty-cent pieces. With detailed cabinetwork and brass hinges, these phones reflect a level of artistry not found today. "Even the sound of the money going in is musical," observes Chronister. Especially if the museum gets to pocket the change.

There are also miniature phones for kids as well as a complete library of historical manuals, books, and telephone company histories. So even if you need more information, you won't get hung up.

The Museum of Independent Telephony
412 S. Campbell, Abilene, KS 67410
((913) 263-2681

LOCATION: **Off I-70, about 30 miles west of Salina**
HOURS: **April 15–October 15; Monday–Saturday 10:00 A.M.–8:00 P.M.;**
Sunday 1:00–5:00 P.M.
ADMISSION: **A nominal admission fee is charged for adults**

↟ La Crosse: THE BARBED WIRE MUSEUM AND THE POST ROCK MUSEUM

Like their namesakes, the Barbed Wire and Post Rock Museums of La Crosse, Kansas, have held up over the years. Barbed wire collecting has stuck around for decades; its museum was established in

1970 and recently moved to larger quarters. Although there are barbed wire museums in Walsenburg, Colorado, and McLean, Texas, and a display at the Ellwood House Museum in its actual birthplace (ouch!) of DeKalb, Illinois, La Crosse likes to bill itself as the Barbed Wire Capital of the World. After all, the Kansas Barbed Wire Collectors Association there hosts an annual festival each May where the faithful come to shop, swap, and see who can do the best job of splicing the prickly stuff.

Although the tiny Post Rock Museum has no such following (imagine schlepping a 450-pound post to a trade show), its history is just as upstanding. Opened in 1964, it tells the story of the steadfast limestone fenceposts that supported the barbed wire on the prairies of North Central Kansas during the late nineteenth century, containing livestock, demarcating property lines, and bringing prosperity as well as range wars to the land. Although cattle ranchers and cowboy types initially had an aversion to any barrier on their free range, farmers, homesteaders, and townspeople *wanted* to be fenced in. All that loose beef on the hoof wreaked havoc in the vegetable garden and on the front porch.

To know barbed wire is to pierce some illusions (to love it, requires a pair of very thick gloves). According to Everett Renberger, a member of the board of trustees for the Barbed Wire Museum, there are over one thousand different types of patented wire, although some's not barbed wire per se "but other types such as knotted planter's wire used to seed corn and cotton crops as well as for fences."

"Back in the 1870s, when the wire first came in use, there was a rush to patent the stuff, so manufacturers were careful not to duplicate each other's designs," he observes. Thus, there's the single-stranded wire with barbs every eight to twelve inches and the four-stranded type with the barbs closer together and the very rare "star" and the menacing-looking "spur rowel" wire. Along with the usual thorn-like prongs, visitors to the museum will find a tangle of leaves, spirals, zigzags, and buckles.

Competitors' dreams were punctured in 1892, when the Supreme Court ruled in favor of Joseph Glidden, the sharp DeKalb farmer who had made the first successful design (double-stranded, with barbs held in place by twisted wire), stating that his patent covered all types of barbed wire. Still, cutting-edge innovations continued:

There are over one thousand different types of patented wire and the
Barbed Wire Museum has most of them. (*Photo courtesy of the museum.*)

Condensed, unforgiving high-tensile wire has been utilized since
World War II; pointed, H-shaped "entanglement" wire penned prisoners in Vietnam. Razor wire, also known as barbed tape, graces the
top of many chain-link fences in larger cities, looking like the Slinky
from Hell.

The museum offers up these and thousands of other types of wire
sliced into standard-length eighteen-inch strips, as well as related
tools. Standouts on exhibit include a line repairman's hammer that
hung from a saddle horn, a steel-studded leather glove that looks
more like a Medieval torture device than something used to install
railroad fencing, and a nest actually constructed from you-know-
what by convenience-minded ravens. "The birds came back every
year to add new pieces of wire," comments Renberger. There's a gift
shop that sells penetrating reminders such as standard eighteen-inch
pieces as well as wreaths for the metal fan who has everything.

Down the block, the Post Rock Museum provides a hard-core
analysis of *its* history. "About forty thousand miles of post rock fence
can be traced throughout our area," observes curator Dorothy
Smith. Much was at stake; at five to six feet in length, the posts usu-

The outside of the Post Rock Museum is as "rocky" as its interior. (*Photo courtesy of the museum.*)

ally measured nine inches square and weighed 250–450 pounds. "Because limestone was so available and abundant, it was also utilized for homes, schools, churches, bridges, decorative stones, and other structures." Rocks were carved into feeders for chickens, dogs, and cats, as well as for larger animals (i.e., troughs for cattle).

Rock was fairly easily quarried out of the hard place by drilling holes into the limestone strata. Feathers and wedges (basically pegs) were placed in the holes and lightly pounded until the rock split into the desired widths. "Sometimes water was poured into the holes in winter so when it expanded and froze, it split the stone," adds Smith.

Nineteenth-century wedges, feathers, chisels, and drills as well as examples of limestone and fence posts (each of which is unique in size, shape, and color) can be found here. "We want to showcase the tools that were used, so [visitors] get an idea of how limestone was mined," observes Smith.

A display of shark's teeth, fossils, clam shells and sea anemones reveals that some things are set in (lime)stone. It's hard to imagine, but "millions of years ago, Kansas lay under an ocean and shells and sediment formed layers hundreds of feet thick," explains Smith. By the time the settlers moved in, the Greenhorn Formation, as it is called, lay close to the surface.

The limestone posts got the shaft in the 1920s, replaced by cheaper wooden and steel usurpers. But you can still purchase miniature versions at the museum. They make great paperweights and bookends and will last forever.

The Barbed Wire Museum and The Post Rock Museum
202 West 1st Street, La Crosse, KS 67548
((913) 222-9900—BARBED WIRE MUSEUM
((913) 222-2719—POST ROCK MUSEUM

LOCATION: The museums are actually a block away from each other although they share a mailing address; 290 miles from Kansas City via I-70
HOURS: Mid-April to Mid-October; weekdays, 10:00 A.M.–4:30 P.M.; Sunday, 1:00–4:30 P.M.; by appointment off-season
ADMISSION: Free

Michigan

✝ Baldwin: THE SHRINE OF THE PINES

If trees could talk, they'd have lots of nice things to say about the late Raymond W. "Bud" Overholzer. He devoted a good portion of his life to building and restoring a memorial to the white pine, king of the forest in Lake County, Michigan. "In the late 1800s, lumberjacks came along and slaughtered a lot of timber," recounts Marie Moore, a dedicated volunteer at the Shrine of the Pines in Baldwin,

OPEN
MAY·1ST
— to —
NOV.1ST
HOURS
10·A.M.
to 6·P.M.
Closed
Tuesdays
and
Fridays

SHRINE
OF THE
PINES

Baldwin
MICHIGAN

Raymond W. "Bud" Overholzer spent days searching for the right piece of white pine to make into household items. (*Photo courtesy of the Shrine of the Pines.*)

Michigan. "When Bud and his wife came here from Ohio in the 1920s, there were roots and stumps all over the ground." Talk about down and dirty.

Rather than letting them rot, Overholzer, who also worked as a taxidermist and fishing guide, salvaged the best and fashioned them into furniture, doors, and accessories for a white pine cabin originally intended as a hunting lodge. "He let the trees dictate the shape of the furniture, instead of the other way around," giving it a rugged, slightly skewed appearance. Even the windows take on the contour of the natural roots, providing a tree's eye view to the wild (as in untamed) Pere Marquette River.

Along with the twenty-five-hundred-square-foot building hand-made by loggers, the shrine includes a table with seating for twelve, beds for a dozen, and a rack to hold the same number of guns at the end of a long day's hunt. Everyone was to sleep in the loft upstairs and share bathroom facilities. "People didn't think much about privacy back then, especially a group of men who were hunting," observes Moore.

There are also tables and chairs for relaxation as well as a matching buffet and candelabra. Mounted deer heads line both sides of the fireplace, making this a spot where Bambi lovers would definitely feel uncomfortable. Above the main room downstairs are the words *Shrine of the Pines* spelled out in (but of course) pine branches. Everything is white pine, except for the stags, the chimney, and the floor, which is red pine.

"Except for glue and a few primitive woodcarving tools, the only investment in the collection was time and thousands of hours of painstaking effort," says Moore. "He used no nails or metal." Doors and drawers swing in perfect balance on hand-hewn pine pegs. The pieces glow, the result of hours of hand rubbing.

Each furnishing has its own story. "It took Bud seven weeks to find alternating tops and bottoms that would fit together for the door," explains Moore. Supported by dowel pins, each piece on top of the door fits into its own notch. It is opened via a pioneer latch with a buckskin pull. An estimated seventy tons of uncut native granite boulders selected by Overholzer dominate the mammoth fireplace. Visitors have claimed to see a lion's head,

The trees dictated the shape of the furniture, instead of the other way around. (*Photo courtesy of the Shrine of the Pines.*)

a wingless grasshopper (a stretch), and in the fan-shaped pine root over the mantle, various letters of the alphabet.

The dining table consists of a seven-hundred-pound stump unearthed by Overholzer himself, roots and all (they serve as legs). It took four winters, but Overholzer sawed and smoothed it down to three hundred pounds, put over sixty inlays on top, and hollowed out a drawer. It is topped by a candelabra that kept falling over until his wife, Hortense, convinced him to remove some of the candle holders to keep it level. And then there's the buffet with swinging doors hollowed out from the same piece of wood and the stairway to the loft made from a single tree killed in a forest fire.

Without any formal training, Overholzer could visualize and execute an object of beauty from an abandoned, gray stump. "He had a picture of the finished article in his mind before he looked for construction materials," observes Moore. He continued to branch out with new items, and by the time of his passing in 1952 at the age of sixty-two, the shrine was deeply rooted in tradition.

Like his wood carvings, Overholzer was a little eccentric. After all, he married a woman twenty-three years his senior, who was his former schoolteacher to boot. But that's part of the charm.

The Shrine of the Pines
M-37, Baldwin, MI 49304
((616) 745-7892

LOCATION: Two miles south of Baldwin
HOURS: May 1–November 1; seven days a week, 10:00 A.M.–6:00 P.M.
ADMISSION: Admission is charged

✦ Beaver Island: THE MORMON PRINT SHOP

St. James, Michigan, on isolated Beaver Island, is thirty miles from the mainland and can only be reached by ten-passenger twin-engine plane or, in April through December, by ferry. Yet the Mormon Print Shop there draws three to four thousand visitors annually. "We're not like other museums," understates director Shirley Gladish.

For one thing, there's a paucity of artifacts. "Most personal papers, written records, clothing, furniture, and other remnants were destroyed when the king was assassinated and a mob drove his twenty-six hundred followers from the island," she continues. "The only thing that remained was the print shop that now houses the museum."

King? Followers? Are we talking about the United States here? "Actually, James Jesse Strang, the only man in America to be crowned king of his people, was ambitious and talented as well as a dedicated Mormon," explains Gladish. Not only was he elected state senator for most of lower Michigan during his "reign" but he authored religious tomes, was responsible for northern Michigan's first newspaper, and even wrote an account of the natural history of the area for the Smithsonian Institution. No doubt he expected royalties.

Led by His Majesty, the Mormons named their settlement St. James. They inhabited the island from 1848 to 1856, building the print shop in 1850. The shop became the source of many of Strang's aforementioned publications. "Strang organized the group shortly after the death of the Mormon founder, Joseph Smith," observes Gladish. "He and Brigham Young both claimed authority as prophet, priest, and leader, although Young led most of the members to Utah." Eventually the rest followed Strang to Beaver Island where each so-called saint, or male Mormon, received an "inheritance" of land.

The Mormons farmed, fished, traded, and provided fuel for passing steamships. As the Mormon's numbers grew, the "gentiles," or non-Mormon inhabitants, were gradually excluded from the island as the Mormons gained economic and political control of the region. Thus the seeds for insurrection were sown.

Discontent and grievances within the colony—some having to do with the polygamy practiced within the group—resulted in a conspiracy and the fatal shooting of Strang in 1856, who himself had accumulated five wives. His death left the Mormons without leadership, and the gentiles, eager to repossess their lost turf, descended upon the island and unceremoniously ousted them from their Promised Land. Monarchy 0, democracy 1.

By the end of the 1850s, the original inhabitants had returned along with a flood of Irish immigrants and developed a thriving community. Around the turn of the century, another extraordinary character, who was much more popular among the natives, appeared. (The *real* natives, Chippewa and Ottawa Indians, had populated the island as early as 700 A.D.) "Doctor" Feodar Protar, a reclusive Russian who kept his true identity hidden, lived in a humble log cabin during the years 1893–1925 and "gave advice and remedies for simple physical ailments, [as well as] offering friendship to the needy," according to Gladish. "Although he never claimed to be a physician, he was knowledgeable and educated and refused to accept money for his services."

Usually the first stop at the print shop is the Strang Room with pictures, memorabilia, and written material as well as a tape for visitors that describes the Kingdom. The Protar Room contains items from the "doctor's" home as well as his medical books and journals. Reprints of Strang's books and annals of the island can also be purchased.

But the icing on this particular cake can be found on the second floor. Along with a Mormon-era white ash and rope bed and chest of drawers as well as other artifacts, the log interior still contains the broad axe marks of Strang's craftsmen. "It hasn't been touched since construction," says Gladish.

"A lot of people come here to try and trace their Mormon and Irish roots," she goes on. "Although Strang had many descendants, they were too embarrassed to admit it until later generations." Given the behavior of modern-day royals, King James Jesse Strang behaved like a prince.

The Mormon Print Shop
Box 263, St. James Harbor, Beaver Island, MI 49782
((616) 448-2254

LOCATION: Plane and/or ferry available from Charalevoix, which is about an hour's drive from Traverse City.
HOURS: Mid-June through Labor Day; Monday–Saturday, 11:00 A.M.–4:00 P.M.; Sunday, noon-3:00 P.M.
ADMISSION: Admission is charged

♠ Farmington Hills: MARVIN'S MARVELOUS MECHANICAL MUSEUM

You enter through a vestibule decorated in early pinball game boards. Antique fortune-telling machines—the Green Ray, Grandmother Predictions, Zelda the Mysterious—are clustered just down the way from a futuristic hologram game and Big Bertha, the "world's largest" slot machine. Nickelodeons, PG (for palm grip) rated love testers, and oversized singing stuffed animals are but a few of the amazements plugged into over nine hundred electrical outlets. An original spotlight from Alcatraz, a pair of enormous overalls, and a conveyer chain with over forty remote-control airplanes dangles from the ceiling. Pass the aspirin, please.

Every inch of Marvin's Marvelous Mechanical Museum reverberates with color, movement, and sound. (*Photo by Frank Curto.*)

Every cubic inch of the 5,500-plus square feet of Marvin's Marvelous Mechanical Museum reverberates with color, movement, and sound. "This is sensory overload," states the creator/curator of the dementia, in real life a Detroit pharmacist known as Marvin Yagoda. "My heart and soul are here," he says. "This is the stuff that pleases me and is unusual enough that people want to see it, remember the past, and wonder where the hell I got it from." A top-of-the-line selection of the latest video entertainments—space simulators, games based on recent movies—should keep even the finickiest trendoid amused. A snack bar with eating tables and two jukeboxes, one of which is embedded in the back of a 1957 Thunderbird, add to the hullabaloo.

Yagoda's latest pride and joy is the Hawtins Hands, invented by four London surgeons in the 1930s. Using beautifully designed art deco hands enclosed in a showcase, players attempt to pick up a toy from a revolving tray. "This is the only machine of its kind in the United States," he says. "It took three years to restore."

Dating from the turn of the century, many of Marvin Yagoda's contraptions were popular on seaside boardwalks during the 1920s and 1930s and are the forerunners of today's pinball and video games. One of the oldest, also from England, is a 1910 series of flip cards of an "execution" (it actually stops before the victim is electro- cuted).

Other things you won't see elsewhere are the Michigan anteater (*Michiganus meshuganus*) that, according to the taped-on explana- tion, "demonstrates the infamous hunting technique that's contributed to its...success as a species" (it misses the ant); a Span- ish Inquisition machine that chronicles the plight of "helpless victims of the secret crypt"; and The Drunkard's Dream, which illustrates the benefits of teetotaling and has various demons popping out of barrels to haunt a beer-swigging gentleman. Those who prefer even more lighthearted fare can watch Merlin the Magician change a frog into a bluebird or visit what claims to be the world's largest display of magic posters. "I'm also a sorcerer," Yagoda half-jokes.

Marvin's obsession with mechanical wizardry began in the fifties while he was still at the University of Michigan. After several nick- elodeons in a canoe livery near the college were sold to the then-new Disneyland, "I decided I wanted [a nickelodeon] of my own, and one thing led to another. Before I knew it, I had thirteen nickelodeons in my house and no place to maneuver." Yet he still found room for slot machines, a self-playing violin, and other as- sorted and bizarre memorabilia.

"People store this stuff in their attics and basements and actually *want* to get rid of it," he muses as if he can't understand why some- one would voluntarily part with anything that blinks, whirrs, and can't be found in the local K Mart. "Now they call me."

"Today people need a place to have old-fashioned fun," he goes on. "I like the fact that they come here and always leave in a good mood." Unless they run out of quarters or the electricity goes out.

Marvin's Marvelous Mechanical Museum
31005 Orchard Lake Road, Farmington Hills, MI 48334
((313) 626-5020

LOCATION: Right outside Detroit
HOURS: Monday–Saturday, 10:00 A.M.–10:00 P.M.; Sunday, noon–
      8:00 P.M.
ADMISSION: Free (but bring plenty of change)

⬆ Gaylord: THE CALL OF THE WILD

Located in an above-ground "cave," the Call of the Wild in Gaylord, Michigan, is for those who like their nature in neat, safe packages. About sixty displays, half of which have sound effects, show stuffed animals in various habitats. Follow the painted bear-track road to moose, elk, deer, bears, various birds, and more. You won't get a single dab of mud on your shoes.

The brainchild of the late Carl William Johnson, the museum was created in the 1950s and is co-owned by his widow and children. "Instead of visiting various tourist attractions, when I was a child we'd go to taxidermy studios around the country, looking for good mounted specimens," recalls his daughter, Janis Vollmer. "My father didn't go out and kill animals to put them in the museum." Whew! What a relief!

Most visitors are appreciative, perhaps because the creatures look realistic enough to spring to life. A wetlands display with a beaver dam includes otter, loons, minks, several types of ducks, and, of course, busy beavers. Two timberwolves pause to look about in another snowy scene, while a pack of coyotes growl and howl in a third.

This cougar's about to spring. Fortunately for visitors, he's stuffed. (*Photo courtesy of the Call of the Wild.*)

Hand-painted by two elderly, self-taught gentlemen, the backgrounds are highly detailed, albeit somewhat romanticized.

You'll find animals indigenous to North America: possums, porcupines, groundhogs, wild turkeys, raccoons (including an albino with pink eyes), flying squirrels, and rust and sharp-tailed grouse (they don't). It's Rocky and Bullwinkle gone native.

Many of the tableaux are dramatic: "things people may never see even if they spent hours hiding in the woods," observes Vollmer. Two bull moose lock horns over conjugal rights to a cow (female moose) who looks on, unperturbed. Push a button and you can hear their mating calls. A doe pauses next to her newborn fawns, while another white-tailed deer pauses in the road, presumably before an oncoming car crosses its path. (They could have shown the moment of impact. But it's a family museum, doggone it.)

According to Vollmer, a scene of a bobcat and coyote snarling over a partridge (not a in a pear tree) elicits the most comments. "People stand around and speculate about who might win." Those who bet should put their money on the bobcat.

Wildlife predicaments abound. A black bear invades a deserted camp and feasts on honey. Utilizing a ledge, a brown bear creeps toward another black bear and her cubs, giving the impression this is not a social call. Their polar cousins are truly frozen in an Arctic tableau.

Smaller animals have their day, too. An owl has a motorized head that continually turns in a 360-degree circle. "In real life, its special neck muscles enable it to swivel its head completely around," states Vollmer. Perhaps she should call an exorcist. A badger exhibit compares and contrasts different species from Michigan and the South—the latter have a longer snout and paler color.

It's not all fang and claw. A shepherd boy in springtime kneels among fawns, sheep, goats, and rabbits. With poetry by Longfellow and Browning, it's a scene straight out of *Bambi*. (Didn't Bambi's mother get killed?) Children can "pet" and have their picture taken with stuffed animals in a walk-in display, an experience akin to standing next to a cardboard Vice-President (See Dan Quayle Museum). There's even a poem nook with nature and family-related verses.

And not all the creatures are stuffed. Along with a miniature vinyl dinosaur diorama of prehistoric Michigan, there's a working beehive for visitors to observe. Exhibits about an early fur trapper, Joseph Bailly, center on his lifestyle (rugged) and his craft (gory).

Some of the local wildlife has said "fangs for the memories" and fled Michigan for the forests of Canada. "They're trying to bring back moose, but have had limited success," remarks Vollmer. Had more animals listened to the call of the wild, they might not *be* in the Call of the Wild.

The Call of the Wild
850 S. Wisconsin Avenue, Gaylord, MI 49735
((517) 732-4336 OR 732-4087

LOCATION: Off I-75 (toward Canada)
HOURS: Hours vary
ADMISSION: Admission is charged

Minnesota

✦ Austin: THE FIRST CENTURY MUSEUM

Austin, Minnesota, is hog heaven: "Although we're a town of twenty-three thousand, you'd be hard-pressed to find someone who hasn't worked for or had a family member employed by the company," observes Paulette Cummings, employee/archivist of the First Century (Hormel) Museum. So it seems natural that the Austin-based manufacturer of DINTY MOORE stews, Cure 81 hams, Little Sizzlers® pork sausage, Kid's Kitchen® shelf stable entrees, the inevitable, infamous SPAM luncheon meat, and many others should have its own museum. And doubly so because it's in the middle of that hub of American consumerism: a shopping mall.

Visitors to Oak Park Mall in Austin won't have any trouble finding the First Century Museum, named in 1991 in honor of the enterprise's centennial. At the entrance is a huge Hormel label, intentionally peeled back to reveal an old-style company logo (progress, get it?). And the four-foot leaded-glass Cure 81 label at the entrance is about the only thing that's not inside a display case in this cute, immaculate museum. With all those years of packaging sausages, hams, wieners, bacon, chili, hash (the legal kind), and spreads, it seems logical that Hormel's artifacts would also be hermetically sealed.

But even though it's company run, the museum contains some juicy morsels of history. One display is dedicated to Assistant Comp-

Advertisements guaranteed that Spam would not be far from the public mind. (*Photo courtesy of the Hormel Company.*)

troller R.J. (Cy) Thomson. "George [Hormel, the founder] helped pay Thomson's way through college so Thomson could get a business degree," recounts Cummings. By 1916, Thomson had risen to the comptroller position, then proceeded to embezzle almost $1,200,000 over the next five years, leaving Hormel nearly bankrupt. Thomson's checks and deposit slips are on view, along with the swindling swine's picture. Although some of his descendants work for the company, "they never mention him." Still, there's no mention of Hormel's bitter and prolonged labor strike of the mid-1980s.

Another exhibit is devoted to marketing materials. Always a big advertiser, Hormel ads appeared in national periodicals like the *Ladies' Home Journal* and the *Saturday Evening Post* and on a radio program featuring George Burns and Gracie Allen. Colorful posters, photographs, and point-of-sale materials reveal changing times and fashions.

According to Cummings, George Hormel's son Jay was an especially inventive promoter. "Jay established the Chili Beaners, a traveling song and dance group to publicize our chili, which was introduced in 1935." That had to have been a gas, because in 1948, the singing, dancing Hormel Girls replaced the company's drum and bugle corps. Uniforms, pictures, and other memorabilia are prominently displayed.

Even statesmen love Spam. Boris Yeltsin received a can from Hormel's president R.L. Knowlton after touring the plant in June 1992. *(Photo courtesy of the Hormel company.)*

Another section contains George's office, with its big desk and his personal business card, an original manuscript of his privately published autobiography, family correspondence, and visual depictions of the company's growth. "Although George worked in nearly every capacity during the company's first few years, he always took time to correspond with his nine brothers and sisters."

The museum also highlights production and manufacturing with artifacts and descriptive illustrations. Products with different variations of the Hormel logo throughout the years and promotional giveaways also catch the eye. The latter include Short Order® (vending victuals) suspenders; chili-can radios and cookers; and clothing items bearing the names of various products. Nothing, however, tops the popularity menu like the Spam memorabilia. "At various times we've had Spam lunch boxes and thermoses, cigarette lighters, baseball caps, blankets, battery operated camping lanterns, radios, flashlights, and two kinds of watches," notes Cummings.

Even she is at a loss to explain the continuing success of Spam, which is basically spiced pork shoulder. First manufactured in 1937, "It was a staple in the American diet during World War II and among the military. And humorists like Monty Python, Johnny Carson, and David Letterman have kept it in the public mind." Over in

Korea, Spam is considered a gourmet treat (next to dog meat) and has spawned many imitators as well as a thriving black-market business. If all the cans ever eaten were placed end-to-end, they would circle the globe at least ten times, and probably wrap around a few other planets, too.

Lest visitors go home empty-handed (after all, this *is* in a shopping mall), Hormel souvenirs are for sale across from the museum. These include Dinty Moore soup bowls, sweatshirts and jackets sporting the company logo, and Spam wall clocks so you can figure out when it's time for your next container of mystery meat.

The First Century Museum
P.O. Box 800, Austin, MN 55912
((507) 437-5345

LOCATION: **Off I-90 at the 14th Street exit; 35 miles west of Rochester**
HOURS: **Regular shopping hours (usually, Monday–Friday, 10:00**
    A.M.–9:00 P.M.; Saturday, 10:00 A.M.–5:00 P.M.; Sunday noon–
    5:00 P.M.)
ADMISSION: **Free**

♠ Minneapolis: THE MUSEUM OF QUESTIONABLE MEDICAL DEVICES

With nearly 250 contraptions, the Museum of Questionable Medical Devices in Minneapolis unearths more quacks than a flock of ducks. Walls lined with gizmos and related advertisements declare cures for everything from abdominal disorders to zits. No medium is too farfetched, and exhibits include devices that work with colored lights, vibrations, radio waves, electrical currents, and even harmful radiation.

Phrenology machines called psychographs measure such characteristics as suavity, executiveness, and sexamity by charting bumps on the head. Although it *looks* like a hair dryer, within seconds of being placed on a head a psychograph produces a printout suggesting vocations like genius, detective, or zeppelin attendant along with more mundane occupations like banker, chemist, and mother.

Dr. Crum's Cotherator claims to grow back amputated fingers and toes with radio waves. For believers not missing any digits (but perhaps a few marbles) it also allegedly kills insects within a seventy-mile radius if a photo of the infested area is smeared with insecticide and inserted into the machine. Another multipurpose device, the electrically powered Nemectron, not only "heals" skin ailments (acne, wrinkles, excess fat) but also "normalizes" over- or underdeveloped breasts *and* strengthens feet, overcoming fallen arches. Whew!

The Ruth Drown Radio Therapy Machine was supposed to diagnose diseases from the "vibrations" of blood samples. Drown, a California (where else?) chiropractor, broadcast "healing rays" to thousands of subscribers at home. An eye exerciser, later marketed as an "aerobic eye exerciser" initially required that users sunbathe nude from 11:00 A.M. to 2:00 P.M. Royal Rife machines presumably sent out rays to zap cancer and other deadly diseases. Acu-Dots, a sort of Band-Aid, "magnetized" iron in the blood, "healing" rheumatism, and the Toftness "radiation detector," sold to chiropractors for $2400, was made of common PVC pipe. Gollee! People sure were gullible back then!

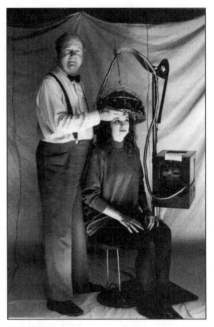

Back then? Except for the Drown machine, which was popular in the 1960s (even actor Tyrone Power swore by it), all of the devices in the previous paragraph "have been marketed within the past decade of so," remarks the P.T. Barnum of this

Through charting bumps on the head phrenology machines measured suavity, executiveness, and sexamity. (*Photo courtesy of the Museum of Questionable Medical Devices.*)

whole array, former steel salesman and professional skeptic Bob McCoy. He even located a reincarnation of Crum's insect exterminating device in a 1989 catalog. Although he's the real McCoy in that he visits medical, library, and other groups to point out the pitfalls of phony panaceas, "people still want to believe in so-called miracle cures." For instance, at a demonstration he gave at a health care organization, "a woman asked where she could get the magnetic Band-Aids." Old P.T. sure knew his public.

Many of the displays are from the early part of the twentieth century when electricity, radio waves, and magnetism were new and mysterious. With its array of colored lights, the Spectro-Chrome could "cure" almost anything. One only had to sit in front of it during certain phases of the moon. Gaylord Wilshire (after whom Wilshire Boulevard in Los Angeles was named) attracted lots of money with his magnetic belt that was said to increase health and beauty by allowing the blood to absorb more oxygen. "Manufacturers made broad claims and guarantees," explains McCoy. "So when people demanded their money back because they hadn't been cured, [the supplier] would say they hadn't used it correctly, or long enough, and proceeded to sell them more."

Some of these products made more than a financial killing. For instance, in the twenties, when radiation was believed to expand sexual organs and prowess, steel mogul and ladies' man Eben MacBurney Byers guzzled about one thousand four hundred half-ounce bottles of Radnithor. Distilled water laced with radioactive isotopes, Radnithor was touted as the "New Weapon of Medical Science." The advertisements were right about the weapon part: by 1930, Byers began to experience headaches and loss of weight and teeth. Eventually both his upper and lower jaw deteriorated. Not surprisingly, he died two years later from radium poisoning. It gave him a glow, but not the one he expected.

Sexuality has always been ripe for strange devices. The strapped-on Vital Power Vacuum Massager was lauded as "the perfect organ developing appliance" for males. The G-H-R Thermitis Dilator, another sexual device, had a light bulb on one end and a nasty-looking probe on the other. It was inserted into the rectum where it heated to one hundred degrees and stimulated "the so-called abdominal brain," aka the prostate gland. And the ring-shaped Timely Warning really clamped down on nightly emissions by "arousing" (as in waking up) the wearer. Then there was "Dr." John Brinkley who built a $12-million empire by implanting goat testes into the scrotums of men to "restore their manhood." "For an extra fee, you could pick your own goat," adds McCoy with a grin. "I think I'd rather be a monk."

Other scams displayed include the Nagelschmidt-Bergonie Apparatus for Curing Obesity (move over, Weight Watchers), the Crosley Xervac hair growing machine for those plagued by baldness (it "worked" by putting pressure on the scalp), and the White Cross Electric Vibrator, a multifaceted device marketed for women that was said to cure "general debility" and is most likely an ancestor of the modern version. A course in "scientific height increasing" employs a torturous-looking gizmo and tells the sad tale of "the belle of the town, pretty, popular" Clarice Young who dumped rich but short Billy Gaston for "fine, tall, healthy, clean-cut" Paul Andrews. ("You, too, can be a big man making others look up to you.... ")

"Many of these things played on people's hopes and insecurities," observes McCoy. Yeah, isn't it great there's a museum devoted to these hilarious gadgets—especially if you're not using them to cure whatever ails you.

The Museum of Questionable Medical Devices
219 S.E. Main Street, Minneapolis, MN 55414
((612) 545-1113 OR 379-4046

LOCATION: Downtown Minneapolis in the St. Anthony Main Section
HOURS: Summers only; Tuesday–Friday, 5:00–9:00 P.M.; Saturday, 11:00 A.M.–10:00 P.M.; Sunday, noon–5:00 P.M. (call for specific appointments or tours)
ADMISSION: Free

Missouri

♠ Independence: THE HAIR MUSEUM

This hair consciousness-raising experience at the Independence College of Cosmetology in Independence, Missouri, offers over 150 wreaths and 500 pieces of jewelry to comb through. It was hair today, gone tomorrow: Everything in the museum contains, or was made of, human tresses and predates 1900. Although there are some crosses, there are no hair shirts or other items of repentance, ensuring a guilt-free visit.

Those who have never heard of hair art—in the nineteenth century and earlier jewelry and other ornamental pieces were crafted from human hair—are hardly alone. If not for Leila (pronounced Le-ay-la)

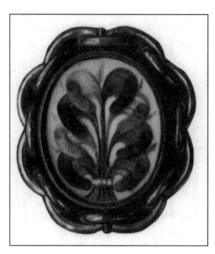

Cohoon, veteran hair stylist, collector, and curator, hair art might have gone the way of snipped-off locks. "I found my first piece thirty-five years ago and fell in love with it," she recalls. "I bought a wreath instead of a pair of Easter shoes." She's been willingly shorn of money ever since.

Intrigued, Cohoon also went to the library in search of information. "Nothing had been written about hair art for decades," she says. She finally located details on braiding watch fobs from the Library of Congress and, through various friends, was

Hair jewelry like this brooch was a popular Victorian ornament. (*Photo courtesy of the Hair Museum.*)

put in contact with a woman in Minnesota who was making hair wreaths. "She learned the steps from an elderly gentleman whose family had done them years ago."

Cohoon is in the process of compiling an instructional video. Hair art isn't exactly Nice 'n Easy. It "requires counting out of each strand, matching colors, and utilizing a tool similar to a knitting needle. It can become tedious." And at times, downright hairy.

Although the earliest pieces date from the 1700s—Cohoon has one homemade family history book with calling cards containing samples of members' hair that covers the period from 1725 to 1900—the exact histories of most of the items remain obscure. "Jewelry clasps and wreath designs tell you something about the general time period, but don't give specifics," she explains. "And few have the artist's or owner's names and dates.

"But we do know that its heyday was in the 1800s, before diamonds became popular around the turn of the century," she goes on. "People would mail postcards with their own hair to family and friends." The jewelry was worn by both women and men, who utilized human-hair watch fobs held together with gold clasps. "There were over 150 different braid patterns." Women donned necklaces, bracelets, earrings, rings, and brooches, although surely the first two must have been scratchy. Rings made from the deceased's locks were sometimes put on during funerals although if the person was balding, it might have caused a problem.

Sometimes worn on the forearm, bracelets with different braiding patterns were sewn together and interspersed with pink, green, or yellow gold, or with other metals. "They were quite ornate and very imaginative," notes Cohoon.

Necklaces with hairballs (not the kind produced by cats) were made by weaving hair around, then removing, ornaments, producing a beaded effect. Others took the form of crosses on gold chains. "Usually (the cross) was made from a loved one's hair, and, more often than not, that person was deceased."

Hair wreaths were also popular. "They hung on the wall and were considered pieces of art," observes Cohoon. Common wreaths included religious designs with crosses, fancy flowers, or horseshoe-shaped numbers with space for additional tresses as a family grew. But as the years passed "many items were put in people's trunks and forgotten."

Among the wreaths on display is one with a stuffed, mounted bird as a centerpiece and others made from the hair of sisters who became nuns. Valued at $10,000, a jumbo forty by thirty-six-inch model features over one hundred one-of-a-kind flowers and perfectly matched, natural colors. "The [estimate] was based on a smaller piece that came from the same museum in Colorado, so it's probably worth more," comments Cohoon.

But the museum is her mane stay and she bristles at the suggestion of selling any of the artifacts. Like hair itself, "the collection's growing every day." It would be a shame to cut it off.

The Hair Museum
815 West 23rd Street, Independence, MO 64055

☎ (816) 252-HAIR

LOCATION: **Downtown**

HOURS: **Monday–Saturday, 8:30 A.M.–5:00 P.M.**

ADMISSION: **Admission is charged**

♦ St. Louis: THE DOG MUSEUM

When a visitor asked Susan Brown, director of the Dog Museum, where the stuffed dogs were, for a moment she thought he was referring to toy pets. "Then I realized he meant taxidermy, as in memorializing Buffy and Sparky," she says. "I informed him that we're a museum of fine arts." These folks mean Sirius business.

The Dog Museum commemorates just about every other aspect of canine life, however. Along with the usual art, artifacts, and literature, its Select-a-Dog service helps potential owners research a breed. The Pedigree Hall of Fame honors canines who have made a contribution to a field other than someone's lawn, and the museum boasts the United State's largest collection of non-X-rated dog collars. And no bone fide museum would be complete without annual Dog Days when family pets are welcome; dogs and owners can compete in a lookalike contest, and there is a Dog of the Week demonstration that highlights specific breeds or talented pooches.

Visitors entering the museum, which consists of an older section, Jarville House, and a larger new section, are greeted by Queen, an antique carousel dog. Rotating exhibits "aim for as much variety as possible," explains Brown. Canine stitchery in needlepoint; artifacts such as clothing and even a pet couch (for a display on pampered pets); and dog-related art and literature for children have been among the offerings. A display on working dogs, such as the K-9 units used in police work, and a collection of championship trophies that dates back through the decades are other recent features.

Jarville House contains a portrait of former "First Dog" Millie and a personal letter from her owner, Barbara Bush. Exhibits cover the dog's history from the seventeenth century until today and range from the classic paintings of Sir Edwin Landseer, artist to English royalty, to thousands of volumes of books on canines, to pampered porcelain pooches on pillows.

The display of about twenty dog collars provides a revealing perspective on how man has treated his "best friend." "The dog collar was often the only thing that stood between the dog and death, and in the case of working and guard dogs, his master and death," remarks Brown. Along with eighteenth- and nineteenth-century brass models, one sterling silver number belonged to the regimental mascot of the Duke of Lancaster.

Engraved with Duke's coat of arms and the words, *Duke of Lancaster's Own*, it has a matching padlock and key. The silversmith who made it probably also produced flatware and tea sets—and hopefully not identical collars—for the Duke's wife and kids.

Also of interest is a nasty-looking bear-baiting collar, a product of nineteenth-century England. With rolled edges and serrated

Queen, an antique carousel dog, greets visitors to the Dog Museum. *(Photo courtesy of the museum.)*

points, "it was supposed to aid the dog when he and others were set upon by a tethered bear during this blood sport," says Brown with a shudder. Unfortunately for Fido, people will do almost anything for a good time.

Those really wanting to go to the dogs should visit the gift shop in the adjoining carriage house. Dog clocks with the tongue as the second hand, sunglasses with 3-D vignettes prancing across the frames, and belts and matching ties with favorite breeds can be found there.

Although this seems like a lot of recognition for a creature with four legs, a tail, and no measurable IQ, "for centuries, people treated dogs in a cruel and inhumane manner," observes Brown. "Yet despite the abuse, they're loyal, work hard, and are always eager to please." It's a dog-eat-dog world, but at the Dog Museum, Rover reigns supreme.

The Dog Museum
1721 S. Mason Road, St. Louis, MO 63131
((314) 821-3647

LOCATION: Queeny Park, in West County
HOURS: Tuesday–Saturday, 9:00 A.M.–5:00 P.M.; Sunday, noon–5:00 P.M.
ADMISSION: Admission is charged

✝ St. Louis: THE NATIONAL BOWLING HALL OF FAME AND MUSEUM

During one episode of *The Simpsons*, the famous cartoon family decided to take a vacation. Homer's choice: the National Bowling Hall of Fame and Museum in St. Louis, Missouri. One of Homer's favorite exhibits there was a car made from a giant bowling pin, built on the frame of a 1936 Studebaker. The collections of shirts, balls, clever badges, gold medals, beer steins, and even a French tapestry no doubt bowled him over as well.

This museum has some serious stuff, too. Along with serving as a repository for bowling history, it houses permanent records for the American Bowling Congress (ABC) and the Women's International Bowling Congress (WIBC). Huge sketches of happenings in the careers of famous bowlers, computer databases with names of hall of fame inductees as well as those who have had 300 games or an 800 series, and busts and oil portraits of respective male and female hall of famers can be found here.

Those who regard bowling as the province of Homer Simpson, Fred Flintstone and their like should look again. "Bowling has been around since 5200 B.C.," explains curator John Dalzell. "Archaeologists found implements for playing a game similar to modern bowling in an Egyptian child's grave. According to many authorities, the sport formally originated in Northern Italy, and was a predecessor to [the Italian pastime] bocce." But despite its likenesses to other games, "bowling as we know it today most closely resembles Dutch ninepins," Dalzell asserts. Tenpins, or its present incarnation, "originated as the result of a law against ninepins in parts of Connecticut and New York." By adding a pin and setting them in a triangle, wily bowlers created a perfectly legal diversion and things have been rolling along ever since. Tenpin Alley, a chronological time tunnel, recreates bowling highlights with life-size dioramas.

Enough history, what about the collection of bowling shirts? "We have close to one thousand, some of which are as old as 1910,"

This car made from a giant bowling pin was built on the frame of a '36 Studebaker. (*Photo courtesy of the National Bowling Hall of Fame and Museum.*)

replies Dalzell. "Men had to bowl in ties with long sleeves and women in ankle-length dresses." Until the 1950s, when the dress codes loosened up, long pants on women would have been about as well received in an alley as evening gowns.

The display includes a hot-pink number with a black, crushed velvet image of the King worn by a team calling themselves Elvis's Crazy Broads. The Zodiac league in New Orleans has a number of eye-popping, glitzy horoscope jerseys, "although they haven't won too many tournaments," notes Dalzell. And there's one from Barry's Funeral Home depicting a coffin with an arm hanging out of it. In the hand is a bowling ball, portraying a true devotee to the end. "We also have some embroidered fringe shirts from the Comanche Squaw team as well as others which remain in boxes as they're from topless bars."

Looking at a bunch of bowling balls and pins may not sound exciting, but the chipped lignum vitae (very hard wood to the uninitiated) models "are some of the oldest around," points out Dalzell. "It wasn't until 1905 that the first successful hard rubber ball was manufactured." Several of the more recent versions are cut open to reveal innards of cork and other materials. "Most balls today are made of polyurethane." How plastic.

Pins include huge mothers over three feet tall used in France as well as pointed, conical, and barrel shapes in mind-bending blues and reds with spots.

Bowling scenes are depicted on German beer steins from two hundred years ago and there's an eighteenth-century Aubusson French tapestry of peasant keglers in the great outdoors.

By now, visitors might be in the frame of mind to try a game. An old-time bowling facility on the lower level of the museum offers lignum vitae balls, hand-set pins, and one lane that's set up with smaller duck pins and a five-inch-diameter ball. "No one's ever had a perfect game," remarks Dalzell of the last. At the opposite end of the room and spectrum are modern lanes that offer the latest technology in equipment and scoring by Brunswick and AMF.

"We rotate displays, using only about 20 percent of the over 100,000 items in our collection," states Dalzell. So you can't pin down what exactly you're going to see on an average visit.

The National Bowling Hall of Fame and Museum
111 Stadium Plaza Drive, St. Louis, MO 63102
((314) 231-6340

LOCATION: Downtown, across from Busch Stadium
HOURS: Seven days a week (except for major holidays and when there
    are special events)
ADMISSION: Admission is charged

Ohio

⬆ Canal Winchester: THE BARBER MUSEUM

"Ours is the oldest legal profession in the world," remarks barber Edwin Jeffers with a smile. "There's even a reference to it in the Old

Testament, in Ezekiel 5:1. It's amazing how few pastors know that." When he's so inclined, Jeffers will give a demonstration haircut at the Canal Winchester, Ohio, museum's licensed barber shop. Or visitors can stop at Zeke's Barber Shop downstairs.

Jeffers has culled about 600 straight razors, 425 shaving mugs, 30 different types of barber poles, 14 wooden chairs, and other wildly assorted memorabilia. The museum fills six rooms on the second floor of an 1880s Knights of Pythias Lodge and, along with being handicapped-accessible, showcases the mostly Victorian-era collection with refurbished wooden wainscoting and high ceilings.

Most of us wouldn't dream of going to a barber to have our teeth pulled or for surgery but "until the 1800s barbers provided these services," states Jeffers. And he has the devices to prove it. For instance, an 1825 bloodletting tool has sixteen small, nasty-looking lancets that were inserted along the inside of the arm. The red and white stripes of the barber's pole derived from this practice: "Blood was let using a white cloth, rinsed, then hung out to dry. Blue, for veins, was added at the turn of the century." Peppermint sticks may never look the same again.

Jeffers has an antique dentist's kit that's basically a lineup of pliers and it's accompanied by a photo of a barber extracting a tooth. The expression of the client sitting in the barber's chair isn't that of someone anticipating a haircut.

The main room of the museum has lined-up barber chairs restored to their natural wood beauty and covered with fresh plush fabrics; spotless antique work stations with mirrors; and display cases filled with mugs, tonic bottles, razors, and other cutting implements. Rotating barber poles add a finishing flourish. "I have two [poles] that still need to be cranked," Jeffers says, giving a demonstration. "Some of the others have been converted [to electricity] but that greatly reduces their value." Along with a one-of-a-kind pole with a clock on top, the museum boasts several rare wooden models.

Shaving mugs are another collectible that have become pricey. "Originally, they were about eighty-five cents each, but now they're coveted by people who see money as no object," Jeffers observes. His collection includes an extremely valuable mug with a lithopane angel on the bottom as well as mugs owned by individuals who kept them at the barber shop. "It was a status thing if you had a mug with your name on it," he explains. "And even more so if it was embellished with your occupation or fraternal organization." Now it's a cachet to own someone else's mug.

Jeffers discusses the evolution of safety razors, which first appeared at the 1900 World's Fair, and shows the clever devices used to

sharpen them. But a look at the display case full of the straight kind reveals a lost artistry. "The Germans decorated both blades and handles," he notes, pointing out one with a brilliant blue peacock and another with an exquisitely etched mermaid. Along with an eight-foot "demonstration" model, other razors have names carved on the blade, such as that of an unknown Englishman who reportedly lived to be over one hundred years old.

One could spend hours scrutinizing the accumulation of hand-blown tonic bottles, hair dryers ("cosmetology didn't come along until the twenties when women started getting their hair

These barber chairs have been restored to their original beauty.
(*Photo by Sandra Gurvis*)

bobbed"), hair creams, and potions (mostly forgotten except for Brylcreem, whose little dab still does whatever), along with the library and the Barber Hall of Fame.

One of the few barbers still licensed to do this, Jeffers also has a complete singeing kit. "People used to think hair was hollow and the oils ran out so barbers sealed hair shut by lighting the wax tapers. And it still helps reduce split ends." A 1920s perm machine that resembles an octopus and a 1950s flattop comb with a built-in carpenter's level aptly illustrate the vanities of each era.

Because he also licenses all the barbers in Ohio, Jeffers only works the museum when he has time. "I clean every Saturday and usually get interrupted by people who stop by and want a tour" and have a little singed off the top.

The Barber Museum
2 1/2 S. High Street, Canal Winchester, Ohio 43110
((614) 833-9931

LOCATION: A few miles south of Columbus, off Route 33
HOURS: By appointment only
ADMISSION: Free

♠ Columbus: THE OPTOMETRY MUSEUM

This is one museum where famous people *really* make spectacles of themselves. A few years ago, Dr. Arol Augsburger, professor of clinical optometry at Ohio State University in Columbus, sent out a hundred letters to local and national luminaries asking them for their old glasses. Most responded positively and Augsburger put them (the glasses) on display.

"Glasses often reflect the personalities of their owners," he observes. Race car driver Bobby Rahal's were broken from a brush with a wall; John Denver's boasted the engraving "Rocky Mountain High"; and Elvis's sunglasses were worth $7,000 (no, he didn't deliver them personally). Writer Stephen King's are appropriately thick, dark, and heavy; Mary Kay (of cosmetics fame) sent a rose-tinted, heart shaped pair in tune with her cosmetics line and pink Cadillacs.

Nearly seventy-five glasses from such diverse personalities as Orville Redenbacher, Gerald Ford, Oleg Cassini, Phyllis Diller, and the late Malcolm Forbes grace display cases throughout the optometry building, Fry Hall. Often the spectacles are accompanied by a photo of the celebrity wearing them (Joan Collins's earrings actually match her frames) and/or a letter. Former President Bush sent a pair with a note explaining they had become warped while he was reading in the sauna.

Sometimes the refusals are as amusing as the spectacles themselves might have been. Columnist George Will wrote that he ran over his extra pair with the family station wagon. Televangelist Billy Graham claimed to have donated his old glasses to charity (does the recipient wear the same prescription?). Talk show host Phil

The Celebrity Eyewear Collection has glasses from race car drivers to singers and presidents. (*Photo courtesy of The Ohio State University College of Optometry.*)

Donahue reportedly kept losing his and thus declined to send an extra pair. And Senator John Glenn refused on the grounds that eyeglasses were incompatible with his public image.

The rest of the Optometry Museum, an assortment of strange-looking gadgets, teaching aids, and spectacles in all shapes, colors, and sizes, occupies a large room in the basement of Fry Hall. There's a turn-of-the-century refractor, a large, owl-eyed contraption bordered with a plethora of numbers. Using this device, computing the correct prescription was a lengthy procedure. Rather than the retinoscope, which looks into the pupil via a flashlight device, early practitioners utilized magnifiers with small mirrors and candlelight. These are also shown.

The spectacle styles on display have also had a number of oddball transmogrifications. In Europe, "the oldest known frames were made of wood, hollowed out to hold the lenses," says Augsburger. Early Chinese frames were "very much like our modern frames" but the temple pieces bent up instead of down. At least they were on the right track.

Around the 1500s, the Italians developed a goggle with leather straps that tied in back to secure the lenses. "They also attempted to tie the lenses around the ears for more stability."

"Not to be outdone, the Chinese hung weights over their ears," he goes on. "These held the lenses on, but wearers ran into problems on windy days and when they shook their heads."

"European countries made attempts at using a wig or hat to anchor the lenses but these designs were fraught with hair-raising experiences," he observes with a smile. Some people went back to holding lenses in their hands, resulting in the fashionable lorgnette, which was popular from mid 1800s to the turn of the century. Made from gold, silver, ivory, and other materials, lorgnettes, along with one-lens quizzlers, were prized by the upper classes.

Monocles, a single lens actually worn in the eye, provided a continental look during World War I. "By the 1800s, basic frame designs had settled down to the types we use today," remarks Augsburger.

"We've come a long way from medieval times when folks tied cows' eyes in a sack around their necks in the hope that sight would somehow be transferred," he goes on. Now we collect famous peoples' glasses.

The Optometry Museum
338 W. Tenth Avenue, Columbus, OH 43210
((614) 292-2788

LOCATION: In Fry Hall on the Ohio State University Campus
HOURS: Monday–Friday, 8:00 A.M.–5:00 P.M.
ADMISSION: Free

Granville: THE GRANVILLE LIFE-STYLE MUSEUM

Petite models clad in underwear prance prettily in front of an admiring audience, bringing a sparkle into more than one septuagenarian's eye. A Civil War period chair shares space with a 1950s TV set and discount-store knickknacks. Visitors actually sit on the furniture. A picture of a Victorian era dress hangs next to the actual article of clothing, along with a matching collar, which is also shown in the portrait.

Located in the Hubert D. Robinson House in Granville, Ohio, the Granville Life-Style Museum has *everything* saved by the Robinson family and their forerunners from the time they moved into the community in 1805 as one of its first settlers. "I left most of the furnishings the way they were when the Robinsons lived here, even down to the window sill clutter," observes director emeritus Gloria Hoover.

Anyone hoping for racy revelations will be disappointed to learn that the undergarments being modeled are geometrically (and vertically and diagonally) opposed to Frederick's of Hollywood. Preserved nearly intact from Victorian times, they cover far more than even an average dress, and can consist of up to nine layers of chemises, knickers, petticoats, stockings, and corsets. "The Victorians were big on concealing body parts," explains the museum's executive director, Marilyn Anderson.

The Robinson family saved everything, even the dress in this picture. (*Photo by Gloria Hoover.*)

The fact that this home became a museum is an accident of birth, or rather, non-birth. "People often remark it's a pity Hubert and Oese Robinson had no children," observes Hoover. "But I tell them, 'If they did, you wouldn't be standing here.' "

Purchased in 1917 by Hubert's uncle as a gift for the couple, the house was originally built around 1870 and is now listed with the National Register of Historic Places. "Oese contacted the previous owners for any information about the house's construction and details about the way it had been decorated," states Hoover. Various photos taken of the home in earlier stages are on display.

Hubert (1877–1960) and Oese (1886–1981) were originally considered outsiders in a wealthy family that valued breeding and education. They inherited all of the family's objects only because they were the last living descendants. According to Hoover, Oese knew where everything was located, down to a single scrap of cloth.

Objects include 116 family hats dated from the 1820s to the 1970s, quilts, china, photographs, furniture, kitchen utensils, clothes, and a lace stockpile of over one thousand pieces. The white organdy dress worn by Hubert's mother, Emma Devenney Robinson, when she graduated from Granville Female College in 1861, and the lavender bonnet used by Hubert's great-grandmother Deborah Sheldon Root when she traveled from Massachusetts to Ohio in 1827 can also be found here. Marcus A. Root (1808–1888), Hubert's step-great uncle, a world renowned photographer and author of the first book on the history of photography (*The Camera and the Pencil*, 1864) has his own little shrine in an upstairs bedroom that includes his daguerreotypes.

"Oese took great pride in her kitchen and garden," states Hoover. The kitchen, remodeled in the late 1940s, is that era's housewife's dream of painted wood cabinets, nifty storage spaces, and a built-in upholstered banquette. "Not only do we have before-and-after pictures, but we've also displayed invoices of the work performed as well as a portrait of the same room in 1907 when it was a dining area." Just off the kitchen is a bathroom with an immense array of cosmetics, creams, soaps, and other toiletries from the twenties through the seventies.

Credited with organizing the county's first garden club in 1929 as well as several others, "Oese would often stop at the post office in small towns and ask if they had a garden club," comments Hoover. Certain areas of the garden at the house replicate the way she kept it in the 1940s.

Hoover is still excavating new "finds." While setting up a picture taken of Oese at a 1950s gardening convention, Hoover wondered if she could locate the hat Oese was wearing. As Oese was in the middle of about five hundred participants, Hoover had to use a magnifying glass to identify the hat. No surprise, it now sits next to the photo on a table.

The Granville Life-Style Museum
121 South Main Street, Granville, OH 43023
((614) 587-0373

LOCATION: About 30 miles east of Columbus
HOURS: Hours vary; tours given by appointment
ADMISSION: Admission is charged for adults

↑ North Canton: THE HOOVER HISTORICAL CENTER

They sit in various places of honor throughout the Hoover Historical Center in North Canton, Ohio. The one hundred or so vacuum cleaners range from the pre-electricity types to the complete line of Hoover cleaners beginning with the first 1908 Model O to a computerized French paragon that speaks four languages. In between, you'll find a sleek black Model 700 (1926) that people are *still* trying to find bags for; the 1956 Walk-on-Air canister that, lifted by its own exhaust, floated behind the user; and 1962's Model 2100, which traveled to a Paris exhibition masqueraded in a light-green plastic suitcase—the Hoover in the Louvre. Like their mostly female operators, they've come a long way.

"People really enjoy seeing the old hand or foot operated devices that date back to 1850," observes Stacy Krammes, the center's director. Several of the early non-Hoovers weighed nearly one hundred pounds. One thankfully obsolete model consists of a platform over two horizontal bellows. "The woman stood on the platform and rocked back and forth," explains Krammes. "A nozzle was attached to the base of the cleaner so she could operate the hose with her hands while generating power with her legs."

Some cleaners worked on the same principle as a water pump; the woman pushed the handle vigorously up and down in order to pick up the dirt. Still others utilized crank operated brush rolls to clean. The 1869 "whirlwind" resembles today's cleaners in that it has a nozzle and dirt bag. But that's where the similarity ends. "The operator turned a crank with a belt and wheel that moved the machine and supposedly removed the dirt," she says. But the only wind it "whirled" was full of dust.

"Between 1850 and 1900, some 250 different types of sweepers were made, none of which worked very well," she continues. But most consumers were practical: "They used a broom or manually beat the dirt from their rugs."

Then J. Murray Spangler filled the vacuum. At the turn of the century, hard times forced the asthmatic Spangler to take a job as a janitor. The dust raised by his heavy cleaning machine worsened his condition so he decided to attach a pillowcase to the cleaner to capture excess residue. He also mounted an electric fan on the sweeper

Hoover vacuum cleaners were a welcome household addition—especially to women. (*Photo courtesy of the Hoover Historical Center.*)

To Every Lover Of Cleanliness:

Note the evident satisfaction of the possessor of this **Hoover Electric Suction Sweeper.** You too, would enthusiastically recommend it to your friends when you had proven our claims as to its being the means of thoroughly cleaning your home and keeping it clean in the simple, sanitary and inexpensive "Hoover Way."

We'll be glad indeed to answer your request for a free demonstration. You will be surprised at results.

Very respectfully,

The Hoover Suction Sweeper Co.

brush to help move the cleaner more easily. From that, he built a prototype for an "electric suction sweeper" made from tin and wood with a cloth dust bag. Although it was crude and cumbersome, it worked.

Unable to draw capital on his own, Spangler went to his boyhood friend William H. "Boss" Hoover, who ran a horse collar, saddle, and leather goods factory in North Canton. Hoover and his sons decided to take a chance on Spangler's contraption. In 1908 Boss Hoover placed a small ad in the *Saturday Evening Post* offering a free ten-day home trial of the cleaner and was swept off his feet with requests. By 1920, the company had shut down its leather business and was producing about 275,000 cleaners annually.

Throughout the years, Hoover vacuums continued to pull in customers, making a number of innovations along the way. Who can forget 1926's Model 700, "the first cleaner offering triple-action cleaning, the principle of beating, sweeping, and suction, a feature which dominates the industry to this day"? 1936 was another revolutionary year: Along with being the first appliance to have parts made from magnesium, the "wonder metal" of the thirties, the Model 150 had a molded hood of Bakelite, the first plastic; a clip-on cord plug; a semi automatic rug adjustment; a time-to-empty signal; a spring-cushioned chassis; and a handle positioner. The list of improvements goes on (and on and on. . .).

Today's vacuum cleaners are so convenient even men might attempt them. The PowerMAX, Hoover's most recent offering, is basically self-propelled, requiring only that the operator guide it with his fingertips. Its top tool connection allows it to be used both as a canister and an upright, it has a power surge feature for tough-to-clean spots, and it comes in several designer colors.

Now, if they'd only invent a cleaner that would open the closet door, propel itself into the family room, and know when to start vacuuming....

The Hoover Historical Center
2225 Easton N.W., North Canton, OH 44720
((216) 499-0287

LOCATION: Outside of Canton
HOURS: Tuesday–Sunday, 1:00–5:00 P.M.
ADMISSION: Free

♦ Plain City: THE BULL HALL OF FAME

With tens of thousands of offspring, these studs put their human counterparts to shame, and that's no bull. The twelve bovine honorees of the Bull Hall of Fame are outstanding in their field or, more

accurately, their stalls. Or they're buried on the grounds of Select
Sires, Inc., the largest artificial insemination (AI) enterprise in the
country. Chosen by the marketing and sire departments for their
"contributions to the overall industry and breed, production value,
and units of semen produced," according to communications coordinator Susan Romines, they represent the cream of the crop, so to
speak.

Welcome to the Bull Hall of Fame in rural Plain City, Ohio, where
such genetic giants as Elevation, Bell, Mark, Duncan, and Big Sky
will be venerated forever—or at
least as long as the company
stays in business. Not too many
employers treat their workers
with such reverence.

A federation of twelve farmer-
owned   cooperatives,   Select
Sires's corporate headquarters in
Plain City boasts large, clean

This husky fellow was a bona fide
Bull Hall of Fame winner and vital
contributor to the Select Sires enterprise. (*Photo courtesy Select Sires.*)

facilities. These include a visitor
greeting   center,   conference
room, collection viewing zone
(where visitors can watch "the act"), laboratories, veterinary treatment area, and sick bay. Six other barns shelter "proven" dairy and
beef sires plus sires waiting to participate in the AI program.
Another nearby barn houses bulls that service the international market. An isolation facility located about ten miles away accommodates
nearly 450 more sires-in-waiting. Rather than hoping for the right
cow to come along, they're awaiting United States Department of
Agriculture (USDA) approval. This can take up to four years.

The Hall of Fame itself isn't particularly awe inspiring. It consists
of sixteen-by-twenty-inch color pictures of inductees on the wall and
fancy carved marble tombstones scattered around the grounds
where late studs are buried, with their full names and the dates of
their birth and demise. (An epitaph might read, "He gave his all.")

Plus, you get a chance to actually meet the bulls, who seem content in their well-lit, roomy stalls. With regular exercise, animals are
kept in top physical condition for amorous encounters. "They're just
like people, with distinct personalities," comments Romines. "For

The Bull Hall of Fame honors bulls that have chewed their last cud, but have produced the most semen. (*Photo courtesy of Select Sires.*)

instance, Rambo pretends to be mean, but he's really pretty mellow." Although you can pet them, you're advised to keep your hands clear should they decide to check *you* out.

Visitors can also watch a fifteen minute video that details the whole procedure, from picking the bulls (the term "elite" is used several times) for AI to the actual mating process. Once sperm is collected, "metabolic processes are basically stopped, allowing sperm to remain fertile for many years," explains Romines. Thus, the bull can continue to produce even after he's chewed his final cud.

The company brochure reads like a manual for a bizarre matchmaking service. "Once a proven...sire enters the active...lineup, he goes on a regular collection schedule.... as [much] as three days per week, depending on his physical...capabilities and semen demand," states the brochure. Bulls with a lower libido can watch, in hopes they'll get into the mood. And men think they're under pressure to perform.

Although some humans may have moral reservations about AI, the bulls appear to enjoy their work. During a recent visit, several matings went smoothly, with one reluctant sire gently led back into his pen. "They'll try him tomorrow," commented Romines.

Select Sires's catalog is a sort of on-the-hoof personals column: the complete bull is pictured, along with age, weight, height, hair and eye color, and strong points ("[Produces] excellent females with good udders"; "Stylish, well-balanced progeny"; "Outstanding frame"). It also includes things you'd *never* find in a Homo sapiens listing—family tree, birth weight, and (really) scrotal circumference.

Since 1965, when the co-ops consolidated, thousands of bulls have passed through the portals of Select Sires. Some have been rejected—put out to pasture, so to speak—others have been steady producers, and a mere dozen have been elected to the Bull Hall of Fame. Of the latter, only Big Sky survives. But the rest, like Mars, who produced ninety-six thousand offspring, will live on through their progeny. It's as close to immortality as we can get and *that's* no bull.

The Bull Hall of Fame
11740 U.S. 42, Plain City, OH 43064
((614) 873-4683

LOCATION: **On the outskirts of Columbus**
HOURS: **Tours conducted by appointment only**
ADMISSION: **Free**

♠ Sandusky: THE MERRY-GO-ROUND MUSEUM

To celebrate their friend's ninety-seventh birthday, the elderly ladies dressed up for a fancy lunch. Afterwards they visited the Merry-Go-Round Museum in Sandusky, Ohio, the only museum in the country with a full-sized, working carousel inside. "I told them that, for safety reasons, no one was allowed to ride sidesaddle," states director Rachel Pratt. "So they hiked up their skirts, slung themselves over the wooden horses, and rode anyway. As they left, the 'birthday girl' informed me she'd be back for her ninety-eighth."

Pratt counts senior citizens among the museum's biggest fans. "They can't wait to go on the carousel and share their memories. Although youngsters enjoy it, they're accustomed to TV and video games for entertainment."

This working 1936 Alan Herschell carousel consists of animals from different manufacturers and owners. (*Photo courtesy of Charles F. Corbell, Sr.*)

This museum has come full circle. In 1988, the issuance of four
carousel stamps in Sandusky sparked tremendous response from
thousands of devotees. "Carousel enthusiasts and community leaders
got together and decided they wanted a museum dedicated to the
preservation of carousel art," recalls Pratt. The horseshoe-shaped
former Sandusky post office was available for a reasonable price.
And two collectors who needed their merry-go-round restored
agreed to lend it to the museum in exchange for its renovation.

Along with the working carousel, the Merry-Go-Round Museum
features master artisan Gustav Dentzel's 1867 carving shop. It contains tools, workbenches, and Dentzel's own partially chiseled
horses. Other acquisitions include works by well-known craftsmen
such as Daniel Müller, M.C. Illions, Charles Looff, and Charles
Carmel; a primitive-looking wooden horse that was part of the first
carousel in the United States; and a stained-glass replica of the
postage-stamp armored steed.

The museum also purchased a 1936 Alan Herschell carousel that
consists of thirty animals and two chariots, many of which are from

different manufacturers and owners, adding color and visual diversity. "We encourage collectors to loan carousel pieces that need reconditioning in exchange for the right to display the finished item," says Pratt. To this end, the carousel museum has its own in-house restorer, Tom Wade.

"Visitors are intense about not only touring merry-go-rounds but also collecting," observes Pratt. As long they're are willing to shell out tens of thousands of dollars for various artifacts, "painted ponies" won't ride off into the sunset.

The Merry-Go-Round Museum
W. Washington and Jackson Streets, Sandusky, Ohio 44870
((419) 626-6111

LOCATION: 60 miles west of Cleveland
HOURS: Monday, 11:00 A.M.–5:00 P.M.; Wednesday–Saturday, 11:00
    A.M.–5:00 P.M.; Sunday, noon–5:00 P.M.
ADMISSION: Admission is charged

♠ Westerville: THE MOTORCYCLE HERITAGE MUSEUM

Bikers. The word conjures up an image of tattooed ex-cons in black leather and chains, drinking beer (or worse) and their "mamas" with mile-high hair in cutoff T-shirts and jeans. And who can forget such B-movie classics as *Biker Chicks from Hell*, *Cycle Savages*, or *The Wild Angels* when a gang roars into town wreaking havoc among helpless, upstanding citizens?

But there's a nice, clean, tastefully designed Motorcycle Heritage Museum in the heart of Middle America, Westerville, Ohio. It belongs to the American Motorcycle Association (AMA), a group of nearly 200,000 law-abiding men and women, including lawyers, doctors, grandmothers, and retirees. For nearly seventy-five years, the AMA has encouraged the education of riders, the proper use of roads and equipment, and has sanctioned over three thousand yearly motorcycle-related events. And there's likely not a Hell's Angel in the bunch.

Visitors to the museum are greeted by an almost life-sized bronze sculpture of a rider on a 1919 Indian factory racer. And he even

Participants in a 1922 motorcycle race drew an admiring crowd. (*Photo courtesy of the Motorcycle Heritage Museum.*)

wears a helmet. But this museum is unconventional in another way: Nearly all exhibits change annually. "For our inaugural year, 1990, we offered displays on Women in Motorcycling and Decades of Development," explains director Jim Rogers. A subsequent presentation included a cornucopia of cycles with four-cylinder engines, ranging from the top-of-the-line new BMW to more workaday Harley-Davidsons and Hondas. It also contained obsolete but still popular brands such as Indian and Henderson and turn-of-the-century models that basically resemble bicycles with engines. "Motorcycles have been around since the late 1860s, when a Mr. Roper invented a steam engine velocipede," Rogers reports. A reproduction of the 1885 Daimler, the first two-wheeler using a gas-powered engine, is on permanent display. The Einspur, another museum fixture, was an early "test bed" for an automobile engine with sort of training wheels on the back that prevent it from falling over when ridden. Still another, a 1949 British Velocette, is a sleek silver model with a spring seat.

Motorcycles really "took off" around the turn of the century. "Prior to 1920, they were the primary form of motorized transportation because they were affordable and rapid," says Rogers. More than two hundred individual brands were manufactured in the United States alone and represented a major export, with motorcycle competition becoming a popular spectator sport. However, the advent of inexpensive automobiles, the establishment of trade tariffs in Europe, and the onset of the Depression eventually caused the demise of all U.S. makers except for Harley-Davidson and Indian. And in 1953, the latter, once billed as producing "the Rolls Royce of motorcycles," shut down production, leaving Harley-Davidson as the lone American manufacturer.

Post-World War II prosperity, leather-jacketed teen idols such as James Dean and Marlon Brando (star of the classic film *The Wild One*), and the influx of Japanese and British-made vehicles like Triumph and Kawasaki signaled the arrival of the "outlaw biker" image the AMA has struggled so hard to overcome. ("Actually, no more than 1 percent of motorcyclists belong to gangs," asserts Rogers.)

"And, rather than being 'cool' or 'hip,' motorcyclists wear leather as a second skin for protection," he goes on, pausing at an impressive-looking Harley (at 260 mph, it was the world speed holder in 1972) and the accompanying red, white, and blue leather uniform worn by rider Leo Payne. "If they fall off their bikes, the animal hide takes a beating instead of their own."

Cycles also line the corridors of the adjacent AMA office. Among others, there's a hooded 1983 Yamaha Heyser that traveled coast to coast in five days on 14.9 gallons of gas, about a tankful in an average-sized car.

"We're here for everyone, not just AMA members," emphasizes Rogers. That includes Hell's Angels, too.

The Motorcycle Heritage Museum
P.O. Box 6114
33 Collegeview Road, Westerville, OH 43081
((614) 891-2425

LOCATION: Near Columbus
HOURS: Monday–Friday, 9:00 A.M.–4:30 P.M., call for weekend hours
    and tours
ADMISSION: Free

Wisconsin

♠ Hayward: THE NATIONAL FRESH WATER FISHING HALL OF FAME

One look at the giant leaping muskie at the National Fresh Water Fishing Hall of Fame in Hayward, Wisconsin, and you're hooked. Who can resist climbing into the four-and-a-half-story structure that's half a city block long and standing in its gaping maw, replete with jagged teeth? It's the biggest fiberglass fish in the pond. Smaller—a relative term here—fiberglass salmon, walleye, and smallmouth bass frolic in a garden below, dedicated to the memory of a human afish-ionado, who had a fondness for those particular species.

The inside of this twenty-five-thousand-square-foot, seven-acre multi-building complex is as ingenious as its exterior. There you'll find four hundred fish mounts representing two hundred species, three hundred classic and antique and outboard motors, and five thousand fishing lures, along with rods, reels, buckets, tackle boxes, and, undoubtedly the world's only collection of hooks that have impaled humans instead of fish.

The more scaled down main museum includes a minnow bucket exhibit. You can see a heated model with a kerosene lamp that was used for ice fishing and a glass number that resembles a minnow trap (not that the minnows can tell the difference). A plethora of tackle boxes traces their development, or decline, depending on one's point of view, from elaborate hand-fashioned leather and wooden containers to K-Mart plastic ones. The fifteen hundred to two thousand hooks that snagged people can also be found here along with the humans' names, hometowns, and where they were fishing. "These [the hooks] were removed and collected by a doctor," explains director Ted Dzialo. In a perfect world, the display would honor the fish they were trying to snare as well as the human body part that was caught.

Famous fishermen, such as Drane Scott (who?) are also represented here. "Along with being a well-known columnist, he collected every conceivable kind of lure and nearly six thousand reels," Dzialo says, answering the unstated question and pointing to a panorama of early wooden plugs and a menagerie of fake mice, frogs, worms, and assorted bugs. Fly fishing is also honored, with a exhibit on Dame

This four-and-a-half-story walk-through muskie is a Moby Dick fantasy come true. (*Photo courtesy of the National Fresh Water Fishing Hall of Fame.*)

Juliana Behners, a sixteenth-century nun who was not only an avid fisherwoman but even wrote a book about it. Louis Spray, who twice held the world record for non-fiberglass muskies, is commemorated with an exhibit of his rods, reels, outboard motors, and photos as well as of the clothes he wore when fishing. Presumably they've been washed.

A World's Record Gallery immortalizes those who have established fresh-water angling records in all tackle and line classes. They accept no fish stories here. Applicants must supply photo and documentary evidence, sometimes even to the point of obtaining species verification from a fish biologist or by producing the (always frozen) fish itself, which can be mounted for taxidermy later. Once accepted, an honoree remains in the Hall of Fame for eternity, even though his or her record may be surpassed.

Those lacking an appreciation of the hundreds of fresh and salt water "trophy mounts" might want to visit the Examples of Poor Taxidermy wall. Here, some fish are disproportionately bloated with plaster of paris while others have truly terrible paint jobs, resembling extras from *Alien* movies instead of dead fish. "We try to include all species, even those that aren't as popular," states Dzialo, speaking of the other, properly mounted trophies. "A fish such as a carp that's undesirable in America is considered a major catch in England." But still, some of the breeds are downright ugly, despite their packaging.

Visitors revving through the outboard motor collection can see a 1909 Evinrude, one of the first commercially made in the United States. "Outboard motors came into use in Europe in the 1890s," Dzialo continues. "By the turn of the century, they were even having races over there." Those who think all outboard motors are created equal should look again. "Older models had no electric starter and you had to crank them by hand. Plus, they were a lot less reliable," a major complication when you're in the middle of a very calm lake. Statues of a hairy bigfoot-type primitive fisherman and his equally unattractive son illustrate how far fishing (and Homo sapiens) have come. A fine kettle, indeed.

The National Fresh Water Fishing Hall of Fame
Hall of Fame Drive, Box 33, Hayward, WI 54843
((715) 634-4440

LOCATION: Near Route 63, 110 miles north of Eau Claire
HOURS: April 15–October 30, Museum and Administrative offices
    open 7 days a week, 10:00 A.M–5:00 P.M. November 1–April 14,
    Museum closed. Administrative offices open Monday–Friday 9:30
    A.M.–4:30 P.M.
ADMISSION: Admission is charged

♠ Mount Horeb: THE MOUNT HOREB MUSTARD MUSEUM

When it comes to mustard, Barry Levenson really cuts it. A self-described "recovering lawyer," he is the creator, curator, and owner of the Mount Horeb Mustard Museum in Mount Horeb, Wisconsin. With nearly fourteen hundred (and growing) different types of mustard, a "Mustard-piece Theater" video featuring British actor Edward Woodward ("The Equalizer" does condiments), and related advertising, sheet music, and film clips, this museum pretty much covers the subject.

And because "man does not live by mustard alone," according to Levenson, there's a food emporium that sells, along with two hundred kinds of guess-what, chocolates, cheeses, cookies, teas, and many other goodies. No ketchup ("persons must pass through a ketchup detector" before entering) or mayo allowed. There's also a newsletter, *The Proper Mustard* ("Yellow journalism at its best") and a catalog ("If you're going to spend money, phone us toll free at 1-800-GET-MUSTARD"). The former includes recipes for meats, sauces, and even cakes, but watch for ringers such as the "Crude Person's Mustard Delight," which basically consists of alternating cans of "very cheap" beer with spoonfuls of mustard.

Levenson received the call for his museum in, appropriately, an all-night supermarket. "I was feeling depressed because the Red Sox just

The Mount Horeb Mustard Museum features a veritable United Nations of Mustard. (*Photo courtesy of the museum.*)

lost the World Series," he remembers. "In my grief, I turned down the condiment aisle, passing the ketchup, pickles, olives, and so forth. When I stood before the mustards, a voice spoke to me, 'If you collect us, they will come.'" Prior to that, he'd been spread pretty (perhaps too) thin as an assistant attorney general for the State of Wisconsin.

The museum sponsors National Mustard Day (August 5) and draws thousands of visitors—including flies and other insects, who aren't welcome. Along with viewing the exhibits, you can sample over one hundred fifty types of mustard on hot dogs, bratwurst, pretzels, and even on apples, french fries, green beans, and ice cream??? ("Really, it's good with sweet honey mustard," Levenson insists.) The museum has even been honored in "everyone's favorite journal" the *Congressional Record* for its contributions to local tourism ("by the same congressman who applied for federal disaster relief").

Where else can you view mustard from Czechoslovakia, Sri Lanka, Japan, China, South Africa, South America, Israel, Turkey, just about every European country, and forty-eight states ("Perhaps Alaska and

Nevada have other things to do?"). It comes in all colors, shapes, and sizes, and has been mixed with fruits (pineapples, cranberries, papayas, etc.) nuts, liquors (whiskey, beer, cognac) and nettles ("for people with sharp tongues").

Mustards have been prepared by Uncle Phil, Fuggle, Arcy Varcy, Dogwrapper, Mucky Duck, and the Duchess of Devonshire. Along with the house brand, Slimm & Nunne, jokingly labeled by Levenson's "long suffering wife" Pat regarding its possibilities for success, you'll find mustard with honey and candied fruits, prickly pear cactus mustard, and habañero mustard, described by its manufacturer as the mustard from hell. "But the hottest is Royal Bohemian Horseradish Mustard, made right here in Wisconsin," states Levenson. "It should have a seven-day waiting period."

The most unusual mustard is a one-of-a-kind jar presented by the Levensons' vet as "a remembrance of the day's procedure, when our cat Ambrose was neutered." Called Feline Nut Mustard, it may or may not contain the genuine article, and Levenson's not about to open it and find out. He never samples the donations.

Throughout the ages, mustard has had other uses, most notably as a plaster to alleviate pain and other ailments, and for snakebites and rheumatism. Although it probably originated in India where the mustard seed was considered a fertility symbol by Hindus, "the ancient Babylonians might have used it on bratwurst," adds Levenson. Still utilized as a bath powder, "it can be very invigorating and refreshing." Plus, "one can dip pretzels into the bath water, if one is so inclined."

Levenson sees a bright future for his favorite condiment. "Along with being low in calories and speeding up metabolism, mustard's most popular on hot dogs, of which Americans consume fifty million a year." Speaking of tube steak, there's a privately owned Hot Dog Hall of Fame in San Francisco. "[The owner] has a modified Oscar Mayer Wienermobile which he calls his Lamborg Wienie." Visitors might want to pass: the exhibits might be kind of green and a mustard museum's hard to top.

The Mount Horeb Mustard Museum
109 E. Main Street, Mount Horeb, WI 53572
((608) 437-3986

LOCATION: **West of Madison at the junction of U.S. 18 and SR 92**
HOURS: **Seven days a week, 10:00 A.M.–5:00 P.M.**
ADMISSION: **Free**

♠ Oshkosh: THE EAA AIR ADVENTURE MUSEUM

The EAA (Experimental Aircraft Association) Adventure Museum, located in Oshkosh "B'gosh," Wisconsin, is more engrossing than your average Chicago to New York hop. The over ninety vintage planes displayed start with a replica of the first self-propelled 1903 Wright *Flyer* invented by brothers Wilbur and Orville (the sand, taken from the beach at Kitty Hawk, North Carolina, is the real thing), and basically follow the evolution of "flying machines" through to combat jets. There are antiques and classics, ultralights, military fighters and trainers, rotorcraft, gliders, and even a seven-ton gondola for a hot-air balloon, the first to cross the Pacific in aviation history. Aerobatic aircraft (in which the plane, and not a person, is the performer) and "home-built" airplanes constructed in basements, garages, or on (rather large) back porches can also be found here.

If peering inside fuselages and cockpits and trying to figure out how the durn things operate isn't enough, through the miracle of modern film technology you can "fly" into the Amazon jungle on a biplane expedition; "brace" yourself during a sensory immersion aerobatic videotape; and be privy to planning a World War II combat flying mission in a Quonset hut. Little crew members can visit Captain EAAgle at the Junior Aviator Theater. A person dressed up as an eagle in a pilot's uniform, the captain makes occasional appearances and has been known to promote the museum from a tree (whether you believe he flew there is a direct measure of IQ and gullibility level).

But the airplanes are the real stars. Five times more powerful than the Wrights' design, the 1911 Curtiss Pusher marked the first use of ailerons (movable surfaces on the trailing edge of the wing, an idea of Alexander Graham Bell's), wheels instead of landing skids, and an actual seat for the pilot. The museum's E–8–75 model was rediscovered in a barn in 1940 and refurbished and flown in exhibitions until 1969. Also included are the Curtiss *Jenny* that gained fame as a

Along with offering airplane rides, the Pioneer Airport displays several
types of early aircraft. (*Photo courtesy of EAA Air Adventure Museum.*)

barnstormer in county fairs of the twenties and thirties; the Stits *Sky
Baby*, once the world's smallest airplane; Henry Ford's Depression-
era *Tin Goose*, the precursor to modern mass air travel; and racers,
such as the *Bonzo*, which looks more like an oversized model than
the real thing. Nearby Pioneer Airport, which is open in the summer, harkens back to the barnstorm era and welcomes classic as well
as newer fly-ins (no jets, please).

In fact, the whole museum's a tribute to unchained model airplane
builders. Replicas of Charles Lindbergh's 1927 *Spirit of St. Louis*
and the 1986 *Voyager 2* "re-create the persistence and dedication of
pioneers who were inspired to step well beyond the accepted norm,"
observes Dick Knapinski, public relations specialist for the museum.
"In the case of the *Voyager*, a handful of people used common
homebuilding technology to construct a remarkable aircraft." With a
110-foot wing span and an unpressured cockpit the size of a phone
booth, the *Voyager* made a nonstop flight around the world in nine
days with pilots Jeana Yeager and Dick Rutan at the helm. The comprehensive Lindbergh exhibit not only features a plane built and
piloted by EAA members for anniversary reenactments of his flight,
but also a diorama of Paris as Lindbergh might have seen it from
four thousand feet, and complete documentation of his voyages.
Another homebuilt innovation, the Aerocar, functions as an automobile when the wings are folded back. "It's a great way to avoid speed
traps."

No visit would be complete without a stop at the irresistably named Propellerama, the air traffic control exhibit, and the cockpit instrument and engine displays. Although not as engaging as some of the other presentations "we try to give enough information so visitors have a complete understanding of airplanes but not so much that they'll go into overdrive," says Knapinski.

The facility has two restoration areas for the museum's planes as well as for larger aircraft. But despite its fancy trappings, the EAA Air Adventure Museum is still a bunch of guys and gals figuring out new and better ways to fly.

EAA Air Adventure Museum
EAA Aviation Center
P.O. Box 3086, Oshkosh, WI 54903
((414) 426-4800

LOCATION: Off Highway 41 at Highway 44 in Oshkosh
HOURS: Monday–Saturday, 8:30 A.M.–5:00 P.M.; Sunday, 11:00
   A.M.–5:00 P.M.; closed major holidays
ADMISSION: Admission is charged

THE
WEST

Arizona

✦ Phoenix: THE HALL OF FLAME

What's loud and red and ever so appropriately located in Phoenix, Arizona? It has helmets, uniforms, ladders, vehicles, and alarms and is the brainchild of the late Chicago industrialist George Getz, Jr. If you haven't Getzed already, Phoenix is the perfect spot for the Hall of Flame, the world's largest fire-fighting museum.

With over 130 restored vehicles dating from 1725 through 1961, the galleries cover almost an acre and have nearly everything relating to fire fighting. Memorabilia ranges from nineteenth-century parade carriages that look great on the Fourth of July but are useless in fighting fires to about 450 rare insurance company marks, a "hot" collectible; from lithographs, photographs, paintings, and drawings to leather hats and buckets from colonial times; and from "hands on" exhibits of a 1916 American La France engine and special safety displays devised for children, to a 1725 Newsham pumper, the first and oldest fire rig in the United States.

Designed to ignite understanding of American's most dangerous occupation, the museum re-creates the history of man's eternal war against conflagration. "In England, fire-fighting brigades were privately run by insurance companies," points out Dr. Peter Molloy, the Hall of Flame's executive director and resident historian. "By the late seventeenth century, the companies began to post fire marks on homes."

In the colonies, volunteers often fought blazes by throwing water on buildings surrounding the one that had caught fire (it was usually already lost by the time the brigade arrived). One rather unimpressive-looking long pole utilized an attached hook to peel first the roof and then the walls from burning structures. "Back then, houses were made of wood and packed closely together, with shingled roofs and wooden or plaster chimneys." Teams of men patrolled the city at

This 1922 American La France Fire Engine serviced the town or Edgerton, Wisconsin from 1922 to 1965. (*Photo courtesy of the Hall of Flame.*)

night, sounding a rotating wooden rattle similar to a New Year's noisemaker to alert the populace of a pending inferno. These are on display along with klaxons, Model T horns and other alarms, making this one museum where visitors don't have to worry about keeping quiet.

According to Molloy, fire-fighting men (and later women) are a pretty inflammatory bunch: "They're tough, aggressive, and see their company as the best in the area. Before the onset of centralized battalions, ethnic-based gangs would often conduct turf wars over who should fight the fire." In order to collect insurance money, a brigade would send bullies to lay claim to the fireplug, giving rise to the expression "plug ugly."

Hence, each brigade tried to outdo the other in purchasing and flaunting glamorous but impractical equipment like the Hall of Flame's delicate, elaborate 1870 Hotchkiss parade vehicle, which is currently valued at about $100,000. "One of my favorite displays is a fancy 1909 gasoline-powered buggy used by a fire chief in Indiana," relates Molloy. "One day a youngster on a bicycle passed him on the way to a blaze." Shortly afterward the chief purchased a Model T Ford.

Still, most of the items on display have seen honorable service and have been painstakingly refurbished. "We've tried to restore them to their original condition, sometimes even researching newspaper archives or contacting descendants of the original designer in our search for accuracy," comments Molloy. The hand pumps are particularly swell: In addition to the Newsham model, which required six firemen to operate the handles, an 1844 pumper used in Philadelphia necessitated a force of *fifty* to get enough pressure into an air chamber to shoot a stream of water two-hundred feet. "It was so arduous that teams had to rotate every few minutes."

Until his early eighties when declining health forced him to quit, George Getz drove a 1930 Ahrens Fox in Phoenix's annual Fiesta Bowl Parade. With 8.5 tons of hose, pump, water tank, and ladders, the vehicle lacked power steering and reminded an often-forgetful populace of those who take the heat. The Hall of Flame continues to carry their torch.

The Hall of Flame
6101 East Van Buren Street, Phoenix, AZ 85008
((602) 275-3473

LOCATION: **Near the Phoenix Zoo; east of Phoenix**
HOURS: **Monday–Saturday, 9:00 A.M.–5:00 P.M.**
ADMISSION: **Admission is charged**

⸸ Prescott: THE BEAD MUSEUM

The Bead Museum in Prescott, Arizona, sticks out like a diamond on a shell necklace. Located smack dab in the center of the state, in the middle of a street full of cowboy bars, it strings along visitors from all over the United States and abroad. "Some, including scholars, even travel to Arizona just to see our collections and research library," claims curator Gabrielle Liese. Where else could you view Tantric Buddhist shaman regalia, pre-Columbian stone and shell jewelry, and Venetian millefiori beads, then go next door and toss down a whiskey?

The museum's beaded gamut runs from a Persian necklace dated several thousand years B.C. to collectible jewelry from the 1950s and represents nearly every country. Most of the beads are from the North and Latin Americas, the African Middle East, Southwest Asia, and the Orient. Made from wood, glass, bone, porcelain, metal, and stone, "they are what the people wore, and not royalty," points out Liese. Perhaps this ornamental museum has more in common with its rodeo (as opposed to Rodeo) drive location than initially appears.

In fact, many of the designs exhibited still adorn tribes today. "Different beads can reveal age, social condition, rank, marital status, and can denote religious occasions," Liese continues. In some cultures, wearing the wrong necklace or headdress can be equivalent to going naked in public and can result in ostracism or worse.

One can learn about a society by studying its beads. For instance, during World War II, the Santo Domingo Indians of New Mexico

Visitors can learn a lot about a culture by studying its beads. (*Photo courtesy of the Bead Museum.*)

used plastic instead of coral in making their necklaces. "Trade was impossible, so the Indians improvised with cheaper, similar-looking materials," explains Liese.

Her interest in art history got her into this sideline in the first place. A retired interior decorator, Liese became intrigued when she learned that beads made off Murano Island in Italy had been used to trade in Africa for slaves. "This bothered me, the fact that human beings were a bartered commodity." Back then, "the early explorers, fur trappers, even Christopher Columbus when he came to America, traded with beads." Like Visa and MasterCard, they were accepted everywhere.

Liese went on a roll, buying native beads, obtaining them as gifts from friends, once even venturing to a warehouse in a dangerous area of Kansas City to bid on the collection of a convicted murderer. Her acquisitions grew into the hundreds (or thousands, depending on how you're counting), and she decided to open a museum.

Exhibits include the Tantric Buddhist regalia that picks more than a few bones. Consisting of a belt with a pendant apron, a pair of armlets, and an upper body ornament, the shaman's getup was made from carved plaques and beads from human skeletons. Many of the donors were alleged to have been executed criminals. "This exercised a powerful effect on the illiterate population," points out Liese.

Other items are as varied and colorful as the beads themselves. Chinese beads and kingfisher feather combinations are incorporated in long pendants, dangling near the ears from a headdress, a sort of fifteen-inch earring without the posts. Oriental prayer strings, consisting of beads, bone, and tassels "were utilized more as wrist ornaments than for religious purposes," like modern-day charm bracelets. And X marks the spot with a shell and tortoise necklace from the Solomon Islands that's worn like a criss-cross harness. It includes white shell *hishi*, a form of currency in the Solomons.

Liese is always on the lookout for new acquisitions and loans. "You get a sense of warmth from something someone wore and cherished. There's a lot more to it than meets the eye." And the wrist, neck, and head as well.

The Bead Museum
140 S. Montezuma, Prescott, AZ 86303
((602) 445-2431

LOCATION: Off U.S. 89 south of Flagstaff
HOURS: Monday–Saturday, 9:30 A.M.–4:30P.M.; Sunday by appointment;
   closed some holidays
ADMISSION: Free, but donations are welcome and memberships available

California

✦ Helendale: EXOTIC WORLD: THE BURLESQUE HALL OF FAME

Although it's in the middle of the Mojave Desert, Exotic World of Helendale, California, reveals the naked truth about burlesque. It's the
largest (and perhaps only) collection of feather boas, elbow length
gloves, breakaway jeweled gowns, G-strings, and pasties from a gone
(but hardly forgotten) era. There's Jayne Mansfield's faded ottoman;
Gypsy Rose Lee's dusty black velvet cape; and an urn with the ashes
of Jennie Lee, founder of the Exotic Dancers League of America,
whose residence this was before she died of cancer a few years ago.

Known as the Bazoom Girl, Jennie Lee had the ability to twirl tassels in opposite directions, a feat accomplished by the use of ball
bearings (don't try this at home, ladies). Along with publishing *Juggs*
magazine, Lee amassed much of the memorabilia that's in the museum today before passing the G-string, as it were, to her close
friend and colleague Dixie Evans, a sixty-something former Marilyn
Monroe impersonator who now manages both the Hall of Fame and
the League.

Covered with photos and paintings of long-legged, bosomy strippers (one topless picture's signed "Breast wishes"), the walls fairly resonate with dreams of fame and glamour amid a lusty sense of humor. Along with the famous (in some circles) Sally Rand, Lily St. Cyr, Blaze Starr, Candy Barr, Tempest Storm, and Chesty "Double Agent 73" Morgan, there are the lesser known luminaries: Teddi Bare and her "sister" Kinda, Lotta Topp, Hope Chest, Helen Bedd, and Honey Bee.

"Exotic dancers do more than take off their clothes," states Dixie Evans, who still flaunts a viable facsimile of Monroe's breathy elocution and kittenish mannerisms. "We entertain and give a little story, and try to do it with class." With that in mind, the six-hundred-member Exotic Dancers League of America hosts an annual reunion in May at the museum to compete for the title Miss Exotic World, show off their assets, and schmooze.

Lest we forget, the Burlesque Hall of Fame keeps alive memories of such luminaries as Sally Rand. (*Photo courtesy of Exotic World.*)

Although the group consists of retired burlesque stars and costume designers, "because burlesque has become more mainstream, each year more nightclub dancers are looking to break in." Or out, depending upon one's perspective. They make the pilgrimage in hopes to lay bare the secrets of the Golden Age of Burlesque and get some pointers from Dixie and any other veterans who happen to be around.

And Dixie's a veritable fountain of information. "Notre Dame football coach Knute Rockne got his idea for the Four Horseman's Back Shift [a famous football move] while watching a chorus line in a burlesque theater," she remarks. "And jazz singer Al Jolson made his first public appearance at another in Philadelphia. Both English royalty and strippers use lead weights in their garments—the queen in her skirt, to keep it from blowing up and the stripper in the ornament that holds her fringe together, so it will go back down after she bumps." And so forth.

Okay, so maybe she's a little hazy about the origins of burlesque, which had its heyday in the twenties and thirties. "It started in the twenties when Hilda Wassau's bra came tumbling down along with the stock market," she has said. (Historians trace it back to the 1860s when a troupe of British actresses in New York satirized Victorian customs in short costumes.) It faded in the fifties with the onset of television, and by the Vietnam era "everybody had seen everything," so the novelty, like many an entertainer's clothes, disappeared. Today if you want to see G-strings, just go to the beach.

But Dixie's more interested in the days when performers dripped rhinestones and furs in dark, smoke-fulled nightclubs. Singers, comics, and magicians opened the shows. "I'm here to preserve the greats," she says.

Although Exotic World only gets about twenty or so visitors a week, Dixie believes burlesque is on the upswing. Recently, she's been featured on *Sally Jessy Raphael* and *Donahue* and has been written up in the *Wall Street Journal*. And she didn't even have to take off her clothes.

Exotic World: The Burlesque Hall of Fame
29053 Wild Road, Helendale, CA 92342
((619) 243-5261

LOCATION: **At the intersection of I-15, Route 395, and Route 58**
HOURS: **By appointment only**
ADMISSION: **Free, but donations are greatly appreciated**

♠ Hollywood: THE MAX FACTOR MUSEUM OF BEAUTY

If beauty is an illusion, then Max Factor was a master magician. What began as a modest shop offering custom wigs, theatrical makeup and related artistry for professional actors exploded into a multimillion dollar enterprise with the emergence of the film industry. The Max Factor Museum of Beauty in Hollywood, California, is a monument to all that glitters.

The Make-Up Salon, as it was called, originally opened in 1928 and "had a very opulent Louis XIV look," explains Linda Jones, the museum's curator. But Max Factor wanted it to be more modern, so he hired renowned architect S. Charles Lee, who redid both the interior and facade in its current art deco form." The building is re-created at Universal Studios in Florida.

The bash that Max Factor threw to celebrate the 1935 grand reopening is still talked about. "Four thousand invitations were delivered by hand, with not one refusal," says Jones. Not just any-body was summoned: The eight thousand attendees included every movie notable of the day. "It was the biggest Hollywood party ever held by a company and drew huge crowds and klieg lights."

Never one to fail to capitalize on an opportunity, Factor had his guests sign a Scroll of Fame, which is still on display at the museum. "It's one of the largest and most complete collections of screen star autographs in existence." Although even bitter rival columnists Hedda Hopper and Louella Parsons added their names to the scroll, "they did so on opposite ends to keep their signatures away from each other."

In his search for the perfect face, Max Factor invented the Beauty Calibrator. (*Photo courtesy of the Max Factor Museum of Beauty.*)

Inside, the museum is divided into several small rooms, each dedicated to a different decade. Max's Office traces Factor's beginnings in Poland to his position as a wig maker and makeup artist for the royal ballet in Czarist Russia to his small enterprise in Los Angeles, where he settled in 1909. "The heavy greasepaint he ordered from suppliers looked thick, shiny, and unnatural under the bright lights and close scrutiny of the camera," points out Jones. "So he formulated a more flexible makeup in a cream form."

Along with examples of early cosmetics and pictures of Factor's original shops, there are letters from grateful clients, not all of them female. "Julian Elting truly appreciated Max's lightening powder," notes Jones. "As one of the first female impersonators, he was one of our best clients." A photo of Julia/Julian in full bridal attire adorns the walls.

But even macho types needed Max. "In 1925, during the filming of *Ben Hur*, Max whipped up several batches of makeup to give thousands of male extras Mediterranean skin tones," recalls Jones. Although Factor hosed them down with the stuff, he forgot one little detail. "When they lift up their arms in the chariot scene to get the horses going, it's dead white."

The original studio was divided into Blonde, Brunette, Brownette, and Redhead rooms, where stars of the day were given their "looks." (this was before Hollywood recognized anything but young Caucasians). The mint-green Redhead Room contains society makeup memorabilia from the mid-twenties to the mid-thirties. Along with the usual samples, there are "liquid nylons" that women could paint on their legs, as well as some not-so-flattering photographs of stars, such as that of a young, pudgy Joan Crawford. Factor knew all their wrinkles—and in Crawford's case, freckles, which she covered up heavily with Factor's cosmetics. "Before appearing in public, she used to run around topless so as not to get the makeup on her clothes." Rita Hayworth greatly benefited from a salon-engineered nose job and electrolysis that furnished her with her famous widow's peak.

Contracts and more star photos line the Main Salon, which touches upon the thirties. Here visitors can view the various lines of makeup used for black and white movies, stage, and the matte-type pan-cake makeup which many found worked equally well off the set. "Actors stole over $2,000 worth because it looked so natural." This and many other products deemed successful were quickly made available to the general public.

The beauty calibrator and kissing machine are also located here. Resembling a medieval torture device, the former measured features within 1/100 of an inch. "Max never found the perfectly aligned face." What sane woman would want to go near it? The mechanical oscillator, or kissing machine, tested the indelibility of lipstick after employees refused to act as guinea pigs. "Max always used workers to see how long his makeups would last." Basically, the machine's a pressure gauge that measures how much lipstick comes off with each kiss. How romantic.

Rather than being a wind tunnel, the powder-blue room for blondes contains artifacts from the forties. "This decade saw great changes in packaging, such as plastic and reusable materials, like trays that could also hold sandwiches or cigarettes," observes Jones. The rose-color chamber for brunettes has Hi-Fi makeup from the fifties, Factor's first liquid offering, and a nod to the burgeoning television industry, for which he also produced cosmetics.

The sixties are covered in the peach-decorated Brownette Room (brownette is a lighter brunette shade with other colors, such as blonde and auburn, mixed in). Who can forget Patent Leather liquid eyeliner that rolled up in a ball if you cried or got caught in a rainstorm? A plethora of false eyelashes is included, in shag and peek-a-boo styles for upper and lower lids. "Models would wear two to three pairs to get the Twiggy look." That, and starve.

This museum reveals the mirrors behind the smoke. Movie stars go fat and bald too, but the public was usually the last to know, thanks to Max Factor.

The Max Factor Museum of Beauty
1666 N. Highland Avenue, Hollywood, CA 90028
((213) 463-6668

LOCATION: **Downtown**
HOURS: **Monday–Saturday, 10:00 A.M.–4:00 P.M.**
ADMISSION: **Free (as is the parking)**
The ownership of this museum will be changing in 1994, so call for
    updated information.

♠ Palo Alto: THE BARBIE HALL OF FAME

What a concept: sixteen thousand Barbie dolls and friends, clothes, cars, airplanes, and other accessories worth nearly a million dollars, all crammed into an eighteen-hundred-square-foot museum. These include the Empress Bride Barbie—*that* can run up to $260—in a costume designed by Bob Mackie; the rare 1988 Christmas Barbie, worth $400–$500 (boxed); and limited edition versions dressed and coiffed by various designers that can cost hundreds of dollars apiece.

"My collection is 99.9 percent complete," says owner/curator/Barbie devotee Evelyn Burkhalter of Palo Alto, California. "I'm only missing six outfits: three Best Buys from '78, two from mod cousin Francie, and one Confetti Cutie for Skipper."

And, unlike other toys and fads, Barbie-mania shows no sign of abating. "She has followed every trend since 1959. There's nothing in the U.S. that hasn't been done by Barbie." (Excluding cheating on Ken, robbing convenience stores, and indulging in mind-altering substances, of course.) When Jacqueline Kennedy became first lady, Barbie got a bubble haircut and wore haute couture; with the popularity of the Gabor sisters a few years later, she obtained a set of wigs (however, Barbie would never dream of slapping a policeman). In 1965, when trousers for women became more acceptable, they showed up on Barbie. That same year, however, Barbie also came equipped with her own doll-sized set of Corning Ware, an ever-so-gentle reminder of her place in society.

Yet, according to Burkhalter, Barbie is neither leader nor role model, which contributes greatly to her lasting appeal. "That gives her an edge over other dolls. Because the minute kids get her, off come the clothes" and their imaginations go to work. "You can put her in any situation—good or bad—and she fits right in."

But, like any other institution, Barbie has had her rough moments. "She almost got stopped by the Beatles and the mod era," states Burkhalter. "So Mattel developed an incentive program whereby for every old Barbie mailed in, you got a discount on the new 'Living Barbie,' who was made of a more malleable plastic, could twist and turn, and had long eyelashes, straight hair, and a psychedelic wardrobe." Far out.

Another failure was 1967's wince-inducing "colored Francie" who was replaced two years later by Julia, modeled after actress Diahann Carroll. 1980 saw Black Barbie and Hispanic Barbie, and a Summit Barbie line that included African-American, Asian, Hispanic, and white dolls. Today, Barbie comes in all skin colors.

And Barbie's been an equal opportunity doll in other areas, as well; serving as astronaut, surgeon, business executive, veterinarian, and in the various armed services (Army, Air Force and Marines). Barbie has also held more traditional jobs, such as nurse, stewardess (American Airlines and Pan Am), candy striper, chef, and teacher. And she's been a ballerina, fashion editor, aerobics instructor, figure skater, rock star (twice), and TV dancer. Her cars have ranged from a Volkswagen to a Mercedes and she's had her own McDonald's, hair salon, and Dream House.

All this and more is divided into sections (brides, ballerinas, etc.) and arranged chronologically at the Barbie Hall of Fame. "This way, visitors get a view of how dresses, hairstyles, and shoes have changed over the years," observes Burkhalter. Although Barbie has evolved from a demure sideways glance and a pout to centered eyes and a big smile "most variations have been in hair and makeup. Mattel has been using the same basic mold since 1977."

And, of course, there's the generic-looking Ken (he's had a few facelifts and body tune-ups over the years too); Midge "a winsome young teenage doll to join Barbie in all of her gay, exciting activities," according to Mattel promotional material; younger sister Skipper and *her* friend Skooter; and Midge's boyfriend Allan. Talk about plastic people....

Sixteen thousand Barbie dolls and friends, clothes, cars, airplanes, and other accessories can be found at the Barbie Hall of Fame. (*Photo by C. Charles. Courtesy of the Barbie Hall of Fame.*)

In over thirty years, some five hundred million Barbie dolls have been sold. "More and more versions keep coming out, almost to the point to where retailers are competing against each other," states

Burkhalter. "And I must have the new ones or I won't maintain youngsters' interest." Barbie would truly understand.

The Barbie Hall of Fame
460 Waverly Street, Palo Alto, CA 94301
((415) 326-5841

LOCATION: **In the Doll Studio, downtown**
HOURS: **Tuesday–Friday, 1:30–4:30 P.M.; Saturday, 10:00 A.M.–noon, 1:30–4:30 P.M.**
ADMISSION: **Admission is charged**

✦ San Francisco: THE OLD MINT MUSEUM

This is one museum where you always carry its souvenirs with you. Along with numismatic and coin-related goodies, it's chock full of mining equipment and California relics. Gold and American Eagle bullion coins surround a glittering pyramid of twenty-eight 99.9 percent pure gold bars, with the whole confection topped by fifty two-ounce gold-leaf specimens. It's not for the light-fingered however: The gold's in a vault enclosed by Plexiglas and guards are everywhere. In fact, security's so tight here that museum administrator Olga Widnes won't even discuss it. They don't give out free samples, either.

Still, visitors to the Old Mint Museum in San Francisco can learn that coins are much more than small change. The first stop is usually the Numismatic Room with its complete sets of proofs. Along with stacks of this year's shiny pennies, nickels, dimes, and quarters, you'll see large plaster casts of the entire coin as well as photographic blowups of current minting processes. Those wanting to view the real thing should roll over to the mints in Denver or Philadelphia. And the big (i.e., paper) money's made at the Bureau of Engraving and Printing in Washington, DC, which also produces stamps. But don't try it at home.

Although the multimillion-dollar gold pyramid's a perennial favorite, one can only drool for so long. So it's off to "meet the press." Through a special trigger attachment, you can activate an 160-ton coin press built in 1869. Out comes your very own 1.5-inch bronze medal with a picture of the mint on the front and a map of the United States on the back. Although it's not your kid, pet, or favorite rock group, it's close enough for government work and only costs one dollar.

An exhibit of U.S. National Medals includes not only coins but Presidential, Army, Navy, and other medallions authorized by Congress that are also for sale. In addition to many others, various sizes of two of the more recent ones, those honoring Generals H. Norman Schwarzkopf and Colin Powell, can be purchased for between two and twenty dollars. "The likenesses are amazingly real," adds Widnes. "Medals often accrue in value over the years." Such a deal.

Most of the exhibits can't be bought, to coin a phrase. Along with a reducing machine that won't help lose weight but has a lot to do with the complicated process of making money, there's a rolltop desk with descriptive photos of nineteenth-century engravers at work, as well as a collection of ancient and rare currency, medals, and tokens.

Built in 1874, the San Francisco Mint was one of the few structures to withstand the 1906 earthquake. *(Photo courtesy of the Old Mint Museum.)*

With a re-created prospector's cabin and 1870s stamp mill for crushing ore, the museum also digs into the other side of the coin: mining.
Four detailed miniatures depict various mining processes and methods. What a (gold) rush.

The rest of the museum is a mélange of West Coast Americana: a
section of a California redwood tree dating back to 1250; a gen-u-ine
circa-1860 stage coach; and the completely restored Victorian-era
mint superintendent's office with its original furnishings. A Victorian
bedchamber, a collection of Victrolas, and other assorted items are
thrown in for good measure.

Even the history of this 1874 federal/classic/revival building is California eclectic. Initially criticized as too spacious, the Old Mint
stayed current with the district's rich mineral finds until 1937 when
inflation (as in space constraints) precipitated a move to larger quarters. The Old Mint's designer, Alfred B. Mullett, committed suicide
because he never received compensation for his later efforts on the
State, War, and Navy Building in Washington. Yet he was recognized
as the premier architect in the post-Civil War construction of government offices. And the San Francisco Mint was one of the few
structures to withstand the 1906 earthquake. As the only financial institution open for business, the mint became extremely popular in
the quake's aftermath.

By 1968, Mullett's structure had been declared surplus and had
begun to deteriorate. Through the efforts of preservationists, it was
turned over to the U.S. Treasury Department for restoration.

After all, they *never* run out of money, and, if they do, they can always make more.

The Old Mint Museum
Fifth and Mission Streets, San Francisco, CA 94103
((415) 744-6830

LOCATION: United States Mint Building, downtown
HOURS: Monday–Friday, 10:00 A.M.–4:00 P.M.; closed holidays
ADMISSION: Free

↑ San Francisco: THE RIPLEY'S BELIEVE IT OR NOT! MUSEUM(S)

The seventeen Ripley's Believe It or Not! "odditoriums" (a Ripley term) are the McDonald's of unusual museums. Rather than specializing in variations on a single item, they offer up a standard menu of human and animal oddities, illusions, and peculiar works of art.

Robert L. Ripley's life and times were almost as bizarre as the collections bearing his name (see The Church of One Tree/Robert L. Ripley Museum, Santa Rosa, California). From the moment you enter the lobby at the Ripley's in San Francisco with its rain curtain and "floating" faucet that's actually suspended in air by a clear glass tube, it's one outrageous thing after another. Be warned: Inquiring minds could go crazy trying to figure it out.

The first gallery illustrates that "one man's or woman's junk is another's art," observes Ian Iljas, the general manager. Here you'll find a dinosaur created from car bumpers, scenes from Super Bowl XVI (San Francisco '49ers versus Cincinnati Bengals) constructed com-

This 1918 cartoon, the first collection of odd facts and feats that Robert Ripley ever created, was originally titled "Champs and Chumps." At his editor's request he changed the title to "Believe It or Not! (© 1994 Ripley Entertainment Inc.)

Robert Ripley with his
favorite oddity, the
Fiji Island Mermaid.
(© 1994 Ripley Enter-
tainment Inc.)

pletely out of folded gum wrappers, and the three-dimensional human and animal figures of kitchen-utensil artist Leo Sewell that were made from items unearthed in the trash heaps of Philadelphia. A one-piece wooden arrow bisects a glass decanter, life-size replicas of famous sculptures have been fabricated from brown paper bags, and the chair fashioned entirely from toothpicks can hold a ton.

From there, it's past a cable car made from 270,000 matchsticks (Got a light?) and on to the "strange people" section. These include a wax figure of the world's fattest man, drafted during World War II at 750 pounds (his final weight: 1069), a true heavy cruiser. There's a portrait of midget Tom Thumb, a P.T. Barnum character and the world's most kissed man. There are worse ways to make a living.

Videos of men twisting their upper torsos 180 degrees, blowing smoke through their eyes, and swallowing then removing a live mouse, abound, as do more wax figures and busts of such people as the world's tallest dude (eight feet eleven inches); the Chinese "unicorn man," with a protruding horn; a four-eyed guy (no, he didn't wear glasses); and still another who roamed the streets of China with a seven-inch candle on his head, inserted in a hole in his skull and held in place with melted wax. Are we having fun yet?

But there's more. Look through the microscope and see the Lord's Prayer on a grain of rice and a crystal with the image of the Virgin Mary and child. A kaleidoscopic mirrored area creates the illusion of being in the middle of a school of sharks and a herd of stampeding buffalo, simultaneous adventures only possible through Ripley.

Looking for an idea for an epitaph? The Graveyard Gallery offers up a parade: "Here lies the body of Jonathan Blake, stepped on the gas instead of the brake." "Here lies the body of Lester Moore, no Les, no more." One presentation gives the impression of being underground with people trying to throw dirt on top of you. What a great way to spend an afternoon.

The travel and culture (if you can call them that) sections offer a painting made from cobwebs and a "fishy" fur-lined fish from Lake Ontario that was a hoax, "but people believed it grew hair because the lake was so cold," explains Iljas. There's also a variety of shrunken heads and torsos (one of which was the property of Ernest Hemingway) and lifelike figures of a Ubangi woman with a huge protruding lip caused by the insertion of discs (not computer), and of the "giraffe woman" of Burma, who elongated her neck by putting bracelets around it. And these people don't even get paid.

Space constraints prevent further description of the exhibits on bizarre eating habits, incredible tales of survival and disaster, an equilibrium-disturbing tunnel, and others. Those wanting to see an "odditorium" up close may not have to travel far "because we're adding new museums every year," reports Iljas. There are also several around the world. As they say in the movie biz: It's coming to a neighborhood near you.

Ripley's Believe It or Not! Museum(s)
175 Jefferson Street, San Francisco, CA 94113
((415) 771-6188, FAX (415) 771-1246

LOCATION: At Fisherman's Wharf
HOURS: Seven days a week, hours vary
ADMISSION: Admission is charged

♠ San Francisco: THE TATTOO ART MUSEUM

This museum may sound like a misnomer, but make no mistake: like the ink injected into your skin, tattooing is here to stay. "Tattooing has been around since Biblical times," observes Lyle Tuttle, the owner of the Tattoo Art Museum in the middle of Fisherman's Wharf in San Francisco. Although no individual lays claim to the invention, Egyptian mummies from 1300 B.C. show blue tattoo marks.

And, throughout the ages, soldiers and sailors, along with royalty, from Russian czars to British princes, have boasted hearts, flowers, or whatever in oh-so-public and private places. So Cher et al., haven't exactly started anything new.

Reaction to Tuttle's enterprise is sometimes mixed. A sign inside states TATTOOING IS MY BUSINESS, IF YOU DON'T LIKE IT, IT'S YOURS. "There are a lot of people who disapprove of what we're doing," he observes. "In fact, several religions prohibit tattooing." Oh, well. They're just thin-skinned.

Compared to the actual tattooing process (piercing small, deep holes into the epidermis, placing dyes into the punctures) walking through this museum/tattoo studio is like dipping a toe into cold water. Consisting of Tuttle's huge private collection, it's a jumble of artifacts, memorabilia, equipment, and drawings. Watching the studio's four tattoo artists work on clients can be kind of fun—from a distance. "In most shops, every available surface—walls, lamps, shades are covered with sheets of flash" (tattoo designs, for the uninitiated). Depending upon its size, each sheet could contain several patterns.

Tuttle has from five to seven thousand sheets, only a few of which have made their way to the oversized flip racks in the museum. "I've traveled around the world looking for this stuff, so I think I can safely say I have the world's largest collection," he observes. "We can reproduce just about anything, or you can bring on your own ideas, which a lot of people do today." Just browsing, thank you.

Tuttle also has an impressive collection of manual and electric tattoo equipment. "Prior to the development of electricity, machines were spring powered," he states, pointing to an electric number that dates to the turn of the century. Yet even today many tattoos are put on by hand "so you can get the desired detail." In collaboration with another artist, Tuttle has created a Texas-sized machine that's four times larger than average. At twenty-seven pounds, "it actually works," he says proudly.

Artifacts and photographs in the Tattoo Pacific section illustrate the interrelationship of the Pacific peoples—Micronesians, Melanesians, Polynesians, Japanese, and others—through similar words and customs, such as tattooing. "The Japanese and Burmese have done the most elaborate tattooing in the world," explains Tuttle. "The Japanese still do a lot today, and in Burma people cover their bodies with designs of plants, animals, and human faces." Patterns once tat-tooed on a South Sea Island chief can also be found here.

African peoples have found ways to decorate their skins as well. "This is effected through scarification, a process by which a keloid scar is produced by causing a minor infection that makes it more pronounced." Is there a reason for this? "If done properly, it can be beautiful." Yet another technique involves utilizing scarification *and* pigment, and is "popular among the medium-dark-skinned peoples, such as Arabs and Africans." Sort of like getting the "works" on a burger, only a lot more permanent.

The museum bristles with odds and ends. Along with lithographs, oil paintings, and antique signs from other studios, there are license plates from four states with TATTOO tattooed on them. What may well be the world's first stun gun, an electrified tennis racket, was rigged by artist "Oakland Jake" who was tired of being bothered by drunks. Apparently they got under his skin instead of the other way around.

"More and more respectable people are into tattooing," Tuttle con-cludes. "There's a charm in its permanency." But if his plans to move the museum to a place with legal parking and earphones that explain the exhibits pan out, he may lose some steady customers.

The Tattoo Art Museum
841 Columbus Avenue, San Francisco, CA 94133
((415) 775-4991

LOCATION: At Fisherman's Wharf
HOURS: Seven days a week, noon–midnight
ADMISSION: Free

San Jose: THE WINCHESTER MYSTERY HOUSE

Was widowed heiress Sarah Winchester a few bricks shy of a full load, believing she'd ward off the spirits of hostile Indians and others by the continuous thirty-eight-year construction of what eventually became her 160-room, $5.5 million mansion? Or was she merely a frustrated architectural genius, the first to discern the value of many late nineteenth-century innovations, who, rather than using a blueprint, sketched as the "spirits" moved her? Her home was among the first in the country to have elevators, wool insulation, gas lights and stove, an "annunciator" intercom with which she could page her many servants from anywhere in the house, and built-in scrub boards and soap holders, which she patented.

This is the puzzle posed to visitors of the Winchester Mystery House in San Jose, California, which was built and rebuilt from 1884 until practically the moment after Sarah Winchester's death in 1922. At twenty-four thousand square feet, it has ten thousand windows, two thousand doors, fifty-two skylights, forty-seven fireplaces (one of which is hand carved), forty staircases and bedrooms, thirteen bathrooms, six kitchens, three elevators, two basements, and one shower.

Only the best was used, and this Victorian home boasts parquet floors with multifaceted inlaid patterns of precious hardwoods; gold and silver chandeliers; exquisite art glass windows; and doors with hinges and designs of silver, bronze, and gold. Storerooms still contain tens of thousands of dollars worth of Tiffany doors and windows, as well as precious silks, satins, linens, and other fabrics. A glass-lined conservatory not only guaranteed sunlight but also had a metal sub-flooring that could be drained to the garden below whenever the servants watered the plants. An acoustically balanced ballroom that cost the then-outrageous sum of $9000 was put together using carpenter's glue and wooden pegs, with tiny nails used only in moldings and floorings.

But the mansion, which rambles over nearly six acres and is four-stories (down from seven before the San Francisco earthquake), brims with oddities. Stairways lead to ceilings and doors open into walls. Pillars on fireplaces are installed upside down, ostensibly to confuse evil spirits. One $1500 Tiffany window will never see the light of day because it's blocked off by a wall. Skylights shoot up from the floor, and a five-foot door, just right for the diminutive (four feet, ten inches, one hundred pounds) Sarah, stands next to a normal sized one that leads nowhere. One cabinet opens up to one-half inch of storage space, while the closet across from it reveals the back thirty rooms of the home.

The number thirteen abounds. Several rooms have thirteen panels with the same number of windows, which, in turn, have guess how many panes. A baker's dozen can be found in the lights in the chan-

The aerial view of the
Winchester Mystery
House illustrates its
massive size. (*Photo
courtesy of the Winches-
ter Mystery House.*)

deliers, in the cupolas in the greenhouse, and in the palms that line
the front driveway. Sarah's last will and testament consisted of thirteen parts and was signed thirteen times, and legend has it that
when she dined, it was on a gold service set for herself and twelve
invisible guests. To further encourage ghostbusting, the house had
only two mirrors.

In order to better understand the house, one needs to delve into the
enigma that was Sarah Pardee Winchester. Born in 1839, in New
Haven, Connecticut, she married William Winchester in 1862. He was
the son of Oliver Winchester, inventor and manufacturer of the repeat-
ing rifle that allegedly won the West. According to several accounts,
Sarah was an attractive, cultured musician who spoke four languages.

But her life was far from normal. Her only daughter, Anna, died in
infancy and a few years later in 1881, her husband succumbed to
pulmonary tuberculosis. "Sarah had never fully recovered from the
first loss, so this further intensified her anguish," states Shozo
Kagoshima, director of marketing for the museum. Sarah was now
incredibly wealthy, thanks to the invention that had the dubious
honor of having killed more game, Indians, and U.S. soldiers than
any other weapon in American history. She inherited $20 million and
nearly 50 percent of the stock in the Winchester company, the latter
of which gave her a tax-free (until 1913) stipend of about $1000 *a
day*. So money was no object.

To ease her grief, Sarah went to a "seer" in Boston, who told her
that "the spirits of all those the Winchester rifles had killed sought
their revenge by taking the lives of her loved ones," relates

Kagoshima. "Furthermore, they'd placed a curse on her and would haunt her forever." But Sarah could construct her own escape hatch, the medium said, by "moving West, buying a house, and continually building on it as the spirits directed." That way, she could escape the hostile ones (particularly Indians), while providing a comfortable respite for friendly ghosts (including perhaps Casper), and possibly guaranteeing eternal life.

So Sarah traveled to San Jose and plunked down nearly $13,000 in gold coins to buy an eight-room farmhouse from a Dr. Caldwell. Thus an exquisite behemoth was born.

Renovated in 1973, the rambling structure has 110 rooms open to the public, about 20 more than were in use when Sarah was alive. "The rest were damaged by the 1906 earthquake or are offices," explains Kagoshima. Other than normal restoration to maintain the status quo "the house is to remain the same as when she died."

"Sarah was an eccentric, although she had many good ideas about building and modern conveniences," sums up Kagoshima. The Winchester Mystery House may never be solved, but it—and everyone connected with it—has had a long, strange trip.

The Winchester Mystery House
525 S. Winchester Boulevard, San Jose, CA 95128
((408) 247-2000

LOCATION: Intersection of I-280, I-880 and Highway 17.
HOURS: Tours given 9:30 A.M.–4:00 or 5:30 P.M. (depending on the season), 7 days a week; closed Christmas
ADMISSION: Admission is charged

↟ San Quentin: THE SAN QUENTIN PRISON MUSEUM

It started out as a convict ship in the 1850s, became one of the nation's most notorious penitentiaries, and now has its very own museum. The recently established San Quentin Prison Museum, in San Quentin, California (across from the Golden Gate Bridge in San Francisco), was "diligently remodeled by a crew of prison inmates," according to a prison news release. This may be the first museum in history created under duress.

Step through the electronic gates, and, to paraphrase a popular beer commercial: It doesn't get any more realistic than this (unless you're an inmate, of course). The museum occupies the home of a former warden and is within shouting distance of cell blocks and death row. Short-timers, aka visitors, sign in on a podium that was utilized during every gas chamber execution except the most recent. It could be worse: You could be strip-searched and fingerprinted.

Most of the nearly 100,000 items in the museum were donated by San Quentin employees and their families, with other "contributions" confiscated from prisoners. "We wanted to illustrate the story of San Quentin," explains associate warden Richard Nelson, who's been with San Quentin for nearly twenty-five years and "in the prison business" a decade more. "So we put a lot of emphasis on history" with plenty of drawings, photos, and text.

Yeah, but what people *really* want to see is the gruesome stuff: a thirty-pound ball and chain that may draw appreciative looks from long-married couples and tortuous looking thumb cuffs, both from the nineteenth century. A four-foot-eight-inch wide, ten-foot-six-inch deep, eight-foot high re-creation of a 1913 cell gives new meaning to

A thirty-pound ball and chain is one of 100,000 items at the San Quentin Museum. (*Photo courtesy of the museum.*)

the term close quarters, especially since it housed two prisoners. There's an impressive collection of firearms dating back to 1849, many of which were employed to put down prison insurrections. Pointing to a machine gun, Nelson remarks, "I used this in '71 to recapture a cell block and recover two corrections officers." (If you're considering any type of crime, this might be a good place to visit.) Restraint equipment such as leg irons, straitjackets, tear-gas guns, clubs, and batons add a final touch.

A display of prison contraband includes an inmate-fashioned pistol, knives, bar spreaders, and an electrical device designed to stall ignition on a garbage scow so one could make a (rather smelly) escape. There's even a shiv that slips inside a toilet paper holder. (Heaven help the poor soul who changed the roll.) A homemade mask employed by another inventive convict attests to the futility of crime: The prisoner hoped to escape by distorting his features and adding facial hair to the mask. "We still have the mask *and* the prisoner," adds Nelson.

But the *ne plus ultra* is the Death Penalty Wing. The faint of heart might not want to hang around after viewing replicas of a gas chamber and gallows; old valves, light fixtures, and a blueprint of the prison gas chamber; a scale that weighed lethal sodium cyanide pellets; and a noose used in an actual execution. Along with grave markers of the unclaimed dead, there's the black blindfold donned by murderess Barbara Graham (remember Susan Hayward in *I Want to Live?*) and a box of miniature nooses. The latter, the personal memorabilia of an employee who participated in 150 executions over a thirty-year period, shares space with a passel of screaming newspaper headlines vividly describing various demises and an executioner's log that records the outcome of the day's work. According to Nelson, "very successful" meant a (relatively) painless hanging, while lesser ratings could indicate that the weights were too heavy, beheading the prisoner.

The good noose is that today's kinder, gentler San Quentin is no longer a maximum security prison with floggings and striped pajamas. Visitors can purchase commemorative belt buckles, coffee mugs, T-shirts, and refrigerator magnets at the museum's gift shop and make donations to the museum on a sliding scale, ranging from "Lifer" ($1000) to "Isolation" ($10) Maybe crime does pay—sometimes.

The San Quentin Prison Museum
Building 106
Delores Way
P.O. Box 205, San Quentin, CA 94964
((415) 454-1460

LOCATION: Just outside of San Francisco, between U.S. 101 and I-580
HOURS: Seven days a week, 10:00 A.M.–4:00 P.M.; other hours by appointment
ADMISSION: Admission is charged

✝ Santa Rosa: THE CHURCH OF ONE TREE/ROBERT L. RIPLEY MUSEUM

Believe it or not: here's a church made out of a single California-coast Redwood tree, now home to the Robert L. Ripley Museum. Not only did Ripley feature the former Baptist chapel in his famous "Believe It or Not" cartoon series but he also worshiped there as a child in Santa Rosa, where he was born during the 1890s and later returned as an adult. Along with a startlingly lifelike figure of Ripley himself sitting behind a counter in the museum, there's a bust of him sculpted by a blind person. Ripley's personal papers and memorabilia on exhibit include original drawings, his battered old suitcase plastered with travel stickers, and items of clothing such as his safari helmet and the Chinese bathrobe and slippers he worked in. The museum also features rotating oddities from Ripley International in Toronto and other Believe It or Not! Museums worldwide. Believe It or Not!

Everything about Robert L. Ripley was a hyperbole. "He was one of the oddest people this country has ever seen," remarks curator John Hacku. Along with his large collection of torture devices, Ripley acquired numerous automobiles but never learned how to drive. Although he was deluged with phone calls, he rarely took them because he feared he'd be electrocuted by the telephone. He traveled to 198 countries; rubbed shoulders with celebrities such as Lou Gehrig, Shirley Temple, and Will Rogers; and was titled "the modern day Marco Polo" by none other than the Duke of Windsor.

Ripley's death at age fifty-eight (or fifty-five, depending on which birth date you subscribe to), which was reported as a heart attack, remains the subject of controversy. "There are as many rumors as people to talk to," notes Hacku. Appropriately, Ripley is buried with his parents at the Odd Fellows cemetery in Santa Rosa. Unlike Elvis, he hasn't been sighted since.

But he had the common touch and along with companion books that sold by the millions, Ripley had a popular radio show, television program, and traveling exhibitions that featured folks who could do some awfully strange things. "For fifteen cents, you could see a woman lift items with a fish hook attached to her tongue or a man who could turn his head completely around," reports Hacku. Ambulances waited outside just in case attendees, in Ripley jargon, "couldn't believe their eyes!"

For over thirty years, Ripley penned more than fifty-five thousand "Believe It or Not" tidbits of amazing "facts" that ran in newspapers all over the world. "Many have been questioned, but few have actually been disproved," states Hacku.

Exactly how the Church of One Tree became the Robert L. Ripley Museum remains somewhat obscure. Built in 1873 from a 275-foot-tall redwood that yielded 78,000 board feet of lumber, "it was originally going to be turned into a parking lot," recalls Hacku. "But then Ripley stepped in and offered to pay [the Baptists] part if the city would match his donation." Although Ripley died before negotiations were completed, the city of Santa Rosa took responsibility for the church, moving it from downtown to its present site in Juilliard Park in 1957.

Made out of a single California coast redwood tree, the Church of One Tree is also the home of the Robert L. Ripley Museum. (*Photo courtesy of the Church of One Tree/Robert L. Ripley Museum.*)

Only about half of the original structure was saved. "The religious school and pastor's study are missing, as are the pews, which were also made from the same tree," observes Hacku. "No one knows exactly what happened to them." A newer pine one covers the original floor.

The oldest organization in Santa Rosa, the current church museum boasts recently restored windows made from the original rare opalescent glass. From its inception as a religious building, it's had its share of Thomases who doubted its veracity. "When they learned their new structure was made from one tree, some Baptists declared it a hoax," recounts Hacku. "A local lawyer went to the lumber mill where it was built and confirmed its authenticity." Ripley's father, a carpenter, supposedly helped build the church.

Some things just seem ordained. In 1937, a young cartoonist sold his first drawing to Ripley for eight dollars. The picture was of a hunting dog that "ate pins, tacks, screws, and razor blades," according to the Ripley caption. The cartoonist's name was Schulz and the dog became the prototype for the "Peanuts" character Snoopy. And that you *can* believe.

The Church of One Tree/Robert L. Ripley Museum
492 Sonoma Avenue, Santa Rosa, CA 95401
((707) 524-5233

LOCATION: Off U.S. 101, 50 miles north of San Francisco, in Juilliard Park
HOURS: March 1–October 23; Wednesday–Sunday, 11:00 A.M.–4:00 P.M.
ADMISSION: Admission is charged

Montana

⬆ Deer Lodge: THE TOWE FORD MUSEUM

About one hundred Fords are in"car"cerated behind the barbed wire, steel bars, and castle-like turrets of the imposing-looking Old Montana Prison at Deer Lodge. They haven't been impounded by the local police—the now-empty prison's a tourist attraction, too—but represent the accumulation of years of devoted collecting by Edward Towe of Montana. And they're actually in a well-lit showroom, along with an early gas station, colorful signs advertising accessories like motor oil and tires, and an accumulation of Ford-Ferguson and Fordson farm tractors.

In the 1950s, banker Edward Towe and his family purchased and restored a Model T, catching the bug that would eventually make Towe's the biggest and most complete collection of Fords in the world, surpassing even that of the larger Ford Museum in Dearborn, Michigan. Towe visited western farms, Iowa barns, and eastern cities, journeying as far as Canada, South America, and Norway in his quest.

"The Ford is the car for the common man and woman," observes Karla (really) James, the collection's curator. "The museum encompasses well-known models from nearly every production year starting with 1903 until 1951, as well as some later and rare designs." The few non-Fords consist of a spacious, two-door 1932 Auburn Cabriolet, a 1932 De Soto roadster, and a bright yellow 1919 Stanley Steamer with a steam tank engine. Towe trucks include some pre-Depression-era fire vehicles and others.

The Towe museum has the 125th issue of the first mass produced auto, the 1903 Ford Model A Runabout. List-priced at a costly (for then) $850, it featured a two-cylinder engine, had two forward speeds and one reverse, and a top acceleration of 30 mph. "It ran well, but like all old cars, produced a lot of smoke," observes James.

In ensuing years, Models B, C, F, K, N, R, and S followed. Ford's first sports car, the 1907 Model K–640 Roadster, came equipped with special springs, low-slung seats, and a showy body style. A financial disaster, this six-cylinder model caused problems for Ford and was rejected by the public. Towe has one of the only sixty units ever made.

A year later, the inexpensive Model T hit the market and by the late thirties, over fifteen million had been produced. "Model T's were dependable, easy to operate, and versatile on rough roads that were the norm in those days," points out James. Through mass production, Ford reduced the price and increased the demand, eventually making the Model T so affordable ($265 in 1924) that it fit the budget to a you-know-what.

The Model A of the late twenties represented a departure from its meat and potatoes predecessors (obviously Ford also ran out of letters of the alphabet). One of Ford's first enclosed cars, it was stylish and low-slung and came equipped with window wing deflectors, electric wipers, and either a trunk or the now-infamous rumble seat—the rendezvous point for many young lovers.

The stylish Model A's of the twenties and early thirties represented a departure from their utilitarian predecessors. (*Photo courtesy of the Towe Ford Museum.*)

"Ford again made automotive history when he introduced the V-8 in 1932," continues James. "His answer to the Great Depression was to produce this powerful engine at a low price." An early V-8 open-cab pickup, station wagon, and Cabriolet are on display.

After helping produce over 275,000 Jeeps for World War II, Ford moved back into the civilian car market with ease. "Most [postwar] cars were improvements upon earlier models, with Touch-O-Matic overdrive, power windows and seats, air cleaner heaters, two-tone paint, and whitewall tires," states James. But an experiment, the Edsel Motor Company, proved a disaster. "Along with a push-button transmission which didn't always work, the Edsels were introduced at a time when the luxury market was saturated." The museum owns two of these increasingly rare vehicles.

Ford models such as the Mustang, Maverick, Falcon, Pinto, and Thunderbird, representing the later fifties and sixties can also be found here. "Our most current acquisition is a large 1978 V-8 Thunderbird," comments James. "Thunderbirds started out small, got bigger, and in recent years, have become more downsized."

The rest of this automotive agglomeration, about 150 other cars, is located at a sister Towe Ford Museum in Sacramento, California. But only Montana has cars behind bars and, as of this writing, no sales tax.

The Towe Ford Museum
1106 Main Street, Deer Lodge, MT 59722
((406) 836-4114

LOCATION: Off I-90, 39 miles north of Butte
HOURS: Hours vary
ADMISSION: Admission is charged

Nebraska

♠ Chadron: THE MUSEUM OF THE FUR TRADE

Although the Museum of the Fur Trade in Chadron, Nebraska, may offend animal rights activists and gun control advocates, it's got a rip roarin' reputation. Along with being one of the world's most comprehensive repositories of facts 'n' artifacts about frontier and Native American life, it has garnered recognition from not only the Smithsonian but from the National Geographic Society as well. The museum contains thirteen thousand volumes of texts and three hundred rolls of microfilm, retains researchers in both England and Canada, and annually handles thousands of technical inquiries.

"We've examined all aspects of the fur trade from 1500 to 1900," states director Charles Hanson, Jr. "And everything here is the genuine article. So when they have questions, collectors, other

museums, anthropologists, artists, and buckskinners come to us."
Buckskinners? "Re-enactors who wear buckskin clothing and shoot
muzzle-loaded guns," he explains. "They rendezvous here periodically." No, thank you.

Located on the site of a trading post on Bordeaux Creek, the museum offers just about everything related to the fur trade from
colonial times to turn-of-the-century Alaska and Western Canada.
Visitors are taken on a chronological journey beginning with the first
settlers. "We have clothing, beads, kettles, knives, and candles that
were used as items of exchange by the English and Dutch." According to Hanson, colonial-era Indians had a fondness for ruffled shirts.
"The typical chief wore cloth leggings, a ready-made shirt, a turban
made from a scarf, and a blanket. The only item of his own manufacture was moccasins." Sounds like a fashion victim.

Traders frequently utilized tomahawks, guns, and swords as currency, obviously neglecting to "axe" questions about their
deployment. One tomahawk doubles as a pipe, with a bowl on one
side and the blade on the other, offering a post-kill smoke. Most uses
were peaceful, however. "People have a mistaken impression of constant wars and racial strife," says Hanson. "In fact, tribes rarely
fought each other and [fought] the white man only when he tried to
take over their land. Along with exchanging cultures, fur traders and
Indians often intermarried."

In addition to Plains, Woodland, and Desert Indians, other galleries cover British traders, Spanish explorers, voyagers, mountain
men, and buffalo hunters. "Each had a specific role," points out
Hanson. "Mountain men were basically white trappers, while traders
handled the business end. Voyagers ran canoes that brought goods in
and out." Visitors will find an abundance of costumes, saddles, horse
gear, and other personal items.

The museum has the world's largest and most complete collection
of Northwest guns dating from 1750 to 1900. "These were specifi-
cally developed for use by Indians," he continues. In addition to a
very rare 1680 firearm, there's a gun that belonged to Chief Tecum-
seh. Pacifists might also want to skip the Bowie knives, other types of
rifles, and assorted frontier weapons.

And, of course, furs such as beaver, wolf, badger, mink, and rare
sea otter abound. Keep the can of red spray paint at home, though:
none are in the form of coats, and most are behind glass.

Metal pipe tomahawks
made for Indian trade,
including one with a
handmade Indian
stem. (*Photo courtesy of
the Museum of the Fur
Trade.*)

Completely reconstructed on its original foundations, a 1833 American Fur Company trading post has a willow bed, kettles on the hearth, and shelves stocked with goods such as bullets, bolts, and beads. Indigenous buffalo hides and deerskins are scattered throughout. "Deerskins sold for a dollar, which is why it's called a buck," adds Hanson. An Indian garden with primitive tobacco, midget corn, and early types of beans, pumpkins, and squash authenticates the ambiance.

"Many people believe [trading] killed off the buffalo, when, in fact, only a small portion were slaughtered for fur. The railroads were responsible because they wanted the Indians off the land and the settlers in." Besides, there are plenty of buffalo around these days to make supplies for a buffalo chip throwing contest sponsored by the museum during Chadron's annual Fur Trade Days.

The Museum of the Fur Trade
HC 74, Box 18, Chadron, NE 69337
((308) 432-3843

LOCATION: Three miles east of Chadron, on U.S. 20
HOURS: June 1–Labor Day; 8:00 A.M.–5:00 P.M., seven days a week (or by appointment)
ADMISSION: Admission is charged

Nevada

✦ Las Vegas: THE LIBERACE MUSEUM

They flock from all over the country and even the world—ladies of a blue-haired persuasion, outrageously clad rockers paying homage to their roots, families with young children. The Liberace Museum, an unassuming, hacienda-style structure, has been the third largest *tour de glitz* in Las Vegas since opening in 1979. Even though Lee, as he was known to family, friends, and fans, passed away six years later, his spirit lives on amidst his glorious stuff.

If he who dies with the most toys wins, then Walter Valentino Liberace hit the jackpot. The world's highest paid musician and pianist, he acquired Emmys, gold records, and stars in the Hollywood Walk of Fame, along with mind-boggling collections of cars, clothing, jewelry, and antiques. He shared his riches with adoring audiences who shelled out hard-earned cash to see what outrageous thing Lee would wear/drive/play on stage next.

Those who scorned the Establishment during his heyday in the sixties and seventies often confused Liberace with the late Lawrence Welk (the Saturday-night-TV snooze with "champagne" music) or condemned him as gauche. But Liberace's rare Moser crystal from Czechoslovakia, monogrammed dinner plates that belonged to John Fitzgerald Kennedy, and miniature piano created by the crown-makers to English royalty hardly seem tacky. Nor do the assorted statuary, elegant art, and rare antiques that dot the corridors and entryways leading to the galleries of his museum.

Okay, so he did go a bit overboard with a candelabra ring with platinum candlesticks and diamond flames, rubies, and other gems and a piano-shaped ring with 260 diamonds in a white and yellow 18-karat gold setting with ivory keys. And the museum does boast the world's largest rhinestone, a 115-karat, fifty-plus-pound monstrosity valued at $50,000 and—surprise!—a gift from a costume jewelry company.

Many of the specialty items used in Liberace's shows were given free or at a discount, such as the glitzy Baldwin pianos rented to him for one dollar a year. "Lee played exclusively on Baldwin and was their best advertisement," states Jamie James, Liberace's close friend and publicist for nearly thirty years. "He sold more pianos than any print or television ad." Early in his career, Liberace refused to perform on a Steinway, insisting the hotel hosting his show get a crane to lift a Baldwin ten floors to the stage.

And the monies from the museum go to the Liberace Foundation, which in turn provides scholarships in the performing arts and grants to colleges and schools. "Outside of entertaining, Lee's pet project was helping people of limited financial means obtain an education," observes his sister-in-law, Dora Liberace. Sure, he could have sold some of his possessions to pay for the scholarships. But think of the goodies we proles would have missed seeing!

One of the world's most conspicuous consumers, Walter Valentino Liberace also founded a nonprofit organization to fund scholarships. (*Photo courtesy of the Liberace Museum.*)

The museum represents a "best of" melange from Liberace's seven homes. Sunglasses are not mandatory, but even the lobby dazzles, with its nude Carrara marble statue and fake-out piano (it's really a desk).

The piano gallery is usually the first stop. "Lee owned forty pianos and eighteen of the rarest are on display here," comments James, indicating an antique model with hand-painted pastoral scenes. "This is a Pleyel used by Chopin at Versailles." Also on view, among others, are a carved Bosendorfer, played on by Brahms and Schuman; a Chicory grand piano owned by Gershwin; and Liberace's trademark Baldwin completely covered with Austrian rhinestones. The latter matched his rhinestone-covered Excaliber Mercedes and costume and was one of six pianos used for a concert in Radio City Music Hall shortly before his death. Still another Baldwin grand with thousands of etched, mirrored tiles sits on a revolving, circular stage. "Chopsticks" anyone?

Adjacent to the pianos is the car gallery. "Look at the tile floor," James instructs. Etched in brass on the black and white checkerboard is a five-foot rendering of Liberace's flowery signature. The lighting is soft and the music from you-know-who. People, especially fans over sixty, speak in the hushed tones reserved for funerals, churches, and Graceland.

Like the pianos, the cars have themes to match Liberace's various performances. The one-of-a-kind collection includes a '57 white English cab with black and white houndstooth panels on the doors; a red, white, and blue Rolls Royce customized for the Bicentennial; and a Bradley GT with solid gold flakes embedded into the body. Standing out, even among these automotive aberrations, are a mirrored Rolls Royce etched with galloping horses and a pink "Volks Royce" also with engraved inlays and mirrored tiles.

Across the parking lot is the library, a misnomer. Although it contains Liberace's personal papers, press clippings, and music, it also has his prized china, crystal, and miniature piano collections, with some of the latter being more expensive than the full-size article. The over three hundred pianos range from an amethyst and pearl encrusted one atop an enamel music box to another made from ten thousand toothpicks to still another fabricated from fused-together nickels. "Fans knew Lee collected these things so they made them for him," notes James, referring to the last two. As if he didn't have enough already.

Next is the wardrobe gallery where costumes and corny jokes abound. When Liberace donned his gold-braided and sable-trimmed Czar Nicholas ensemble accompanied by two Russian wolfhounds, a visitor is informed, he warned people not to eat in front of the dogs, lest they be tempted by food and jump off the stage. "Lee always wore larger shoes during performances because he changed his socks to match the costume," recalls James. "Then he'd lift up his pants leg and show the audience." His costumes were also notoriously heavy, the most massive being a mink and rhinestone number weighing two hundred pounds. Liberace may have played in Peoria, but his museum thrives only in Las Vegas.

The Liberace Museum
1775 E. Tropicana Avenue, Las Vegas, NV 89119
((702) 798-5595

LOCATION: 3 miles east of the strip on Tropicana Avenue
HOURS: Monday–Saturday, 10:00 A.M.–5:00 P.M.; Sunday, 1:00–5:00
    P.M.
ADMISSION: Admission is charged

New Mexico

↟ Albuquerque: THE NATIONAL ATOMIC MUSEUM

See Fat Man and Little Boy, the first nuclear bombs ever deployed during World War II, part of a timeline of authentic Army, Navy, and Air Force weaponry—the world's most comprehensive display! *Experience* the complete history of U.S. nuclear development, from the discovery of fission in Germany in 1938 to the improved delivery methods and related technologies of the eighties and beyond! *Learn* about nuclear weapons safety, an oxymoron if there ever was one! And best of all, IT'S FREE!!!

"People sometimes misunderstand and think we're here to promote nuclear weapons," comments Joni Hezlep, director of the National Atomic Museum at Kirtland Air Force Base in Albuquerque, New Mexico. "But the goal of our museum is to preserve an extremely important part of American history." Still, she admits with a smile, "When I go to conferences, people call me the Bomb Lady and ask if I glow in the dark."

Opened in 1969 in a former missile-repair facility, the museum started out with a simple display of unclassified weapons and has been stockpiling them ever since. "Blasts from the past" include:

• Little Boy and Fat Man. The first nuclear warhead ever used, Little Boy was dropped on Hiroshima, Japan, on August 6, 1945, devastating four square miles of the city and killing more than seventy thousand people. Uranium-235 was utilized in a gun-type weapon, with two amounts of active materials shot together, causing them to reach critical mass and explode. Three days later, Fat Man fell on Nagasaki, creating about forty-five thousand fatalities and two square miles of devastation. Unlike its predecessor, Fat Man was an implosion device that used Plutonium-239 surrounded by TNT. A chain reaction resulted when the explosives were detonated. Fat Man served as the prototype for subsequent bombs.

• Mark and Lulu. The "Smith" and "Jones" of missiles, Mark, or MK, followed by a number has designated warheads from an early

These nuclear antiaircraft missiles guard the former bomb repair facility that houses the National Atomic Museum. (*Photo courtesy of the museum.*)

modified Fat Man clone (MK–5) to an atomic projectile for am-
phibious landings (MK-23). According to a museum fact sheet, the
MK-17 was the first droppable thermonuclear weapon (did they vol-
ley the others?). An atomic depth charge designed to rupture hulls
of ships and submarines, Lulu was among the first nuclear weapons
developed by the Navy.

• Genie, Davy Crockett, and Honest John. Development on
Genie, a smaller missile devised for use with aircraft, began in 1945.
The bazooka-type Davy Crockett "was designed to bring atomic
warhead capability to the front-line infantry," according to the Department of Energy fact sheet. The oldest field artillery rocket
system still utilized by the United States, Honest John "supposedly
has accuracy and firepower previously required [of] an entire battal-
ion of artillery." No wonder they don't name these things after real
or living people. With the explosion potential of thousands and millions of tons of TNT, most of the above have been "retired" and
replaced with more effective devices that may not be found in museums until after they've done their damage (if there are still museums
around then).

A wall-mounted history of the Manhattan Project details how
American scientists turned the concept of a nuclear bomb into a $2-
billion reality during World War II. Black-and-white pictures depict
the first mushroom clouds on the Trinity site in White Sands, New
Mexico, three weeks before Hiroshima and other exhibits document
the "new" delivery methods of the fifties and sixties. The development of early airdrop systems, the H-bomb; and energy-related
topics such as hazardous waste isolation and the use of particle-beam
fusion accelerators that may eventually replace nuclear power plants.
Throughout the museum, strategically placed TV sets provide ex-
planatory videos with the touch of (really) a red button.

Along with an outside weapons exhibit, the museum has a program on nuclear weapons safety. In the "very remote" event that a
terrorist attack, theft, or other accident results in the detonation of a
nuclear weapon "[persons] should stay in the sturdiest room in the
house and use tables, mattresses, and other bulky furniture as protection devices," advises the DOE fact sheet. And kiss their rears
good-bye. Maybe this museum's not such a bargain after all.

The National Atomic Museum
Kirtland Air Force Base
P.O. Box 5400, Albuquerque, NM 87115
((505) 845-6670

LOCATION: East of downtown
HOURS: Seven days a week, 9:00 A.M.–5:00 P.M.; closed New Year's
    Day, Easter, Thanksgiving, and Christmas
ADMISSION: Admission is free

⚑ Albuquerque: THE POTATO MUSEUM

For nearly twenty years, Tom and Meredith Hughes have had their
"eyes" on the potato, whipping up a collection of books, pamphlets,

"SPUD MURPHY" ESQ
MONARCH OF ALL HE
SURVEYS

World War I postcard from England,
when potatoes for civilians were rare.
(*Photo courtesy of the Potato Museum.*)

technical materials, artifacts, and
ephemera; even publishing a
tome for small fries, *The Great
Potato Book* (Macmillan). Their
avocation sprouted in Brussels—
Belgium, that is, from a class-
room project started by Tom
when he was teaching at the International School there. "Hundreds of museums are devoted
to weapons, battles, and wars
and few, if any, to food," explains
Meredith, a freelance journalist
and, like her husband, a Quaker
and pacifist. From that seed
grew this, a planned World Food
Museum, and a sporadic newsletter, *Peelings.*

The Hugheses acquired some
tubular stuff during their travels throughout South America,
Europe, and China. Spudabilia

Potatoes were made to
look "larger than life"
in these 1909 Ameri-
can pictures. (*Photo
courtesy of the Potato
Museum.*)

ranges from sweet potato remnants from 1800 B.C. (*way* past the
mildew stage) to Victorian postcards proclaiming "Like the potato is
true, I am fairly mashed on you" to the complete line of Mr. Potato
Head offerings. "He was far from the first potato head toy," points
out Meredith. "Earlier versions were made out of magnets and papier-maché." The museum has those too, along with the Spudmatic,
a British air pistol that shoots potato pellets.

There's an 1850s rounded, striped potato-bug mandolin; Spanish
cooking utensils for *churros*, a potato flour delicacy; and a potato-
digging tool from the Andes mountains made from hand-wrought
iron and wood and held together by llama skin. Along with ornate
nineteenth-century letterheads from potato merchants, the
Hugheses even unearthed a 1930s art deco wrapper from a loaf of
potato bread. Talk about hitting pay dirt....

A Tater Time Clock runs on guess-whats and they're also a home
curative for acne, sunburn, and frostbite. The first color photography
process utilized autochromes, dyed potato-starch granules. And in
Germany, 'taters also doubled as fuel. What a spud.

The museum also pays homage to the tuber in books, art, and
song. "After all, we have van Gogh's *The Potato Eaters*, and the
potato-faced blind man in Carl Sandburg's *Rutabaga Stories.'* "
Meredith cites two better-known examples. Weird Al Yankovic's "Ad-
dicted to Spuds," Louis Armstrong's "Potato Head Blues," Tom
Paxton's "Don't Slay that Potato," and the Kinks's "Hot Potatoes" attest to the spud's broad-based musical "apeel." And there's always
the "Potato Mambo," "The Potato Bug Boogie," the "Potato Peelings
Polka," and that baby boomer classic, the "Mashed Potato." An

amazing accumulation of recipes dates back to 1581 (boiled potatoes with bacon fat and milk).

Instead of baked or fried, the Hugheses take their spuds seriously. "You put *potato* and *museum* together and people laugh," observes Meredith. "But I don't mind the humor because it draws attention to the way food has influenced history and our lives. Youngsters especially need to learn about the things we eat and understand that it involves much more than going to the supermarket." For instance, potatoes have been domesticated for over seven thousand years, grow from sea level to fourteen thousand feet in a wide variety of soils and climates, and are considered one of the most nutritionally valuable comestibles.

"The more people know, the more likely they'll support farmers or new research or techniques that will continue to feed our incredibly burgeoning population," she goes on. "Americans in particular think they have an endless supply, when in fact the opposite is true." To this purpose, the Hugheses are planning the World Food Museum and have enlisted the help of heavy-hitting scientists such as Norman E. Borlaug, a Nobel Peace Prize winner, and John Neiderhauser, who was awarded a World Food Prize.

Whatever the Hugheses concoct, it will likely cover all bases. After all, they're not starting exactly "tuber" rasa.

The Potato Museum
4 Tumbleweed NW, Albuquerque, NM 87120
((505) 899-0588

For information about the Potato Museum, and the planned World Food Museum, contact Meredith and Tom Hughes at the above address.

✦ Portales: THE WINDMILL COLLECTION

Don Quixote could have learned a few things from Bill Dalley. Rather than attacking windmills, he should have collected them. Of the seventy-some examples of antique and modern devices in his collection, Dalley, of Portales, New Mexico, has restored about twenty to their original whirling glory.

A retired high school counselor, "I got into this by accident," explains the sixtyish Dalley in response to a question about his switch from troubled teens to the chaotic contraptions. "Several years ago I found a strange looking piece of junk in an old homestead building and, based on a description from an elderly man, was able to put it back together." That uncovered even more windmills from golden agers who'd stored them in their barns for years. "They just told me to come by and pick them up."

According to Dalley, who has a background in woodworking and construction, windmills are fairly easy to assemble. "They were meant to be put together by the farmer in the field, so the instructions are straightforward." If you're not afraid of heights, that is, and can nail two boards together. The trick is in making sure they don't fall down. "A strong wind can come along and blow them apart, particularly the older wooden models. During a storm, the rancher has to turn off the mills, otherwise they go around too fast and self-destruct."

Windmills are still utilized in remote areas of the United States. "The newer ones are self-oiling, made of metal, and equipped with a device that automatically pulls water to the surface," he says. "They can pump water with very little breeze." Plus, there's no bill.

According to Dalley, windmills have been around since around 600 A.D. "For centuries they were horizontal, powered by the wind to drive a single pair of millstones." They appeared in Europe five hundred years later and "developed in a variety of directions. The best known were actually 'wind pumps,' used by the Dutch to drain low lying lands." The term *windmill* is a misnomer: "The modern multivaned windmill introduced in America in 1854 mostly pumped water, rather than actually serving as a mill."

Dalley's tallest windmill towers at thirty-two feet, the largest wheel stretches to eighteen feet across, the oldest dates back to about 1870, and his most recent model is from the 1930s. The wooden Railroad Eclipse in the collection was one of the first made in the United States. "It was named after the locomotives, as it supplied boiler water for steam engines." From the 1860s to the 1920s, the smaller Eclipse was "manufactured throughout this country and abroad and was the most commonly found antique windmill in this area."

Metal mills were introduced as early as the 1880s but production didn't really gear up until the early part of the twentieth century. "These were much sturdier and more reliable and are the precursors of what's in use today." Many of the models overlap, such as the Challenge Self-Oiling Vaneless and the Challenge Vaneless with wooden arms and metal parts. With all the different manufacturers and types, it's enough to make one's head spin.

And then there are the homemade windmills and power mills. "Although not overly successful, they reduced backbreaking work for many families," observes Dalley. So-called power mills cut wood, shelled corn, and helped with other daily chores. Made from any available materials, the collection's peculiar-appearing homemade numbers include a Depression-era oil drum windmill that was assembled from the differentials and drive shafts of junked automobiles. "Not only did it alleviate having to purchase a windmill but also the expense of repairs." Still another bizarre mishmash even had Dalley chasing windmills: "At first I thought I had something very rare, but further research revealed it was parts from different manufacturers pieced together by a farmer."

Dalley and others have started a movement of similar souls who provide grist for the newly formed International Windmillers Trade Fair Association. Each June, collectors get together and shoot the breeze, swapping ideas and parts. Like its namesake during a thunderstorm, the group appears to be gathering momentum: "As time goes on, more and more people have been coming from all over the United States and abroad," he remarks. It's good to know that, unlike the Man of La Mancha, Dalley's efforts haven't been in "vane."

The Windmill Collection
E. Star Route, Box 7, Portales, NM 88130
((505) 356-6263

LOCATION: Take US 70 to Portales and go one mile east to Kilgore Road and turn south
HOURS: By appointment; call first
ADMISSION: Free

Oregon

✦ Redmond: THE WORLD FAMOUS FANTASTIC MUSEUM

It certainly ranks among the universe's weirdest agglomerations: a red double-decker English bus; Hitler's stamp collection; the petrified remains of Olaf, a nine-foot-tall Viking warrior; Elizabeth Taylor's lavish dressing room from the movie *Cleopatra*; military artifacts from the Gulf War; sports memorabilia, such as a rubber batting circle stolen from Dodger Stadium; a '38 Cadillac in which John Fitzgerald Kennedy allegedly learned to drive; and the pressure gauge from the zeppelin *Hindenburg*. Plus, there are over one million buttons, seven thousand matchbooks, two hundred clocks, innumerable antique arcade games and toys, and God-knows-what-else paraphernalia jammed into this seventeen-thousand-square-foot Western-style storefront museum.

Okay, so maybe some of it's not *exactly* authenticated. "Sometimes you go to an auction and [the sellers] say it is what it is, so you have to believe it," states James Schmit, a wealthy Lake Tahoe developer who, along with partner Tom Fields, has spent the last few decades gathering the stuff that forms the collection of what is now known as the World Famous Fantastic Museum in Redmond, Oregon. "It's a business transaction, so you assume it's on the up-and-up."

Take 750-year-old Olaf, for instance, who came with the onetime Jones Fantastic Museum in Seattle, purchased by Schmit several years ago. "A circus had him and he's pretty well preserved inside his glass case. I had a couple of doctors look him over and they said he was real. But the only way to truly tell whether Barnum and Bailey extended his legs to make him taller would be to open him up and check the skeleton." And deprive all those children of this cultural excursion?

Der Fuhrer's stamp collection? "It's a bunch of different stamps with Hitler's mug on it [sic], found in the desk in his office. When the troops came in, they took it out and it's been around since the

One of Elvis's Cadillacs. (*Photo courtesy of the World Famous Fantastic*

war." The gauge from the *Hindenburg*? "It was inherited by the son of a man who was a security guard at the site of the explosion." Listening to Schmit's stories about how he got this stuff is half the fun.

Take one of his newer acquisitions, the licorice-dispensing Mirthmobile from the movie *Wayne's World*. "A young lady from Oregon won the car in an MTV promotion. After she went to New York to claim her prize, she decided she wanted to sell it to have money for college." Schmit offered her ten grand, and before she hung up, he'd sent a truck to pick it up. "Anything and everything's for sale. A lot of it comes along at the spur of the moment."

Schmit has acquired nearly five hundred items of Bing Crosby's, from mud-caked fishing boots and hunting gear to clothing to photo albums. "His family sold everything. They wanted to share these pieces of Bing with the world." Yes, and it's raining money in Las Vegas. Elvis's silver tour bus "was one of his last vehicles. He got a thrill from taking it out at three o'clock in the morning and tooling around." Schmit also has a '57 pink Cadillac owned by the King "but it's no big deal because there are a lot of those around."

In some places, the museum almost makes sense. With pots, pans,

and other staples, the old-time general store features a full-sized period mannequin ringing up a sale. A turn-of-the-century schoolhouse
was re-created from a Norman Rockwell painting. The clock collection covers time from the 1800s to the 1950s and related pieces
include an hourglass from the 1300s and pendulum from the seventeenth century. The transportation display consists of about half of
Schmit's forty antique cars as well as bikes, trains, and related articles, such as blow torches and an early gas pump, circa 1910.

Some of it's just plain bad taste: a World War II–era game using
fleeing Japanese soldiers as the target and a postcard of an alligator
gobbling a black man. Oh, and along with the million-button-filled
buckboard wagon and not-yet-counted marble collection, Schmit
claims to have the world biggest accumulation of business cards.

Space prohibits further discussion of a dune buggy from the movie
Megaforce, James Dean's motorbike, Sammy Davis, Jr.'s dance shoes,
and many other items. For those preferring more coherent entertainments, the museum offers miniature golf, carriage rides, and go-carts.

The World Famous Fantastic Museum
3290 S. Highway 37, Redmond, OR 97756
((503) 923-0000

LOCATION: About 120 miles east of Eugene
HOURS: Seven days a week, 10:00 A.M.–5:00 P.M.; open later in summer
ADMISSION: Admission is charged

Texas

↟ Dallas: THE OLDE FAN MUSEUM

How totally cool: Six-hundred fans of all shapes, colors, eras, and sizes sitting on the shelf of a Dallas, Texas, museum cum repair shop. Plug 'em in and you've got the biggest breeze this side of the border. A tornado at the very least.

But although all of them operate, these fans aren't meant for general consumption. In fact, some are so valuable they're worth thousands of dollars. Besides, their owner, Kurt House, aka the Fan Man, spent years collecting and fine-tuning his babies, "turning" them into a museum only a few years ago.

He's acquired fans and "fans" from all over the world, connecting with people from Yap in the Caroline Islands, Italy, Japan, Puerto Rico, and the Virgin Islands and founding the four-hundred member American Fan Collectors Association (AFCA) in 1980. He's even authored a book, *Antique Mechanical Fans*, now in its third printing. One fan-hunting expedition to Arizona blew in what is apparently the world's largest collection of oscillating fans (306), while another trip to Boston drew in amused looks when he handcarried three expensive fans onto the air-conditioned plane for the flight home.

Fans, he's found, cut across all racial, ethnic, and social lines. "People will do just about anything to cool off, and get very creative." He cites an example of an elderly fellow who, as a child, attached a Tinkertoy blade onto an old motor. "It ran for years." Powered by a rocking chair, a pre-Civil War number flapped its blades like a bird.

The museum's fans range from four- and six-inch diameter personal versions to a huge five-foot-wide, three hundred-pound

Six hundred fans of all shapes, colors, eras, and sizes line the shelves of the Olde Fan Museum. (*Photo courtesy of Kurt House.*)

Cyclone used in the movies that, if faced to the wall, will propel itself into it. That's one forceful sucker. Although, according to House, mechanical fans date back to the 1700s, his oldest model is a circa-1860 spring-powered number. "I set an arbitrary cutoff date of 1960 for the collection."

In between, there's a lot of hot air. "In addition to electricity, fans can run by steam, water, alcohol, kerosene or other fuels, springs, batteries, and even via vacuum and air," he points out. Examples of these include a 1916 Lake Breeze that's propelled by kerosene or alcohol, a 1880 Dayton steam-powered fan, and a 1930 Ribbonaire with blades made out of ribbon for safety. This contrasts to Edison-era fans in which the "guard" or protective cover cost five dollars extra, big bucks in those days.

Along with Edison's DC electrical originals (as opposed to the AC current employed today), House has the first Emerson fan ever manufactured, as well as a rare English Verity brand that goes up and down in addition to oscillating back and forth. Among his one-of-a-kinds is a two-foot-tall, 1902 spring-wound fan. It's a Victorian beauty, with pinstriping, claw feet, and painted flowers. "I've been offered $15,000 for it, but it's worth more." Touch it, and you break into a sweat.

Perfume fans of the twenties utilized canisters to not only cool the place off but make it smell nice. "These were often found in restaurants." For a nickel, patrons in hotels could chill out with coin-operated fans of that era also. "One fan from a hotel with a questionable reputation came with a bullet hole in it," adds House.

"If only it could talk." Yeah, but House and his collection would no doubt have to enter the Federal Witness Protection Program.

Still another model, a lighted, brass-bladed funeral-parlor fan kept flies from paying their own type of condolence call. Fly fans were also used on kitchen and picnic tables to keep bugs away from the food.

According to House, the most fan-tastic piece in his collection is a 1915 American Electric, the only remaining remnant of this short-lived company. The head goes completely around in a circle, while it bobs up and down, somewhat resembling a spastic Kewpie doll.

Along with offering repair of common household fans, House has a line of antiques and reproductions for sale so you can adopt one of your very own.

The Olde Fan Museum
1914 Abrams Parkway, Dallas, TX 75214
((214) 826-7700

LOCATION: Near downtown at the Lakewood Shopping Center
HOURS: Monday–Friday, 9:00 A.M.–6:00 P.M.; closed Sundays and holidays
ADMISSION: Free

✝ Plano: THE COMBAT COCKROACH HALL OF FAME

Only in America could the "roach" to riches be paved with the most originally dressed cockroach, and only from Texas could there emanate a search for the world's largest roach with a bounty of $50,000. In keeping with the patriotic spirit, only *Periplaneta americana* (the American cockroach) need apply. That's the winged, reddish brown, Palmetto bug of at least an inch in length and diameter who scuttles around basements, sewers, and moist, wooded areas. It is not to be confused with the punier German cockroach, who has two racing stripes; the Oriental version, a mostly wingless, mahogany colored water bug; or the nearly seventy-five other species of cockroach indigenous to the United States. Oh, and the contestant must be dead and preserved in alcohol—no squishing, stuffing, stretching, or steroids allowed.

Life's a beach at the Combat Cockroach Hall of Fame. (*Photo courtesy of Michael Bohdan.*)

Those who wonder what buggy mind cooked up this bizarre quest need look no further than exterminator Michael Bohdan, the field director for Combat Roach Control and owner of the Pest Shop, a Plano, Texas, enterprise that not only gets rid of insect nuisances but serves as home base for the Cockroach Hall of Fame. "I've always been interested in bugs, fossils, and nature," explains Bohdan, who looks and acts normal, despite his affinity for creepy crawlies. "After I graduated college, I figured out I wanted to be in pest control." When he first started the business in Plano, he began collecting bugs, "particularly roaches. Everything's the biggest in Texas, so why not have the world's best cockroach collection?"

Basically, the Combat contest has two categories, one for the world's largest roach and the other for "sensational roach art." Entrants for the first must be submerged in a plastic vial filled with rubbing alcohol that is sealed with tape and then packed securely in a box. "Some people just stick them in a baggie and mail them, and, believe me, they smell," observes Bohdan. Entries are judged by "expert roachologists" who utilize a digital electronic calibrater and measure from the tip of the head to the tip of the abdomen or wings, whichever is longer.

In order to qualify for the $50,000 jackpot, roaches must be at least 2.09 inches, larger than the 2.08-inch winner of the 1987 contest that was nabbed in a Florida school (hopefully not in the cafeteria). Regardless of size, the largest roach each year—or rather, its owner—will receive $1,000 and a year's supply of Combat Bait Trays. The winner—roach, not owner—also has a twelve-month reign on a glittery, three-tiered throne in the Hall of Fame. "It's not the Miss America pageant, but it's pretty close."

Occasionally Bohdan receives a contestant for the "sensational roach art" category who's still among the living. "Sometimes the roach escapes, and the person who sent it becomes upset because its being alive was an integral part of design." With $1,000 at stake and guaranteed placement for the winner and selected runners-up in the Hall of Fame, "people get pretty involved. They spend hours on their submissions. They'll call me up and ask if I have any extra roaches." (Those who are interested should submit their entries by June 15.)

Roach art runs the gamut from former presidential hopeful Roach Perot standing on a pile of money to Marilyn MonRoach complete with blond hair, white dress, and spiked heels. How do you put high heels on cockroach? "Very carefully," replies Bohdan. A beach scene with bikini'd roaches on surfboards and in lawn chairs submitted by employees at a Honolulu morgue was a recent winner. Bohdan gets a lot of submissions from the southern tier states like Florida, Mississippi, and Alabama "although California and Hawaii have been pretty strong the last couple of years," and estimates that he receives over two thousand submissions annually from both the United States and abroad. Understandably, they're not returned. "It's hard enough on the mailman as it is."

The Hall of Fame has Batroach, Elvis Roachley (in his "fat" phase), and a "roach coach" mobile-food dinette with the critters acting as both servers and consumers. Roach ranchers cook out at a Texas barbecue, a roach lies enshrined in a lined coffin, and a string of Tiffany pearls boasts a roach as a clasp. Some of these, along with other exhibits, travel with Bohdan when he goes on the road to promote the contest, which is held each August in a different city. Still, Bohdan's bread and butter, so to speak, comes from the exterminating business. Man cannot live by cockroach alone, especially when he has a family to support.

"At first people thought [the contest] was crazy, but it's done a lot of good," insists Bohdan. "It helps educate the public about insect control. Researchers at Combat alone are studying a million cockroaches." If they ever run out, they'll know where to turn.

The Combat Cockroach Hall of Fame
The Pest Shop
2231-B West Fifteenth Street, Plano, TX 75075
((214) 519-0355

LOCATION: A few miles north of Dallas, off US 75
HOURS: Weekdays, noon–5:00 P.M.; Saturday, 10:00 A.M.–2:00 P.M.
ADMISSION: Free

Washington

♠ Stevenson: THE DON BROWN ROSARY COLLECTION

Jesus Christ. Not in the profane sense of the word, but if He were to be resurrected today one of the first places He might want to visit is the Don Brown Rosary Collection. With about four-thousand rosaries (and still growing), it is the largest agglomeration of its kind. They hang in row after glorious row in a specially designed room at the Skamania County Historical Society and Museum in Stevenson, Washington. Talk about bearing a cross.

For the uninitiated, rosaries "are used by Catholics to keep track of the number of times they have said a repetitive prayer," explains Sharon Tiffany, executive director of the museum. "They [rosaries] are not to be worn like jewelry, but rather are part of a religious ritual. Only nuns, priests, and other church officials are permitted to have rosaries as regular attire. These are usually knotted at the waist." Fashion police, take note.

Rather than being considered a place of worship limited to believers, "the rosary collection is open to anyone," emphasizes Tiffany.

"It's an almost universal art form, with prayer beads used in Eastern religions and pre-Christian-era Jews utilizing a similar form of reckoning their prayers." There's even a menorah "given to Don by some Jewish friends," a touch of affirmative action among the brass relic holders, statuary, and other candelabras on the altars.

The items in this collection also include an organ and a white-pine American flag formed from thirty-nine guess-whats, definitely *not* separation of church and state. A statue of St. Dominic, the so-called "propagator" (interesting choice of words) of the rosary smiles benevolently at his propagees. "According to Catholic legend, St. Dominic was admonished by the Virgin Mary to preach the rosary as a special defense against heresy and vice," states the museum's brochure.

The rosaries gleam enticingly from behind glass cases, giving the room a jewel-box effect. "The counting beads can be made of almost anything—glass, bone, precious metal, ivory, semi-precious stones such as rubies and opals," points out Tiffany. Most, however, are neither glamorous nor expensive and consist of such humble items as olive pits, exotic nuts, wood, knotted leather, and, in one case, bullets.

Don Brown had truly Catholic tastes, as evidenced in his rosary collection, the world's largest. (*Photo courtesy of the Skamania County Museum.*)

The latter—No. 2757—"was sent to Don by a young medical student in Yugoslavia," she continues. Made of small and large brass rifle shells, it commemorates Russia, Bulgaria, and Serbia around the time of the World War I.

Who was Don Brown, and how did he get so many rosaries, anyway? By all accounts, he was as plain as his name—unmarried, a devout, converted Catholic who lived a simple life and didn't even drive a car. "He always loved rosaries and was afraid [the tradition] would be some day be deleted from common Catholic practice," observes Tiffany. "He dedicated all his time and concentration to the collection." Brown passed away in 1975 at the age of eighty.

"One of the few times he asked [for a rosary] was in 1960, when Senator John F. Kennedy decided to run for president." And it was given. The rosary had been carried by JFK during World War II and is considered the collection's most valuable acquisition. A wooden rosary left in a West German church by Robert Kennedy was sent to Brown after RFK's assassination, and the collection also has one used by Al Smith, the first Catholic to run for president, in 1928.

Rosaries range from miniatures with beads the size of a pin head to rings to a jumbo sixteen-foot-three-inch number made from styrofoam balls used in a school play. In between there are chaplet rosaries, about the diameter of a bracelet or choker; necklace length rosaries; belt-style rosaries; and, finally, wall hangings. "Many have been blessed by various members of the Catholic clergy, including several popes," adds Tiffany.

The oldest, an ebony wooden cross with beads of amber glass, came from Bavaria, circa 1770. Several are affixed around a picture of Columbus (the explorer, not the city), commemorating his travels. Made from Trapa seeds, also called Jesuit nuts (really), No. 4 hails from the Fontaine Monastery in Rome. Trapas are also known as water chestnuts, so that might explain the sudden urge for Chinese food after examining it.

No. 98 was created from catalpa seeds and staurolites, the naturally occurring "fairy crosses" found only in Virginia. With beads covered in purple silk thread and tassels of tiny glass, No. 287, from an ancient Orthodox monastery, definitely has a Russian flair. No. 723 was hand-carved entirely from deer horns, and No. 1961 boasts a different portrait of the Virgin Mary on each bead. But perhaps the most "illuminating" one is No. 2870, which has large, hollow double-capped pyrex glass dividers, "the contents of which is [sic] a secret formula of inert gases and mercury...and last a life time [sic]" according to the museum's brochure. Move it around in the dark and it will glow red, possibly to ward off vampires and assist in exorcisms.

Although they're in the process of building a new museum, the Skamania County Historical Society continues to accept rosaries (and donations, too). "We recently received fifty different rosaries from a collector in South Carolina," reports Tiffany enthusiastically. But even they have their limits. "We had to turn down one that was three hundred feet long made in honor of the pope's visit to Florida. There was no room." Sorry about that, Don.

The Don Brown Rosary Collection
Skamania County Historical Society
Box 396, Stevenson, WA 98648
((509) 427-5141 EXTENSION 235

LOCATION: Until mid-1995, it will be at 170 Vancouver Avenue; after that it will be housed in the Columbia Gorge Interpretive Center, 90 S.W. Rock Creek Dr.
HOURS: Monday–Saturday, noon–5:00 P.M.; Sunday, 1:00–6:00 P.M.; closed legal holidays
ADMISSION: Fee will be charged in new location

CANADA

Ontario

✦ Niagara Falls: THE DAREDEVIL HALL OF FAME/NIAGARA FALLS MUSEUM

Although it's actually in Canada, the Niagara Falls Museum is a hop, skip, and jump from the New York State border. But rather than leap, go over the Rainbow Bridge to get there. Otherwise, you might end up as part of the Daredevil Hall of Fame.

A timeline with photographs and artifacts, this Hall of Fame celebrates "the adventurous, indeed, the foolhardy, [who] defied death and attempted to conquer both the mighty Cataracts and the rampaging rapids of the lower river," gushes the museum's flowery, dated brochure. Regardless, the whole thing started in 1829, when Sam Patch dove off a ninety-foot platform into the falls. The next amazing feat occurred forty years later when the French tightrope walker Blondin (real name: Eugene Francois Gravelet) crossed the Niagara gorge on a rope set up over the whirlpool rapids. Both went on to fame and fortune.

This is an equal opportunity Hall of Fame. "We include all categories of daredevils, from barrel plungers to platform divers to swimmers to one young boy who accidentally tumbled over the falls in 1960," explains Jacob Sherman, the congenial director of his family-owned museum. The child in question, Roger Woodward, was fishing with his sister and uncle when their boat capsized. The uncle was killed and the sister was, according to the brochure, "snatched from the arms of death" by two tourists as she started to plunge over the falls. Seven-year-old Roger rode the crest with "only a fragile life preserver sharing the ordeal with him." He survived with a few scratches and a desire to forget the whole experience. "We call him the Miracle of Niagara," Sherman adds reverently. Although Roger Woodward now resides in Florida and "doesn't like to be associated with the daredevils," his name's up there anyway.

Women, too, have barreled their way to success. Teacher Anna Edison Taylor was the first to survive this type of attempt. "On the morning of October 24, 1901, her bruised and battered frame

142—Niagara Falls Museum

[emerged] from a now-historic barrel some three hours after it had been loosed in the Upper River," proclaims the brochure. The Hall of Fame displays a rather tacky-looking wax reproduction of Taylor inside her famous keg.

Along with the original wooden models, daredevils used steel cylinders (Bobby Leach), a sealed rubber ball with oxygen (Jean Lussier), and two giant Greek pickle barrels surrounded by inner tubes (Steve Trotter). In the last, dealing with the odor alone must have required great fortitude. Most of the specimens on exhibit reveal nicks and dents from their perilous travels.

The Daredevil Hall of Fame celebrates those who tumbled over Niagara Falls, whether accidentally or on purpose. *(Photo courtesy of the Niagara Falls Museum.)*

The Hall of Fame also honors those who died trying, such as George Stathakis, Charles Stevens, William "Red" Hill, Jr., and Miss Maud Willard "a Canton, Ohio, lass whose [barrel voyage] abruptly ended with her demise." Triumphant swimmers and divers such as Patch, Lord Hamilton, Cecil Baring, and Bill Kendall share space with the not-so-lucky Captain Matthew Webb and John Lincoln Soules.

Although "the majority of daredevils feel conquering the falls will catapult them to stardom, they're not suicidal and won't attempt to ride the American side of the falls which has huge bolders and shards of fallen rock," observes Sherman. Also, Park Rangers put a damper on things by fining those performing "unauthorized" (i.e., any) stunts several thousand dollars. What a downer.

The rest of the Niagara Falls Museum (and there's a *lot* of it) includes an Egyptian collection, a Hall of Dinosaurs exhibit, an Indian lore gallery, freaks of nature, ancient arms and weaponry, a mineralogical collection, and an Oriental curios gallery. With 700,000 exhibits, it's also one of the oldest museums in North America. Established in 1837 by Thomas Barnett "it originally displayed items of a largely historical nature," comments Sherman. "But it's always been family owned."

Through the years, the museum has also attracted famous visitors—Abraham Lincoln, King Edward VII, Ulysses S. Grant, and Mickey Mantle to name a few. Just seeing everything can be an act of daring.

The Daredevil Hall of Fame/Niagara Falls Museum
5651 River Road, Niagara Falls Ontario, L2E 6V8 Canada
((416) 356-2151 (CANADA) OR (716) 285-4898 (U.S.)

LOCATION: **Right across the Rainbow Bridge from the United States**
HOURS: **Call to confirm hours**
ADMISSION: **Admission is charged**

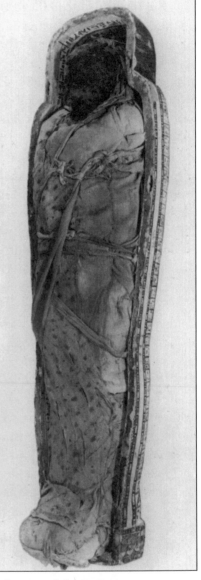

The star of the Egyptian mummy collection is thirty-four-hundred-year-old General Ossipumphnoferu ("Ossi" for short), whose red hair, beard, and facial features are still intact. *(Photo courtesy of the Niagara Falls Museum.)*

♠ North Bay: THE DIONNE QUINTS HOME AND MUSEUM

In their pictures, the Dionne quints of Corbeil, Ontario look like five identical little dolls. Because they practically grew up in a fishbowl and were put on display in their government-subsidized home and playground, Yvonne, Annette, Emilie, Cecile, and Marie struggled with the realities of adulthood. The only identical quintuplets to survive in over five hundred years, "they weren't famous because of anything they accomplished," observes Sharon Clark-Berard, director of the Dionne Quints Museum in nearby North Bay. "They were farm girls, not Hollywood starlets." Now approaching sixty, only three—Yvonne, Annette, and Cecile—are alive today. None are married (although there have been several divorces and children), and "they've expressed a desire for privacy."

But you can relive their glory days of the 1930s and 1940s at the Dionne Quints Home and Museum. The original birthplace of the five girls, the one-and-a-half-story partial log farmhouse was built by their paternal grandfather around the turn of the century and relocated to North Bay to fit in with a million-dollar tourist information center (or centre, as they say in Canada). Walk in, and you're accosted by fives: five baby carriages, five St. Christopher medals, five tiny eyedroppers that fed them their first meals (for obvious reasons, breast-feeding was not an option), five bottles, five undershirts with red maple leaves, five rocking chairs. There are five toothbrushes, five sets of dark brown pigtails, five prayer books, even five perfectly preserved frilly white dresses and bonnets worn on the day in 1939 when they met King George VI and Queen Elizabeth, when the quints were (really) five years old. They eventually appeared in three movies and like all true celebrities wrote a tell-all, *We Were Five*.

Of course not every item has four clones. There's the wooden bed where the girls (and many of the family's eight other children) were born in 1934; the old washing machine and stove that served the infants' multiple needs (in the true sense of the word); an incubator and butcher basket that held the swaddled babies (combined birth weight: 13 lbs, 6 oz); a scale; toys and sports equipment; and other items used by the Dionne parents and Dr. Allan Dafoe, the country physician who delivered them. Dafoe's medical library and, for some obscure reason, collection of license plates are also on display. He

Annette   Cecile   Dr. A.R. Dafoe   Marie   Yvonne   Emilie

Shown with the doctor who brought them into the world, the Dionne quints captured the imaginations of people the world over. (*Photo courtesy of the Dionne Quints Home and Museum.*)

has his own personal shrine in the North Himsworth Museum a few miles away in Callander, across the street from the former Dionne mansion, now a nursing home called Nipissing Manor.

Family and news photos and advertising endorsements line the walls. "The quints were big business," relates Clark-Berard. Thus their likenesses on Palmolive soap, Colgate dental products, Karo syrup, Quaker Oats, Carnation Milk, and many other products meant big bucks for all concerned. "The government of Ontario set up a trust fund and hired a manager to handle their affairs."

Although the girls lived in the farmhouse for the first few months of their lives, it had neither electricity nor running water, "and the family was unable to support five other children and the girls, who were not expected to live," she goes on. "When the father considered exhibiting [them] at the Chicago World's Fair, the government stepped in." And proceeded to declare the quints wards of the state and construct a glass playground where *they* put them on display. Although there was no charge to see the little darlings, millions of people flocked to the Dionne mansion annually, bringing an estimated $20 million in tourist revenue to the province during the first two years.

Raised by nurses and Dr. Dafoe, the quints could only visit their family for a brief period each day. Eventually, their father, Oliva Dionne, took the government to court and won his daughters back, and they lived not-so-happily ever after.

Today quint collectibles, such as coins commemorating the fiftieth anniversary of their birth and dolls manufactured in 1935 by the Madame Alexander Doll Company of New York City, have become hot items. One wonders though, could anyone ever *really* tell the five girls apart?

The Dionne Quints Home and Museum
North Bay Chamber of Commerce
P.O. Box 747, North Bay Ontario, P1B 8J8 Canada
((705) 472-8480

LOCATION: Off Highway 17 on Seymour Street in North Bay (about 80 miles east of Sudbury)
HOURS: Seven days a week; mid-May–mid-October, 9:00 A.M.–5:00 P.M.; July and August, 9:00 A.M.–7:00 P.M.
ADMISSION: Admission is charged

♠ Toronto: THE GEORGE SCOTT RAILTON SALVATION ARMY HERITAGE CENTRE

In 1881, Salvation Army leader George Scott Railton missed the boat back to England and, having a few days on his hands, started a branch of the Army in Canada. Accompanied by seven "Hallelujah Lassies," he preached the gospel in the streets, held open-air services to convert the unchurched, and laid the foundation for what would become a mainstay for the needy and homeless. "Founded in 1865 by William and Catherine Booth as the Christian Mission, the Salvation Army had already taken hold in England and in the United States," explains Major William Brown of the Heritage Centre in Toronto.

People who model their flag after the blood of Christ and the fire of God's Holy Spirit; adopt uniforms, ranks, and military terminology in carrying out their duties; and name their newspaper the *War Cry* are not to be messed with. Although they are basically peace-loving missionaries, one wouldn't want to incur the wrath of *their* Commander-in-Chief.

Before Alcoholics Anonymous and the Betty Ford Clinic, there was the Salvation Army. "In the mid-1860s, only 2 percent of the working class in England attended worship, but thousands flocked to saloons," observes Brown. "It was a degrading and desperate milieu." The Booths spread the Word through gospel meetings and songs and stirring band music ("Onward Christian Soldiers," etc.) A few years later, William Booth started calling his followers the Salvation Army.

Along with sepia photos and written materials depicting nineteenth-century England, there are artifacts such as William Booth's walking cane, fountain pen, and sermon book; the now-familiar deaconess bonnet that uniformed female Salvationists wear when ringing that bell at Christmas time; and a "mercy seat" where people knelt in the middle of the chapel and "surrendered to God." No private confessions for these folks; as a part of the Christian Church, the Salvation Army had its roots in English Methodism.

The museum covers Canadian Salvation Army development as well. The lives and times of various leaders; the Battle of the Basilica, a riot against Salvationists in Quebec; and the Dawson City gold rush are depicted here. A painting portrays sinners repenting at an open-air gathering in Toronto in 1895. Old telephones and typewriters, as well as copies of *This is My Story* and *The Living Word*, radio and TV programs, respectively, are available. (Those ripe for an evangelistic trip down memory lane can view an original *Living Word* film after the tour.)

Another exhibit centers around Salvation Army brass bands. "Music is a big part of our heritage, although we did not set out to form bands," comments Brown. "Our members enjoyed playing instruments," many of which are on display. During the 1914 *Empress of Ireland* disaster, most of the Canadian band perished when a Norwegian freighter struck that ship broadside. Over one thousand two hundred people went down, including about 130 Salvation Army Members (records are not exact). Sandwiched between the *Titanic* (1912) and the *Lusitania* (1915) catastrophes, "the *Empress* tends to be somewhat forgotten." But not at this museum. Along with pictures, lists of passengers, and other memorabilia, there's a tablecloth that had been thrown around a bandsman after he was pulled from the icy waters.

Various social services are also covered by exhibits, such as the League of Mercy in which Salvationists helped prisoners and their loved ones; Rescue Homes for women and halfway houses for convicts; Children's Shelters for orphans; and more. Coffee and socks (not necessarily in that order), ambulances, and prayer assistance were provided by Salvationists during both world wars.

Today the Salvation Army is found in over ninety countries and offers assistance from birth to old age and for diseases from leprosy to alcoholism. Its cornucopia of charities provides counseling for suicides, a missing persons bureau, camps for underprivileged children and much more. One can forgive the fact that their museum's a bit preachy, and doesn't include any member of the Army being parodied in the Broadway musical *Guys and Dolls*.

The George Scott Railton Salvation Army Heritage Centre
2130 Bayview Avenue, Toronto, Ontario M4N 3K6
((416) 481-4441

LOCATION: In the suburbs, halfway between Eglinton and Lawrence
HOURS: Monday–Friday, 9:00 A.M.–4:30 P.M.
ADMISSION: Free